Literacy in the Digital University

Literacy in the Digital University is an innovative volume which brings together perspectives from two fields of enquiry and practice: 'literacies and learning' and 'learning technologies'. With their own histories and trajectories, these fields have seldom overlapped either in practice, theory, or research. In tackling this divide head on, the volume breaks new ground. It illustrates how complementary and contrasting approaches to literacy and technology can be brought together in productive ways, and considers the implications of this for practitioners working across a wide range of contexts.

The book showcases work from well-respected authorities in the two fields in order to provide the foundations for new conversations about learning and practice in the digital university. It will be of particular relevance to university teachers and researchers, educational developers and learning technologists, library staff, university managers and policy-makers, and, not least, learners themselves, particularly those studying at postgraduate level.

Robin Goodfellow is Senior Lecturer in Teaching with New Technology in the Institute of Educational Technology at the Open University, UK.

Mary R. Lea is Reader in Academic and Digital Literacies in the Institute of Educational Technology at the Open University, UK.

The Society for Research into Higher Education (SRHE) is an independent and financially self-supporting international learned Society. It is concerned to advance understanding of higher education, especially through the insights, perspectives and knowledge offered by systematic research and scholarship.

The Society's primary role is to improve the quality of higher education through facilitating knowledge exchange, discourse and publication of research. SRHE members are worldwide and the Society is an NGO in operational relations with UNESCO.

The Society has a wide set of aims and objectives. Amongst its many activities the Society:

• is a specialist publisher of higher education research, journals and books, amongst them Studies in Higher Education, Higher Education Quarterly, Research into Higher Education Abstracts and a long running monograph book series.

The Society also publishes a number of in-house guides and produces a specialist series "Issues in Postgraduate Education".

• funds and supports a large number of special interest networks for researchers and practitioners working in higher education from every discipline. These networks are open to all and offer a range of topical seminars, workshops and other events throughout the year ensuring the Society is in touch with all current research knowledge.

• runs the largest annual UK-based higher education research conference and parallel conference for postgraduate and newer researchers. This is attended by researchers from over 35 countries and showcases current research across every aspect of higher education.

SRHE

Society for Research into Higher Education
Advancing knowledge Informing policy Enhancing practice

73 Collier Street
London N1 9BE
United Kingdom

T   +44 (0)20 7427 2350
F   +44 (0)20 7278 1135
E   srheoffice@srhe.ac.uk

www.srhe.ac.uk

Director: Helen Perkins
Registered Charity No.313850
Company No.00868820
Limited by Guarantee
Registered office as above

Society for Research into Higher Education (SRHE) series

Series Editors: Lynn McAlpine, Oxford Learning Institute
Jeroen Huisman, University of Bath

Published titles:
Intellectual Leadership in Higher Education: Renewing the Role of the University Professor
Bruce Macfarlane

Strategic Curriculum Change: Global Trends in Universities
Paul Blackmore and Camille B. Kandiko

Reconstructing Identities in Higher Education: The Rise of 'Third Space' Professionals
Celia Whitchurch

The University in Dissent: Scholarship in the Corporate University
Gary Rolfe

Everything for Sale? The Marketisation of UK Higher Education
Roger Brown

Forthcoming titles:
Feminism, Gender and Universities: Politics, Passion and Pedagogies
Miriam David

Literacy in the Digital University

Critical perspectives on learning, scholarship, and technology

Edited by
Robin Goodfellow and Mary R. Lea

Routledge
Taylor & Francis Group

LONDON AND NEW YORK

First published 2013
by Routledge
2 Park Square, Milton Park, Abingdon, Oxon OX14 4RN together with the
Society for Research into Higher Education (SRHE)
73 Collier Street
London N1 9BE
UK

Simultaneously published in the USA and Canada
by Routledge
711 Third Avenue, New York, NY 10017 together with the Society for
Research into Higher Education (SRHE)
73 Collier Street
London N1 9BE
UK

Routledge is an imprint of the Taylor & Francis Group, an informa business

British Library Cataloguing in Publication Data
A catalogue record for this book is available from the British Library

Library of Congress Cataloging in Publication Data
Literacy in the digital university : critical perspectives on learning, scholarship,
and technology / edited by Robin Goodfellow and Mary R. Lea.
    pages cm
    1. Learning and scholarship—Technological innovations. 2. Education,
    Higher—Effect of technological innovations on. 3. Academic
    writing—Computer-assisted instruction. 4. Digital communications.
    I. Goodfellow, Robin, 1947– II. Lea, Mary R. (Mary Rosalind), 1950–
    AZ195.L58 2013
    001.2—dc23
    2013004285

ISBN: 978-0-415-53796-4 (hbk)
ISBN: 978-0-415-53797-1 (pbk)
ISBN: 978-0-203-07451-0 (ebk)

Typeset in Galliard
by Swales & Willis Ltd, Exeter, Devon

MIX
Paper from
responsible sources
FSC
www.fsc.org   FSC® C013056

Printed and bound in Great Britain by
TJ International Ltd, Padstow, Cornwall

Contents

Illustrations

Figures

Tables

Contributors

David Barton is Professor of Language and Literacy at Lancaster University, UK. His research interests are in all aspects of language online, the interaction of words and images, multilingual issues, changes to vernacular practices and learning. He is especially interested in language on the photo-sharing site Flickr. His interests also include methodology, especially ethnographic approaches to literacy research.

Siân Bayne is Senior Lecturer in the School of Education at the University of Edinburgh. Her research is concerned with higher education and museum learning, with a particular focus on visuality and multimodality in assessment practices, posthumanism and sociomaterial understandings of online education and digital scholarship.

Helen Beetham is an independent consultant, researcher, and author in the field of e-learning in UK Higher Education. Since 2004 she has played a leading role in the Joint Information Systems Committee (JISC) e-learning programme. She co-edited *Rethinking Pedagogy for the Digital Age* (Routledge 2007) and *Rethinking Learning for the Digital Age* (Routledge 2010). She was a member of the expert panel for the Department for Children, Schools and Families (DCSF)-funded Beyond Current Horizons programme (2009).

Jude Fransman is a Postdoctoral Research Fellow at the Institute of Education, where she focuses on 'the politics of method and representation in research' and teaches modules in research design, social theory and visual methods. She has published in the fields of literacy studies, academic practice, and multimodal practices of representation in community activism and community based research.

Robin Goodfellow is Senior Lecturer in the Open University's Institute of Educational Technology. He was principal investigator for the Economic and Social Research Council (ESRC)-funded seminar series *Literacy in the Digital University* between 2009 and 2011. He is co-author of *Challenging E-Learning in the University – A Literacies Perspective* (McGraw Hill/Open University Press 2007).

Lesley Gourlay is Senior Lecturer in Contemporary Literacies in the Department of Culture, Communication and Media, and Director of the Academic Writing Centre at the Institute of Education, University of London. Her research focuses on digital mediation in higher education, media theory, actor network theory (ANT), textual practices, and digital literacies.

Mary Hamilton is Professor of Adult Learning and Literacy in the Department of Educational Research at Lancaster University, UK. She is an associate director of the Lancaster Literacy Research Centre and a member of the Centre for Science and Technology Studies, The Centre for Gender and Women's Studies and the Centre for Ageing Research at Lancaster.

Caroline Haythornthwaite is Director and Professor, School of Library, Archival and Information Studies (The iSchool@UBC), University of British Columbia. She has an international reputation for research on social networks, computer media and e-learning, and is a founding member of the Society for Learning Analytics Research (http://www.solaresearch.org/). Major publications (with Richard Andrews) include *E-learning Theory and Practice* (Sage, 2011), and the *Handbook of E-learning Research* (Sage, 2007).

Jane Hughes is an academic developer and researcher and a HEDERA founding partner. She was previously a lecturer in learning technologies at University College London (UCL) and a teacher of English in schools. Her research interests include technology mediated collaboration and communication and open education.

Chris Jones is Professor of Research in Educational Technology at Liverpool John Moores University. His research focuses on the utilization of the metaphor of networks in the understanding of learning in higher education. He has edited two books and published over 70 journal articles, book chapters and refereed conference papers connected to his research.

Mary R. Lea is Reader in Academic and Digital Literacies at the Open University, UK. Both her research and practice are concerned with writing, knowledge, and meaning-making in a wide range of higher education contexts, including the digital landscape. She is co-editor of *Student Writing in Higher Education: New Contexts* and co-author of *Writing at University: A Guide for Students* and *Challenging eLearning in the University: A Literacies Perspective*.

Carmen Lee is Assistant Professor in the Department of English at the Chinese University of Hong Kong. She has published and carried out projects on social aspects of language and literacy, linguistic practices on the internet, and multilingual literacy practices. She is co-author of the book *Language Online* (Routledge 2013).

Allison Littlejohn is Director of the Caledonian Academy, a research centre exploring technology enhanced professional learning in the public and private sectors, and Professor of Learning Technology at Glasgow Caledonian

University, UK. She was Senior Researcher with Royal Dutch Shell 2008–2010 and founding Series Editor for the Routledge Connecting with eLearning and Advancing Technology Enhanced Learning book series.

Alison Mackenzie is Dean of Learning Services at Edge Hill University. Until recently, she was Chair of the SCONUL Working Group on Information Literacy and she continues to champion the importance of information and digital literacy and its contribution to student success.

Lou McGill is an independent consultant and writer in the areas of technologies for learning and teaching. She has worked on a range of studies on digital repositories and learning materials, eLearning transformation, digital literacies, open educational resources and open courses. She also works as a researcher for the Caledonian Academy.

Colleen McKenna is a higher education researcher and founding partner of HEDERA, and a visiting research fellow at the Institute of Education. Previously, she lectured in academic literacies at University College London (UCL). Her research interests include digital writing, open education, and postgraduate writing and identity.

Lindsey Martin is Assistant Head of Learning Services (Learning, ICT and Media Technologies) at Edge Hill University. She is secretary of the Heads of eLearning Forum Steering group (HeLF), a national network of senior staff having a strategic role in the enhancement of learning and teaching through the use of technology in UK higher education institutions.

Martin Oliver is Reader in ICT in Education at the Institute of Education, University of London, working in the London Knowledge Lab. He researches the use of technology in higher education, particularly curriculum design and students' study practices. He is currently president of the Association for Learning Technology.

Jen Ross is a lecturer in the School of Education at the University of Edinburgh, and the programme director of the MSc in Digital Education. She is part of the Digital Cultures and Education research group, and her research interests include digital futures, cultures, feedback, assessment, and writing.

Candice Satchwell is Lecturer in Education at the University of Central Lancashire. Previously she worked as a Senior Research Associate in the Literacy Research Centre at Lancaster University, and lecturer in English and Linguistics at Blackpool & The Fylde College and UCLan. Her publications cover literacy and education in a variety of settings.

Bronwyn T. Williams is Professor of English at the University of Louisville. He writes and teaches on issues of literacy, identity, digital media, and popular culture. His recent books are *New Media Literacies and Participatory Popular Culture Across Borders* and *Shimmering Literacies: Popular Culture and Reading and Writing Online*.

Series editors' introduction

This series, co-published by the Society for Research into Higher Education and Routledge Books, aims to provide, in an accessible manner, cutting-edge scholarly thinking and inquiry that reflects the rapidly changing world of higher education, examined in a global context.

Encompassing topics of wide international relevance, the series includes every aspect of the international higher education research agenda, from strategic policy formulation and impact to pragmatic advice on best practice in the field. Each book in the series aims to meet at least one of the principle aims of the Society: to advance knowledge; to enhance practice; to inform policy.

The convergence of technological change with structural reorganization has affected post-compulsory education worldwide. This edited book by Robin Goodfellow and Mary R. Lea explores some of the manifestations of this upheaval, from the perspective of teachers, learners, researchers, educational developers, policymakers, and managers, all of whom are likely to be experiencing – and some of whom are responsible for initiating – the introduction of new technological practices across the higher education sector.

Lynn McAlpine
Jeroen Huisman

Introduction

Literacy, the digital, and the university

Robin Goodfellow and Mary R. Lea

Background to the book

The last decade has seen a proliferation of applications of information and communication technologies (ICTs) in all educational sectors. This volume responds to this broader context and to the convergence of technological change with structural reorganization that has affected post-compulsory education worldwide. The impact of new technological practices in colleges and universities can be seen right across the spectrum of professional activity, from the digitizing of management information, to the use of virtual learning environments (VLEs) in teaching and learning, to the development of digital scholarship in academic research. The nature and scale of this impact varies from institution to institution. In one setting, for example, we might find frustrated learning technologists bemoaning the existence of academic 'dinosaurs' who continue to resist using VLEs or the internet. In another, there are teachers who pride themselves on being early adopters of the latest technologies, but who are now finding that the innovative nature of what they are doing – in both their teaching and their own scholarship – is being undermined by institutional policy. For example, they may be facing a requirement to teach using digital tools and materials developed elsewhere and 'bought in' for primarily economic, as opposed to pedagogic reasons. Elsewhere, teachers, researchers, and administrators are quietly getting on with using technologies, day to day, and developing new ways of working, which, whilst seemingly unremarkable to them, are potentially very significant in terms of change in the production of knowledge in the institution as a whole. Digitization thus makes its mark in many different ways: on research and teaching; course design and assessment; professional and academic development; enrolment, registration, and ongoing student support processes; budgeting and marketing. Moreover, structural reorganization has made it increasingly possible for other interest groups with different agendas outside the university to reach in and effect changes that reflect their own interests and those of wider political and economic communities. Employers directly influence the knowledge curriculum, as the content and orientation of professional courses is prescribed by external professional bodies working in collaboration with private service providers to offer professional accreditation. Global media and IT companies directly shape conditions of teaching and learning through the design of applications and online environments that rapidly become indispensable to the flexible learning required in the modern age. Developments of this kind, as we have argued elsewhere (Goodfellow and Lea 2007), can serve to conflate aspects of pedagogy with administrative and managerial activity, concealing, at the same time, critical differences between the social practices of different institutional communities.

The digital university

It is this broad context of technological and structural change in the post-compulsory sector that we are looking to encapsulate in the concept of the 'digital university' – an emerging context in which fundamentally different forms of social practice around learning and technologies jostle together and strain the boundaries of institutions and the professional communities who inhabit them. It is the intention of this book to explore and critique some of the manifestations of this upheaval, from the perspective of teachers, learners, researchers, educational developers, policy-makers, and managers, all of whom are likely to be experiencing – and some of whom are responsible for initiating – the introduction of new technological practices across the tertiary sector. Many of these groups and individuals are bearing the brunt of technology-driven change in their work with little support, as their institutions have often been slow to engage with broader questions concerning the way this 'new communication order' (Snyder 2001) impacts on social relations. In part, the lack of institutional engagement with the social and cultural implications of new technological practices has been because of an overriding focus on the role of these technologies in organizational change required to meet wider societal and governmental objectives. Such objectives include the 'massification' of higher education, the development of flexible provision, and the introduction of greater competition in a global market. We have seen considerable technical and managerial effort and resource put into the creation of VLEs to supplement or replace bricks-and-mortar infrastructure, but far less corresponding attention paid to professional and educational development in terms of understanding and supporting the practices of staff as they begin to adapt their teaching and learning to the conditions of digital information and communication (McAvinia 2011). Similarly, we have seen considerable investment in the digitization and electronic delivery of information about the institution, the curriculum and its procedures, leading to increased accountability and audit, but much less in researching the particular challenges that technologies present to learners and teachers pursuing learning goals in particular subjects and disciplines (Goodfellow and Lea 2007).

Literacy

We believe that the absence of a critical social perspective on the digital in post-compulsory education is due to a more general sidelining of the issue of *literacy* at this level. This may be because many associate the concept with the development of print-based reading and writing skills in primary and secondary education, and view the emergence of digital modes of communication at tertiary level as a different (and perhaps more fashionably up-to-date) issue. In contrast, many of the contributions to this volume have a particular interest in the way in which the new communication order in the university is actually bound up with established literacy practices, in research and publication, teaching and assessment, management and academic service, public engagement, and external relations. By literacy practices we mean activities around textual production – texts and practices which taken together are recognized as typical and purposeful for a community. Although it is true that the word 'literacy' is increasingly being used to refer to different aspects of communication in the wider world (media literacy, emotional literacy, business literacy, etc.), it is in its association with the production of knowledge in textual form that it remains central to educational practice, whatever the media and material dimensions involved.

Researchers coming from a tradition of critical applied language studies in education have long argued for a recognition of the role of literacy practices in meaning-making throughout the university (Ivanič 1998; Jones, Turner and Street 1999; Lea and Street 1998; Lea and Stierer 2000; Lillis 2001; Turner 2011). They have stressed the essentially social character of textual communication, its complexity and diversity, and its ultimate provenance within the practices of all members of an institutional and/or disciplinary community, not just the students (Lea and Stierer 2009; Lillis and Curry 2010). This continues to be the case when the notion of text is broadened to encompass meaning-making in and around the multiple modes associated with digital media (Bayne 2006; Lea and Jones 2011; McKenna 2012; Williams 2009). Academic literacies in digital contexts encapsulate a multiplicity of social practices involved in creating, communicating and evaluating textual knowledge across this range of modes (Goodfellow 2005; Lea 2007; Lea and Jones 2011; Goodfellow 2011; McKenna 2012). Other voices from 'new literacy studies' (e.g. Barton and Hamilton 1998), 'multiliteracies' (Cope and Kalantzis 2000), and 'new media literacies' (Lankshear and Knobel 2003) have shown how participants in academic learning communities are also informally engaged with meaning-making communities outside their institutions, whose digital practices may be quite removed from those of the school or academy. For all these researchers and practitioners, the concept of literacy has broadened far beyond the notion of an individual learner's acquisition of skills in the decoding and encoding of printed language.

Broadening the 'literacy' debate

In tertiary education, however, much of the policy-informed activity around professional development, pedagogy, and the assessment of learning outcomes continues to embrace a predominantly normative individualistic cognitive skills agenda (see Goodfellow 2011 and Lea 2013, for discussions of this position).

It is in recognition of this tension between 'literacies' and 'skills', and out of a belief that the latter perspective actually sells short learners and teachers who are required to operate across a variety of digital practice settings, that this volume brings together researchers and practitioners from different disciplinary backgrounds to explore the changing and expanding meaning of literacy in the digital university. Our starting point was to identify groups of researchers who have been involved in research projects that approach issues of literacy, learning, and technology through contrasting conceptual and methodological lenses, identified broadly as critical applied language and literacy studies, learning technology, and cultural media studies. A group of such scholars and practitioners came together for a series of seminars with the title 'Literacy in the Digital University', funded by the UK Economic and Social Research Council between October 2009 and April 2011 (ESRC 2012). This volume builds on the discussions and debates that took place in these seminars, supplementing them with more recent relevant, topical, and related work in the areas of media and information literacy and e-learning. This has enabled a dialogue across the volume between contrasting approaches, and the potential development of new thinking and methodologies for researching practice in the digital university. There is inevitably some contested space in the positions of these contributors and this emerges most strongly around the notion of what literacy means in digital contexts. But despite differences in theoretical and methodological assumptions, there are also major points of agreement. The notion of learning practices, for example, emerges as a key concept which cuts across different approaches and supports different pragmatic agendas. Similarly, there is much agreement about the implications of the concept of the 'digital university' for understanding the shifting boundaries between and within existing institutions. In its attempts to circumvent differences in disciplinary and practical orientation and bring contrasting perspectives together, the book offers innovative conceptualizations of the institution and its texts, technologies, and practices. Many of these are reflected in the integration of familiar terms such as 'literacy' and 'the digital' into new and hybrid concepts such as 'digital scholarship', 'the borderless institution', and 'posthuman pedagogies'. In all cases, the discussions and insights of the authors of the chapters in this book have a direct bearing on the way that literacy and the value placed on it at tertiary level is conceived of in response to the changing communications environment, and offer a new lens on existing research and practice.

The structure of the book

All the chapters included here were specially written for this volume, and relate to ongoing work in the tertiary sector. The authors have addressed many of the issues and topics discussed above, each from their own particular disciplinary and practice perspective. This presented a challenge for us as editors as to how to organize the contributions and the relationships between them in a meaningful way that did not perpetuate divisions between disciplinary, theoretical, and practical orientations. Since one major objective of the volume has been to highlight both agreements and differences about the meaning of literacy, understandings of the digital, and the nature of the university, and all the chapters relate in some way to all of these themes, we have decided not to attempt to group them according to topic but instead to arrange them in a way that allows the main focus to shift across the themes in successive chapters. In the following synopsis we take each of the themes 'Literacy', 'the Digital', and 'the University' and discuss how the different chapters address them. We hope that readers may find this useful in help-ing them to determine which of the contributors are addressing topics that are of most immediate interest to them, but also which are dealing with other topics which have an unexpected connection.

Literacy

Framing this book with a literacy lens has not been without its problems. Literacy as a term is often elided with a generalized skill and capability and no more so than in the arena of digital literacies (see Goodfellow 2011; Lea 2013). This approach underpins the orientation to literacy in some of the chapters. An alternative is offered by those who intentionally use literacies in the plural in order to signal the multiplicity of contested and contextual, social, and cultural practices around reading and writing (see the discussion on 'literacy' and 'broadening the literacy debate' above).

Adopting the 'literacies' theoretical and methodological perspective, Colleen McKenna and Jane Hughes highlight how authorship is key to understanding literacy practices in the digital university. They explore this in terms of commodi-fication and intellectual property and point to the potential of digital authorship to subvert conventional print-based literacy practices. Central to their argument is the provisional nature of digital texts; the ease with which they can be changed, copied, dismantled, and reassembled. They discuss the implications of this for understanding literacy practices in terms of what technologies actually do to writing practices. Taking the example of plagiarism detection software (PDS), they argue that the technology dominates; the result being that complex textual practices embedded in the notion of what it means to plagiarize are now largely hidden from view for students. In short, literacy practices become masked by attention to the software, to the technology. In addition, PDS acts as a constraint because, they argue, it is premised upon an outmoded print literacy paradigm. Its design makes it impossible to recognize multimodal meaning-making – interac-tive multimodal texts cannot be captured and uploaded in PDS – and practices which happen all the time in digital scholarship, for example the use of blogs and Twitter. They argue that it is important to locate, name, and scrutinize lit-eracy processes and actions before they become naturalized, fixed, and invisible, and lost in a network of technology and regulation. Robin Goodfellow picks up some similar themes around authorship in his exploration of digital scholarship. He looks in detail at the ways in which scholarly texts are constructed and how they speak to particular audiences and claim authority. In an effort to identify the values and beliefs behind approaches to digital scholarship he draws on analytical perspectives from the fields of new literacy studies and rhetorical studies, with a focus upon rhetorical practices within academic texts. He identifies openness as an increasingly common academic practice in the arena of digital scholarship but it is the scholarly texts themselves, their structure and the kind of moves that are taking place within them, which are central to his argument. He contrasts the ways in which the authors, whose work he examines, construct their audience, conventionally as an academic audience of scholars or speaking to the reader as a relative newcomer rather than a member of any particular academic community. The chapter articulates how textual practices enact these approaches and positions and illustrates the work they do to construct the different approaches to academic practice and knowledge which are embedded in the authors' work. It suggests that notions of openness and scholarship not only commit to a certain kind of digital transformation but they also commit scholars as authors to a decision about truth and use, and to engaging in literacy practices that accord with the values of the community they are speaking to.

Carmen Lee focuses on literacy from a linguistic perspective and, in this respect, she foregrounds language and its association with 'literacies as social practice' research. Although she looks primarily at texts, she is also concerned with practices in and around digital media and their implications for pedagogy. The chapter is orientated towards methodology, including text-making practices and discourse-centred online ethnography, both of which underpin her work on hybridity and creativity in digital texts. It offers detailed research into multilingual text-making practices amongst undergraduate students in Hong Kong, exploring digital spaces where relatively controlled academic discourse meets and interplays with interpersonal, hybrid, and informal discourse styles. Lee's contribution to the volume is from the perspective of a discipline specialist and she illustrates how undertaking research on student engagement with digital text-making practices has had particular implications for her own teaching.

Creativity, hybridity, and fluidity are all key elements of the literacy practices foregrounded in this volume and are evidenced in the practices of post-compulsory college students explored by Candice Satchwell, David Barton, and Mary Hamilton. They take as their starting point the need to look beyond the text and to consider what people do with literacy. Their concern here is with how literacy practices are subtly altered as they cross the boundary from one domain to another, for example, when college students incorporate their experience of multimodal multimedia texts into their coursework. They argue that notions of agency, identity, and power are always fundamental to the ways in which different ways of doing literacy are embraced or resisted and that practices from one context do not migrate simply into another even when technology is in place to facilitate this.

There are close similarities with Satchwell, Barton, and Hamilton's work in Mary Lea's chapter. Taking an academic literacies approach she illustrates a misalignment between student practice and assessment practices, illustrating how students' practices of meaning-making and use of resources in digital contexts are rarely reflected in their completed assignments. Lea builds on this empirical research context to examine the development of academic literacies as a field of study as it grapples with a digital higher education. She argues that the theoretical and methodological orientation of academic literacies may not be robust enough to help us understand literacies in the digital university and suggests that we need to interrogate the categories and binaries that the field has taken for granted, for example, the distinction between academics' and students' practices. She believes that we need to bring in and integrate perspectives from other intellectual traditions, in particular actor network theory. This moves away from the propensity of academic literacies research to see issues of agency, identity, and processes only in terms of what particular people do. It involves reassembling academic literacies in order to examine the workings of institutional networks over and above the activities of specific groups of people, for example students and teachers. This means asking different kinds of questions around texts and practices and also recognizing that it is our ability to see and capture them which is changing in the shift to the digital. Lea argues that bringing together the critical, contested approach from academic literacies with an actor network approach can offer a counter to the relentless drive of higher education to stabilize the digital and align it uncritically with literacy as individual capability. Such an approach might help us to think differently about literacy and in particular academic literacy in the digital university. This will mean moving from a focus on accounts of individual practice to explorations of network practice, how networks come into being and how they are sustained. She illustrates her argument through exploring the idea of 'digital literacy' and its power to configure institutional practice within and outside the university.

The digital

As with their approaches to literacy, the contributors to this volume bring different assumptions and points of focus to their conceptualizations of the digital, although only Chris Jones attempts an explicit definition of the term. He does this by contrasting contemporary digital technologies with their technical predecessors, arguing that the new generation of digital sociotechnical systems is distinctively different by virtue of features such as replicability, mutability, instantaneity, connectivity, portability, etc., all of which have consequences for new sociocultural practices. His chapter is motivated by the desire to understand the implications of 'digitality' in this technical sense, and to use this understanding to characterize the digital university as a distinctive kind of educational institution. The other contributors, by contrast, use the term 'digital' to highlight a variety of different phenomena: specific devices, networks (or 'assemblages' in the more theorized accounts), technical affordances, modes of text and textuality, types of skills and competencies, practices, and environments, depending on the kinds of motivations discussed below. Inevitably, perspectives overlap, and any attempt to categorize these different approaches to the digital in mutually exclusive terms will fail to do justice to some aspect or other of their authors' intentions. However, in accepting the different emphases that the authors put on theoretical and pragmatic features of the digital we can perhaps come to a better understanding of 'digitality' as a complex phenomenon, and hopefully to a better appreciation of its role in the social construction of the universities of tomorrow.

For some of the contributors to this volume, it is policy (governmental or institutional) that is the principal shaper of the digital in the university. Allison Littlejohn, Helen Beetham, and Lou McGill, for example, locate their understanding of the digital against the efforts of the UK higher and further education policy and practice community to deliver an 'entitlement agenda' for twenty-first century students. From this perspective, they discuss 'digital literacy' as the capability to engage in new kinds of economically productive work and learning practices, arguing that this is becoming 'essential for participation within society'. Lindsey Martin and Alison MacKenzie, and Colleen McKenna and Jane Hughes conceptualize the digital from the perspective of institutions currently focused on the creation and reuse of open educational materials (OERs) with both philanthropic and self-interested motives. Such materials implicate the digital both in their means of production and their modes of use – an issue which can be seen as having professional development implications, both practical (Martin and MacKenzie), and normative (McKenna and Hughes). Candice Satchwell and her colleagues locate the digital in the artefacts and practices that distinguish informal from formal contexts of work and study for the further education students whose learning was the focus of their publicly-funded research. Lesley Gourlay and Martin Oliver explore their expansive concept of socio-material practice through a study of students' 'digital literacy', as required by the terms of the national research and development programme that funds their work.

Despite his concern for a technical definition of the digital, Jones concludes his chapter with a critique of the role of technically determinist accounts of the digital and its users in providing simplistic solutions for policy-makers, and argues for a socio-material understanding of the digital that takes account of the way that it can constrain as well as afford human intentions. The critical dimension is very important for some of the other contributors to this volume, for whom the digital poses significant theoretical problems for current ideas about pedagogy and literacy. Gourlay and Oliver, Siân Bayne and Jen Ross, Mary Lea, and Jude Fransman, for example, all position the digital as a socio-material phenomenon – an aggregation of networks or assemblages of actors and devices whose role in the shaping of pedagogy and the outcomes of learning needs to be accounted for in theoretical terms. For Bayne and Ross in particular, the capacity of digital devices to generate and operate on an 'uncharted space of flows' (quoting Castells 1999) independently of any knowledge of individual human actors, creates the possibility of an entirely new kind of institutional and pedagogical space for online teachers and learners. To account for the transactions that go on in this kind of space, they argue, it is necessary to move beyond the individualist and humanist framings of the social that we are used to. They pose a conundrum for those wishing to assess students' work in highly digital contexts, by drawing attention to the role of non-human agents such as feeds and content aggregators in shaping what is eventually 'submitted' for assessment by the students on their own Master's in Digital Education. The posthuman perspective on the digital is also explicitly referenced by Gourlay and Oliver, whose view of the digital as constituted by 'assemblages' of devices and actors (human and non-human) is convincingly illustrated in their account of students and others using technologies for study purposes in a variety of locations and social contexts. Lea's consideration of new thinking about the socio-material derived from actor network theory problematizes the taken-for-granted viewpoints on human interactions and transactions that underpin literacy and learning. Fransman's exploration of the affordances of the social media application Twitter shows how its materiality determines the way that its users are constructed for research purposes. Such problematizations signal the capacities of digital devices to unpredictably disrupt practice, not only to enable or empower practitioners and learners. As these accounts remind us: issues around new forms of authoring (Gourlay and Oliver, McKenna and Hughes, Lea), new informational forms and social memory (Bayne and Ross, Jones), and new institutional spaces (Gourlay and Oliver, Lea, Fransman, Bayne and Ross) can raise doubts and uncertainties as well as hopes about the benefits of the digital world that the university is being propelled towards.

Against a background of these wider problematics, some of the contributors are concerned more immediately with specific technologies and their relation to the digital practices of their users. Bronwyn Williams, for example, focuses his consideration of the digital on the course management platform Blackboard, as it is used in his own and other American educational institutions. His analysis of the way that power is materialized in the design of 'efficient' and 'convenient' systems is used to make the argument that a critical perspective on the digital is an important goal for learners as well as for researchers and developers. Robin Goodfellow addresses the technologies that are implicated in the 'opening up' of academic publishing and scholarly communication in general. His consideration of the affordances for actual scholarship of print versus online books about 'digital scholarship' raises the question whether the assumed association between the digital and openness is as reliable as we imagine. Carmen Lee explores the social media and messaging systems that her Hong Kong students use to create a social dimension to their university studies. Her discussion of the text-making practices that she and the students develop during this study leads her to suggest that teachers need to bring their own personal digital practices into pedagogy more explicitly, a conclusion that is reinforced by Littlejohn *et al.* in their argument for digital academic literacy. Caroline Haythornthwaite discusses applications that support the creation of online communities, and suggests that the e-learners of the future will learn to 'be' their 'particular definition of a distributed, online learning community'. Chris Jones invokes Säljö's notion of 'social memory' constructed for online communities through the increasing capability of devices to carry out 'analytical, cognitive-like operations that were previously made by people' (Säljö 2010).

Many of the authors take an implicit position on the issue of the digital as textual, although only Bayne and Ross and Goodfellow use the actual term 'textuality' as such, the former to problematize the assessment of hypertextual and visual assignments, the latter to compare and contrast 'print' and 'digital' approaches to academic writing. Digital text-making as a novel form of practice is foregrounded by Gourlay and Oliver and Bayne and Ross, and by Lea in her discussion of students' 'hybrid' texts produced in the course of integrating digital resources into assignments. It is also addressed by McKenna and Hughes in identifying the contradictions inherent in using PDS in an arena dominated by hypertext, and by Lee addressing the creative and bilingual use of short message systems by Chinese students. Several of the chapters raise the issue of multimodality. Jones, for example, discusses the role of multimodality in Gunther Kress' notion of 'reading as design' (Kress 2003, 2010) – a principle further illustrated in Littlejohn et al.'s discussion of digital knowledge practices involving remixing resources, sharing across global sites, and 'crowd-sourcing' solutions to problems. Fransman gives an illustrative description of the way an automatically generated visual diagram of Twitter users and their followers comes to determine which features of the network are salient and which are 'othered' for the purposes of understanding the phenomenon at hand. Bayne and Ross, and Gourlay and Oliver both introduce visual data to illustrate their discussions of their own students' digital practices, which provides an interesting counterpoint to Williams' critique of the lack of affordance of Blackboard for multimodal communication. Martin and MacKenzie, and Satchwell et al. discuss the importance of non-textual artefacts, both digital and actual, in the practice of their professional colleagues and their vocationally oriented students.

Finally, some of the contributors are motivated to interpret the digital in terms of a futuristic 'vision' of some kind, whether of newly empowered learners, or of transformed institutional values and practices. This is perhaps to be expected in the current context of perpetual digital innovation and the uncertain future of conventional boundaries between authors and readers, designers and users, sellers and buyers, teachers and learners, etc. For Caroline Haythornthwaite, the whole question of the digital is elided with the emerging practices of 'e-learners', creating for us a vision of a technologized future in which learning is a constantly reiterated response to the 'perpetual beta' conditions of a digital environment in which tools and procedures are constantly changing, and new practices are constantly emerging. Haythornthwaite shows us quite explicitly where she thinks we have come from and where we are heading, in her comparison of the 'then' and 'now' of e-learning. For her, the digital has gone from being a thing of wonder and some trepidation for the first learners to venture into online discussion forums, to an all-pervasive communicative context, in which 81 per cent of US students preparing for exams check their email and Facebook accounts every hour while they are studying. Ahead lies a world of participatory practices amongst formal and informal learning communities, of open resources and innovative credentialing, of learners who continuously invent and enact the new literacies of their online environments. Martin and MacKenzie, and Littlejohn *et al.* also provide accounts based on envisioning the digital teachers and learners of the future. Martin and MacKenzie, from a pragmatic perspective, offer solutions to a scenario where teachers are required to develop new digital skills and competencies consistent with a burgeoning world of open educational resources (OERs), wherein processes of locating resources and adapting and repurposing them begin to take over from the more traditional activities of researching and writing teaching materials. These perspectives reflect the discourses of transformation that have characterized the penetration of the digital into contemporary institutional practice and the construction of the university 'of the digital age' but McKenna and Hughes have a somewhat more critical take on the goal of the funders of the OER movement to use digital technologies to 'equalize access to knowledge for teachers and students around the globe', questioning the implications of unrestrained reuse and remixing for concepts and values of authorship and ownership. Littlejohn and colleagues also temper their discussion of future digital ways of working and employability, based on the transformation of knowledge work and the dissolution of disciplinary and sectoral boundaries, with a critical view of the 'competence framework' approach to the development of digital skills.

From the more empirical perspective of the digital in the everyday social life of post-compulsory education, all of the contributors to this volume highlight in different ways the mutual shaping of digital technologies and educational practices, and the day-to-day material engagement of educational practitioners and the local negotiation of their practices.

The university

Finally we turn to the nature of the university in a digital age. The chapters in this volume deal with this sense of the university in contrasting ways, which in part reflect the differing intellectual, disciplinary, and practice-based perspectives of their authors. McKenna and Hughes are concerned specifically with values in higher education within the digital domain and, in particular, what this tells us about power, control, and trust as functions of digital writing and publishing. They illustrate this through their explorations of OERs and PDS, arguing that both these aspects of higher education practice raise questions about issues of values and trust. For example, they argue that a core value of higher education, trust between students and teachers, is severely undermined by the use of plagiarism software. Simultaneously, the development of OERs challenges some long-held beliefs about power and control, traditionally held within the bounded university. Goodfellow also pays particular attention to values in his discussion of the nature of digital scholarship and scholarly communication. In making visible the rhetorical practices of scholars he compares digital scholarship and its manifestation in two different contexts. He questions what scholarship might mean in a university with more permeable boundaries and what then counts as scholarship, intellectual enquiry, and academic knowledge. He suggests that the question of digital versus open scholarship may well be the defining dichotomy for the shape of the university of the future. In so doing he raises issues related to McKenna and Hughes' point that dominant values around academic authorship and ownership of knowledge, which have historically underpinned the university, are being reconfigured through practices associated with Twitter and blogging.

Bayne and Ross are also concerned with the unbounded university in an exploration of a web-based open course. Taking a posthuman perspective, they offer a challenge how we think about institutional space and may take for granted the flux and flow of the university. Their interest is in the ongoing tension between the demands of assessment and openness of the work that students are undertaking through participating in their Master's course. Littlejohn, Beetham, and McGill's chapter takes a related stance in looking at changes in knowledge-making practices. It illustrates how the notion of the university is leaking outwards to take account of wider policy agendas – such as employability – on the one hand and, on the other, the proliferation of student engagement in social online networks. Their interest is less with the nature of the university per se and more with how it might sit within wider social and cultural online activity. Gourlay and Oliver throw further light on this as they adopt a socio-material lens when looking at the detailed practices of a group of postgraduate students' engagement in academic, professional, and personal practice. They illustrate how students are engaging with the digital creatively in working around the limitations of institutional provision and in effect are moving their practices outside of the spaces and places bounded by the university. Lee is also concerned with student practice; her interest is in terms of the changing relationship between teachers and students in a more digitally orientated university. As an applied linguist, she reports upon her research in this area but also reflects upon her own experience of using digital technologies in teaching and the concomitant issues of teacher and lecturer identity that this raises. Satchwell, Hamilton, and Barton broaden debates to take account of post-compulsory education. They contrast the perspectives of students in a further education college with those of academic staff in a conventional university. Boundaries and identities are to the fore in their discussion. The chapter contrasts students' demands to bring aspects of their identity – around day-to-day multimodal, digital text-making practices – into their college study with the ways in which academic staff continue to build boundaries to enable them to undertake academic writing work away from the ever-growing institutional demands of their university, many of which are enacted through the digital.

To differing degrees all the accounts signalled above contribute to our understanding of the nature of the university in a digital age, without necessarily explicitly interrogating this in depth. In contrast, Jones puts the digital university centre stage in examining what the term might mean. He makes the case that as yet it does not actually describe any real or existing university. Nevertheless, he argues, the future of the university appears to be dominated by two related phenomena:

first, the construction of young people, students, as digital natives and second, the existence of a strongly deterministic rhetoric which articulates how universities should respond to the experiences and perceived demands of these students in a networked social world. He suggests that such simplistic accounts are unhelpful in our understanding of the digital university. Haythornthwaite points to the ways in which today's e-learners are continually learning to enact their environments and makes the case that universities need to understand and respond to this in supporting their learners to learn how to talk, to be present, and how to retrieve information and to navigate across platforms. At the heart of her chapter is a belief that universities are being transformed by ICTs as the university is increasingly encapsulated in its learning management systems, blended learning, and learning analytics. Williams takes a more explicitly critical perspective to these kinds of developments in his exploration of the ways in which course management software has come to dominate university practice and is indeed called into service as a collaborator in the project of digitizing the university. In this respect, he highlights how technology has been measured in terms of revenue and efficiency, but rarely in relation to pedagogy. In considering the small number of powerful and dominant players in this context, Williams suggests that this rush to put VLEs at the heart of the university has been driven implicitly by ideological imperatives of proficiency, control, and surveillance which he argues are central to the workings of the contemporary university.

Jude Fransman also takes a critical lens but rather than engaging directly with the nature of the university in a digital age her interest is in researching an aspect of this context, namely academics' use of Twitter. She explores what lies behind the choice of particular methodological approaches, arguing that interrogating these can show up hidden ideological agendas that each research approach embeds. The chapter makes a compelling case that we need to keep to the fore the explicit recognition of these different framings when we are researching academic practice in a digital age. Lea also asks questions about researching the university. She suggests that relying on the categories and binaries that literacies researchers have taken for granted may be blinding us to the complexity of practice, which cannot be adequately captured in the individual accounts of students and teachers. She is concerned that the digital circulation of texts enables powerful networks to colonize particular conceptions of practice and use them to promote and serve policy agendas which enact strong versions of the university. She sees this as a consequence of the power of networks to bring things into being in particular ways, which are then hard to challenge. This resonates with Williams' critique of VLEs. She argues, therefore, that a network approach to researching practice may be better at making visible the messiness of the university in a digital age. This potentially chimes with the practice-based scenarios explored by Martin and MacKenzie around the use of OERs and their argument that curriculum design using digital content requires a rethinking of traditional roles and a broad acceptance of new professional partnerships using multi-professional teams, which they believe characterize today's university.

Although the chapters in this collection offer contrasting perspectives from practice, theory, and research, the connections between them are evident. Indeed they often resonate in quite unpredictable ways given the very different concerns and orientations of the authors. The nature of the university in a digital age and the concomitant changes in practice are evidenced in discussions of values, boundaries, the curriculum, social online activity, what counts as academic knowledge, and who controls it. Not only do these signal changing practices and relationships, for example, between students and teachers, academics and other professional groups, learning technologists and library staff but they also raise fundamental questions about literacy and the embedded nature of power.

This volume has attempted to problematize constructively the relationships between digital communication, literacy, learning, and scholarship in post-compulsory education. We see it as the first step in establishing a critical pedagogical research and development agenda that is capable of shaping the 'digital university' as an academic as well as an economic enterprise. We believe that the breadth of contributions in the book make visible the complexity of the relationship between learning and social practice in a digital higher education. Whilst on the one hand many of the chapters expose the inadequacy of skills-based conceptualizations of literacy to support principled pedagogical approaches at tertiary level, others point to the need to take a critical lens to established perspectives on literacy as social practice if we are to adequately account for the textuality of the digital domain and its relationship to learning, teaching, and scholarship in the university of the digital age.

Chapter 1

Values, digital texts, and open practices – a changing scholarly landscape in higher education

Colleen McKenna and Jane Hughes

Introduction

Digital technologies and environments offer many affordances in terms of texts and practices. Texts can be reproduced and distributed. They can be searched for and made searchable, and they can be fragmented, reconstructed, and curated. But what are the implications of this new textual world in terms of authorship, commodification, and intellectual property? What values are brought to bear in this writing, production, and distribution of digital work and how are conventional literacy practices being disrupted?

The role of values in higher education (HE) has a certain currency in the literature on academic practice. Macfarlane (2004) argues that the discourse on academic practice is largely concerned with competencies and skills and generally fails to engage with the 'ethical complexities' of HE teaching. Little in higher education is 'value-neutral' and yet conversations about the ways in which personal and professional values frame or inform practice are infrequent, particularly in relation to e-learning where the metaphor of the computer as 'tool' produces a veneer of objectivity devoid of human agency. (Goodfellow and Lea 2007 offer a compelling critique of this metaphor.) In the field of higher education studies, the exploration of values and ethics in the academy is gradually gaining purchase, with Harland and Pickering (2011) addressing values in HE teaching. However, neither Macfarlane nor Harland and Pickering consider values within the digital domain, nor (with a few notable exceptions, to be discussed below) can the topic be found in much of the literature on e-learning or digital literacy.

In this chapter, we consider *values* – particularly in relation to power, control, and trust – as functions of digital writing and publishing. We discuss different ways in which values are embedded – whether recognizably or not – in practices that have grown up around digital texts. In the first section we consider the conflicting impulses within the HE sector of, on the one hand, the Open Education movement and its commitment to sharing academic resources and opportunities, and, on the other, universities' increasing interest in branding and commodification. In the second section, we explore plagiarism detection software (PDS) and the values implicit in its use. In particular, we consider the way in which practices surrounding PDS construct both the student–teacher relationship and a particular model of student writing predicated on texts as products. Finally, we discuss new forms of authorship resulting from distributed, ephemeral, and multi-voiced texts. Specifically, we ask whether digital authorship subverts conventional print-based literacy practices.

Throughout, we are informed by an academic literacies paradigm, a theoretical framework which views writing as a social practice (Lea and Street 1998). An academic literacies approach enables us to think about issues of power, context, and identity in relation to digital literacy, with an emphasis on practices (Lea and Street 1998; Lillis 2001; Ivanič 1998; Goodfellow and Lea 2007.)

Open Education

Open Education illustrates a values-led approach to educational practice as well as an instance in which tension between old and new models of providing access to higher education might arise. Values underpin this movement, and principles of transparency, shared development, and equality of access inform the open practices that have evolved over the last 20 years. The Open Source movement shares development of software transparently with a community that creates, offers feedback, and engages in further development. The Open Educational Resources (OER) movement (see Martin and Mackenzie in this volume for a discussion of its development) applies similar principles to learning, opening up courses, and releasing learning materials via social networks and institutional, national, or disciplinary repositories. Alongside this, work towards supporting learners, providing credit for study, and embedding open practices in mainstream academic practice is ongoing. There is not yet a clear picture of how resources are being reused: 'Something, but not enough, is known about *who* reuses *what*' and 'Almost nothing is known about *the* h*ow* and *the why* of reuse' (JISC OER Impact Study blog 2011b). Investigating reuse and repurposing (for example, Lane 2012 and Pegler 2012) is an ongoing effort.

These developments have unfolded in an increasingly marketized HE environment (Hemsley-Brown and Oplatka 2006; Molesworth *et al.* 2009) in which universities seek to trade on their brands and there is pressure to commodify courses and materials. These aims may appear incompatible with open educational values such as sharing, benefit of a common good, and widening access, but universities have engaged in open practices in order to promote their brand; by releasing open resources they can showcase teaching by 'star' academics with a view to attracting students. In doing so they give away some, but not all, in the same way that a free software application may require users to pay for more advanced features. The discourse around institutional OER adoption in the UK (for example in the JISC OER InfoKit 2011c) has tended to foreground reputational gains but in the wider Open Education movement values are more visible, as in the OER University's wiki description of itself as 'rooted in the community service and outreach mission' and the Hewlett Foundation's aim to: 'Equalize access to knowledge for teachers and students around the globe through Open Educational Resources' (Hewlett Foundation Values and Policies).

Reputational gains such as increased visibility and more frequent citation of publications are also claimed for individuals (Downes 2007). However, personal and professional values are also being shown to play a role in motivating academics to write and share open texts (see Martin and MacKenzie in this volume). Masterman and Wild (2011) found some evidence of an association between an academic's holding 'open educational' values and being disposed to engage with OER. Interviews with teacher-creators of OERs by Hughes and McKenna (2012) tend to support this position, with interviewees speaking persuasively about the values that inform their practices:

> It [Open Education] just seems a very natural extension of the fact that if through my whole teaching career if anybody had wanted to use my handbook or teaching materials or anything, they'd ask me and I'd always say 'yes'.

This interviewee felt that OER authoring and publishing enabled her to participate in an education 'movement' whose values she already embraced. The digital dimension of Open Education meant, however, that her texts could be shared much more widely and they were formally 'attributed' to her, so what had been a part of her 'everyday practice' (after Lea and Stierer's 'everyday writing', of which more below) was now formally recognized. Another interviewee in this study suggested that participating in Open Education had a transformative effect upon her practice and allowed her to articulate values, particularly within a professional context in which there were competing values in operation. For example, she spoke of using Creative Commons (CC) licences to signal publicly her values: 'I have a colleague who always puts a copyright notice on every slide, so I've started putting the CC logo on my slides. It has had an impact on me' (Hughes and McKenna 2012). So, early research into Open Education is suggesting that it offers colleagues an opportunity to realize and/or publicly enact their values.

Moving beyond these examples, to look at academic practice as a whole, a concept particularly relevant to the creation of digital texts is that of the 'open scholar', who is according to Weller (2012c: 3) 'almost synonymous with the "digital scholar" so closely aligned are the new technologies and open approaches'. (Conceptions of digital scholarship are examined elsewhere in this volume by Goodfellow and by Jones.) Weller, as Goodfellow (this volume) indicates, fits the 'open scholar' profile he sketches. He contrasts 'open' with 'traditional' scholars, describing the latter as 'exclusive', available only to students registered on specific academic programmes, publishing via access-controlled print media. 'Open' scholars, on the other hand, will create open resources and share outputs, do open research and comment openly on other people's outputs, build and contribute to a network, evaluate and adopt new technologies for professional use, and support open learning. Formal publications will be in open access journals but the open scholar will also produce a variety of informal publications such as podcasts, tweets, and blog posts, often engaging the audience by mixing the personal and professional in these texts. Weller does not claim that digital scholarship has replaced traditional academic practice. However, he presents a convincing picture of diversifying practices that might be considered in relation to the Open Education literacies framework proposed by Martin and MacKenzie in this volume. One might also ask how – or whether – these changes are reflected in the disciplinary practices to which students are exposed.

This leads to a consideration of authorship, which is explored more fully in section 4. Developing open resources involves negotiations around the rights of the creator; a CC licence asserts rights as well as granting them. The inclusion of 'attribution' – acknowledging the author or creator – in all CC licences implies that this is a fundamental value. However, as already stated, our knowledge about reuse and repurposing of open educational resources is still limited. The vision of an OER community in which a text will repeatedly be reused, changed, and shared again raises questions about who the author is and perhaps also about other kinds of creativity that might need to be acknowledged. For how long in the lifetime of a resource will the notion of an original author be meaningful? Do we perhaps need to acknowledge the kind of creativity that Weller points to, that of someone who makes no changes to a text but finds a new context for its use? Again, how does reuse and remixing relate to students' textual practices and to the academic values they are asked to embrace at university?

The aspects of being digital that support open educational practices may also be the ones that increase concerns about student plagiarism: digital material that can be found easily via a search engine and downloaded. In both cases, too, the provisional nature of digital texts is important: they are easy to change, copy, dismantle, and reassemble. In relation to both Open Education and plagiarism, the value issues are around authorship and particularly attribution – the rights of the author and what the finder feels able to do with the found material. As we have suggested here, the Open Education movement makes explicit the values embodied in its practices; however, in the use of electronic plagiarism prevention/detection systems values are less explicitly articulated, as we explore in the next section.

Plagiarism: systems and practices

Probably nothing conjoins technology, texts, processes, and values more sharply and contentiously than the use of plagiarism 'detection' software (PDS). In this section we will consider several studies that have explored the *practices* that are evolving in conjunction with plagiarism detection systems as well as the *implications* of the routine scanning of student texts for evidence of copying. These implications include:

- potential changes in the relationship between student and teacher, especially in terms of academic trust;
- the increased sense of writing as a product;
- the reframing of the understanding of plagiarism from the student perspective; and
- a view of writing which demonstrates little awareness of texts that are multimodal, hypertextual, or dialogic.

Conversations about plagiarism are fraught even without the presence of technology. Discussions on the topic tend to be characterized by accounts of fraud, transgression, control, immorality, and dishonesty, with rather less attention paid to the writing practices of novices including those writing in new languages, educational contexts, and subjects (Zwagerman 2008; Hayes and Introna 2005). Furthermore, discourses on plagiarism often fail to acknowledge the complex nature of student writing development and the ways in which disciplinary, linguistic, and national contexts can play a role in perceived plagiarism (Gourlay and Deane 2012; Hayes and Introna 2005). Rather the nuances tend to be elided and the more simplistic equation of 'plagiarism = cheating' obtains, often with little recourse to the complexities of entering a textual conversation with other scholars.

Of course, these issues are magnified when PDS becomes an integral part of writing and assessment practices in universities. Arguably, a range of values features in decisions and assumptions surrounding the use of such technologies, yet these often remain unarticulated. However, evidence is emerging that the introduction of technology into the process would seem to lessen the awareness of the complexities around writing and plagiarism, reducing an understanding of plagiarism to the technical act of copying text (Introna and Hayes 2011; Lea and Jones 2011).

One value that is foregrounded by the use of PDS is that of trust between teacher and student and between institution and student. Academic literacies research has shown that student writers operate in a nexus of regulation and power held by tutors, institutions, and disciplines (Lillis 2001; Lea and Street 1998; Ivanič 1998). The practices growing up with the introduction of PDS into the assessment process are likely to intensify these power differentials as Zwagerman suggests, with trust and dialogue between students and teachers one of the early casualties:

> . . . plagiarism detection treats writing as a product, grounds the student–teacher relationship in mistrust, and requires students to actively comply with a system that marks them as untrustworthy . . . Surveillance technology . . . reinforces rather than interrogates social roles and power differentials, as if they are natural and immune to scrutiny.
>
> (Zwagerman 2008: 691–2)

Zwagerman's extended critique of PDS is strenuous and compelling. In the extract above he labels such software 'surveillance technology' and elsewhere he draws on Foucault and a broader discourse of surveillance, to demonstrate how such technologies and practices construct the reader/writer or student/teacher or even student/institution relationships in terms of control, power, and distrust. As other observers have noted, requiring students to submit coursework to a third party for detection of plagiarism before a copy even goes to their assessor undermines any sense that students are to be trusted as writers and valued members of the academy. However, our broader point is that issues of trust, control, and surveillance are at best implicit in the practice of plagiarism 'detection'. Our experience is that these values are not discussed or even acknowledged but that rather the introduction of technology lends an air of objectivity and neutrality to proceedings – such that, a process by which departments, faculties, and institutions require all students to submit all assessed coursework through a detection system is increasingly and unquestioningly seen to be part of the practice of assessment, with little or no debate about what values are being communicated to students and indeed teachers

Additionally, it appears that this integration of PDS into the assessment process reframes the concept of plagiarism for students (Lea and Jones 2011; Introna and Hayes 2011). Students in Lea and Jones' study not only had a diminished sense of plagiarism as being solely about copying text (rather than a failure to attribute ideas), they also saw it as a quantifiable act; they believed that they were 'allowed' a certain amount of plagiarism. In the example below, two students (at a prestigious university) discuss plagiarism with a researcher:

> Don: What is the extent to which we're allowed to plagiarise, 17% or something?
>
> Mark: No, it's just like 20%, but I mean that's all with just the bibliography or literally a couple of words which they highlight and you just ignore that, but obviously if you've got a paragraph then . . .
>
> (Lea and Jones 2011)

As Lea and Jones go on to discuss, these students view plagiarism as largely about copying text. The use of the word 'allowable' suggests an ignorance of the definition of plagiarism: they 'show no broader understanding of why one might want to avoid plagiarism . . . or any wish to explicitly acknowledge whose ideas and words one is drawing upon. For them, plagiarism has been reduced to a technical issue of percentages of reproduced text.' (Lea and Jones 2011: 389) This flattening of the understanding of plagiarism means that even the most basic ideas of writing within a community of scholars and acknowledging their contributions seem not to have been grasped.

It would seem from this exchange that the introduction of technology into the process has led to an abdication of responsibility on the part of both the student and the teacher. The technology, by default, becomes a sort of arbiter of what is allowed and the whole practice becomes understood as being about percentage of copying rather than one of attribution of ideas. How can we expect students to enter into disciplinary conversations if they fail to understand the basic rules of such engagement? Yet, as Zwagerman and others have suggested, the practices that are developing around these technologies are at risk of normalizing this diminished understanding of plagiarism.

Another of Zwagerman's observations that is worth further examination is his objection to the product-oriented construction of academic writing. In the above example, essays are recast as digital artefacts to be uploaded to a plagiarism detection system (the arbiter) for scrutiny. So, processes and drafts become subjugated to technology and product in this approach. This shift is also value-laden – with writing viewed as a commodity to be judged. For years, teachers of academic writing have tried to effect a move to valuing process-oriented writing, and have viewed the emphasis on drafting as a way of discouraging plagiarism. The privileging of drafting also makes space for peer and self-review, which again would seem to be negated by an overreliance on digital detection practices.

Finally and of particular relevance for this book, one can argue, as Kress 2010 has, that these systems are premised upon an outmoded print literacy paradigm, which fails to acknowledge the potential of and increasing enthusiasm for academic digital texts. (See also Williams' observations about the conservative, print literacy assumptions on which the Blackboard virtual learning environment (VLE) is based.) PDS is predicated on text matching and cannot, for example, evaluate images, animation, colour, or other modes of meaning-making. Indeed, potentially, the growing popularity and internalizing of these detection practices might inhibit the use of multimodal forms in academic scholarship at the very moment such new genres have become possible. Web-based, multimodal, interactive texts are much less easily 'uploaded' for 'originality' checking.

Plagiarism is a vexed and complex concept even before we bring technologies into the frame. However, the introduction of technology constructs literacy practices in particular ways, such as, in an example discussed here, foregrounding the copying of words. We should ask, what conversations are therefore not being had and what is the potential loss, to build on Gourlay and Deane's theme, to university students' understanding of entering a disciplinary conversation and to the relationship between student and teacher, in terms of trust, seemingly a core value of higher education. We should also be mindful of Zwagerman's warning that 'the better this technology works, the more likely it is to become natural, invisible, and permanent' (Zwagerman 2008: 692). In this rapidly changing digital arena, it is important to locate, name, and scrutinize literacy processes and actions before they become naturalized, fixed, and invisible, lost in a network of technology and regulation.

Authorship and digital texts

While PDS is designed to pin down, fix, and identify copying as transgressive, the textual practices in operation in spaces beyond the formal academy boundaries are increasingly characterized by sharing, co-creating, and reproducing (for example, through retweeting) ideas (albeit with attribution). Building on the above discussion of open scholarship, this section will address the reconfiguring of authorship in online spaces and potential implications for the ways in which the sector values these texts which are 'academic' yet unstable, fragmented, and multi-authored.

Digital texts, environments, and practices

Social networking spaces (e.g. Twitter, Wordpress, Flickr) are giving rise to alternative ways of articulating and responding to academic knowledge. The resultant texts tend to be open, intertextual, and reliant upon audience engagement. Indeed, in certain environments, such as Twitter, 'texts' are co-constructed to the extent that they resemble loosely structured, digital conversations with actors entering and exiting the discussion at various points. The exchanges are ephemeral yet semi-permanent, leaving a searchable digital footprint that defies erasure. They are also multimodal and hypertextual. Significantly most of these networking spaces exist outside the university jurisdiction and thus, staff and students are interacting in digital environments that the university cannot regulate (Weller 2012c).

Taking blogging and tweeting as examples, we might ask 'to what extent is this writing academic'? As suggested above, there are similarities here with what Lea and Stierer (2009) have termed 'everyday writing' – texts that are part of professional practice, yet often go unmarked. As Lea and Stierer observe, these 'everyday writing' texts do not merely 'index' academic activities, 'they are central to them' (Lea and Stierer: 426), and we believe that the same holds true for many academics in relation to this type of digital writing. Furthermore, we suggest that the digital texts described here should not only be valued as part of the 'identity work' (Lea and Stierer; Ivanič 1998) of scholars, but their contribution to research should be acknowledged, particularly in terms of the impact of digital texts upon a scholar's profile, public engagement, and on the discipline itself. As Weller (2011) suggests, higher education is in a transition phase in relation to digital scholarship, but increasingly, academics see blogging and tweeting (and similar practices) as a core part of academic discourse. For example, Thoma (2011) argues that blogging is changing the way that economics is practised. Published research on the impact of blogging/microblogging upon academic scholars is sparse, but recent studies suggest tentatively that it has a positive effect on both the dissemination of research and influence on policy (Ross *et al.*, 2011; McKenzie and Ozler 2011; Terras 2012). A useful indicator, perhaps, of the changing status of online discourse (and its perceived academic value) is that the

Modern Language Association (MLA) recently issued guidance about how to cite tweets in printed texts (MLA n.d.).

Alternative models of authorship and scholarship

Of course, academic scholarship is closely aligned to print literacy especially in terms of format, distribution, and authorship (McKenna 2012a, 2012b; Bayne 2010; Goodfellow and Lea 2007; Kress 2010) and the culture of print literacy privileges certain models and values, as Williams suggests elsewhere in this collection in his analysis of Blackboard. Exploring the concept of an 'uncanny digital pedagogy', Bayne (2010) argues that digital text-making defamiliarizes print-based writing practices, particularly with respect to authorial identity: 'the digital text, in its many forms, is volatile where print is stable, fragmented where print is bound, distributable where print is fixed, *and often doubtful in its mode of authorship, in contrast to the tight association of author and text within the print mode* (Poster 2001; Bayne 2006 cited in Bayne, 2010)' (emphasis added). As Bayne suggests, the conventional notion of authorship is being disrupted and undermined as new forms of textual collaboration and co-creation emerge. In part, this is due to the nature of digital texts which tend to be more fluid and open than printed items, as we suggest above. Additionally, these textual formats and practices encourage collaboration and dialogue, and even online texts that begin life as single author works, such as blogs, invite reader contributions and links to other writing. Indeed, even the categories of 'reader' and 'writer' are blurred in these environments: readers quickly become authors (of blog comments, tweets and retweets, and wiki editing, for example) and vice versa. The literacy practices emerging in these sites involve much joint writing and rewriting of texts, but often in a model of collaborative writing that bears little resemblance to print-based processes. As Kress (2010) argues, when considering multimodality, contemporary communication, and Wikipedia, 'authorship' is 'in urgent need of theorizing'.

   This instability of digital texts and changes to textual production and distribution challenge our notions of authorship and help construct new scholarly alignments and communities. However, what might they mean for writers, particularly those who are judged by their 'output' according to a print literacy paradigm? This paradox was recently articulated by Weller in an article for *The Chronicle of Higher Education* in which he observes that since he began blogging he has published less in academic journals and that this is perceived to be a 'negative impact'. Yet, blogging has had an immensely positive impact on his own sense of scholarship and peer recognition: 'However, it has led to so many other unpredictable benefits—such as the establishment of a global peer network that helps me stay up to date with my topic, increased research collaboration, and more invitations to give talks—that it's been worth the trade-off' (Weller 2012d). One might well ask why a shift in the balance of writing towards digital publication (particularly with its large and diverse readership) has to be framed as a trade-off at all.

Sitting outside current modes of regulation and control

This discussion of authorship as a function of digital, dialogic texts speaks to our other themes of Open Education and the technologizing of plagiarism. In terms of the former, the scholarly practices growing up around social networking accord with the openness movement in terms of establishing community, sharing ideas, and co-authoring/reauthoring texts. In terms of the latter theme, the sheer openness of these spaces (in that anyone can view others' unprotected tweets and blogs) subverts the monitoring and surveillance culture that PDS represents and a monitoring culture is increasingly part of many academics' professional experiences.

The concept of control can also be interrogated with reference to authorship and readership. For example, universities tend to assess academic performance in ways that assume a fixed, regularized authorial identity to which certain types of countable, closed texts can be assigned for purposes of quality assurance and funding mechanisms (such as the UK Research Excellence Framework). Such processes are almost wholly based on print literacy models and fail to recognize and accommodate the potential of online identities and digital discourse, as a number of academic bloggers and commentators have observed.

Furthermore, reader access for such academic work has traditionally been controlled by publishers – although the Open Access movement is starting to reverse this trend. For example, Harvard University has recently publicly challenged the traditional model of journal publishing and has encouraged its academics to publish in open access journals, rather than those which operate paywalls (Sample 2012b). Furthermore, from 2013, it will be the UK Research Councils' policy that publicly funded scientific research will be made openly available (Sample 2012a). Nonetheless, generally speaking, formal writing and publishing practices for academics are heavily regulated – by both universities and academic publishers – in terms of access and genre. So one could also interpret the popularity of these dialogic, social networking spaces and textual practices discussed above as a reaction against the limited, prescribed, and bounded opportunities for academic expression. (See, for example, Weller 2011, who argues that freedom of expression is one of the chief appeals of blogging and microblogging. See also, Lievrouw 2010, who explores the rise of 'little science' communities – which sit outside the boundaries of more formal, institutionalized 'Big Science' – through social networking.)

The largely unregulated digital spaces and practices discussed above are characterized by textual variety and disruption. Frequently a Twitter feed can resemble Bakhtin's noisy, anarchic carnival – with its heteroglossic mix of modes, tones, and genres, not to mention subversive humour and even anger. Lievrouw (2010), considering scientific blogging and microblogging, has suggested that such writing has a provisional and at times epistolary quality that she associates with the type of conversational, personal writing that characterized early scientific journals. Frequently with blogging and tweeting, the personal and the sociopolitical merge with the professional in a manner not often seen in sites of formal academic discourse. In this way, such writing offers a challenge to more dominant, conventional modes of academic writing. If we consider Lillis' 2003 extended academic literacies framework, these digital texts and practices undoubtedly feature at the 'oppositional' end of her typology: they challenge and make visible (through their difference) dominant discourse practices (Lillis 2003). Although this theoretical framework is concerned with student writing, we feel it has applications to academics' writing and the values implicit and explicit in the making and reception of such work.

Conclusion and implications

There are a number of implications for practice that grow out of the work described here.

In terms of writing and identity, one implication is the need to develop new ways of acknowledging authorship that take into account the shared creation of texts over time. This changing concept of authorship is relevant to both academics and students and will inform ideas about writing texts for Open Education, assessment, and publication. Open Education complicates authorship for an individual but also has a complex relationship with the 'bounded' university. As Open Education and Open Access movements develop, it will be interesting to see how tensions between openness and ownership (from the perspectives of individual scholars, universities, publishers, and the broader community) are managed.

Additionally, universities will need to develop mechanisms by which they can recognize and value digital contributions that are more fragmented and less fixed than print-based texts. Questions that might be explored in relation to this would include how can multi-authored textual spaces, such as blogs, or Twitter feeds be credited? How can the academic identities and reputations that emerge through such work be valued by an institution? And, building on the Open Access and Open Education movements, how can a culture of sharing and community be fostered in HE?

Many of these questions hold true for student texts too and here we need to think what values we want to embrace in relation to student writers. One of the implications of the literature on PDS on which we have drawn is that a more nuanced approach to plagiarism and associated practices is needed. In particular, academics and managers must realize that the use of technology may result in students having a reductive view of plagiarism as being merely the verbatim copying of text (Introna and Hayes 2011; Lea and Jones 2011). Additionally, the signals about trust in student writers communicated by the blanket use of PDS should be considered. Do we really want to imply that students are cheating until proven otherwise?

Finally, in this fast-changing arena of digital literacy, much more research is needed into the writing practices of professional academics. While some research is being done into the academic writing of students in digital domains, the practices of academics remain under-researched. This is a particularly pressing need, given how much depends on the ways in which an academic's written 'output' is valued by institutions, publishers, and disciplines. The rise of digital scholarship in its many forms is challenging our existing models of what it is to be a student, an academic, and even an institution. In particular, as we have suggested here, many of the assumptions and practices that are based on print literacy paradigms are being undermined. It is, therefore, an important moment to articulate, celebrate, and critique the values that underpin these new digital practices.

Chapter 2

Researching academic literacy practices around Twitter

Performative methods and their onto-ethical implications

Jude Fransman

Introduction

Though undoubtedly a contentious concept, the notion of 'digital literacy' has gained currency in recent years. Intrinsically linked to research within the fields of library and information studies (e.g. Borgman 2007); educational technology (e.g. Pearce *et al.* 2010; Weller 2011); academic literacies (McKenna 2006; Lea 2007; Goodfellow 2011; Lea and Jones 2011); and the emerging field of 'digital humanities' (Schreibman *et al.* 2004; Unsworth 2000). This recent proliferation of academic studies into the design and use of digital technologies and texts has focused both on general practices spanning the use of multiple digital resources and on practices specific to particular digital resources, such as the microblogging platform Twitter. In the context of higher education, research into Twitter practices has focused on user identities and the micro-dynamics of use (e.g. Reed 2005; boyd *et al.* 2010; Marwick and boyd 2011); use of the resource for teaching and learning (e.g. Fernandez-Villavicencio 2010; Rinaldo *et al.* 2011; Junco *et al.* 2011; Kassens-Noor 2012); and use of the resource in domains such as libraries and lecture halls (e.g. Cuddy 2009; Elavsky 2011; Tyma 2011).

It is important to note that this proliferation of academic studies on the use of Twitter in universities occurs against the backdrop of a similar proliferation of commercial research tools available for personal use online. Such tools draw on methods such as psycho-social personality profiling (to describe and classify users); textual analysis (to quantify frequently used terms and topics); and network analysis (to describe relationships between users focusing on variables such as the size of a network and relative influence of individuals within a network). While these commercial tools may not carry the same authority as academic methods, they nevertheless generate significant data that is often subsequently 'mined' by academics. The methods they use are also sometimes reproduced in academic studies by academics familiar with the tools. The most popular tools such as 'Klout' (which measures Twitter users' 'online influence') play an arguably *performative* role (Barad 2003) by influencing as well as reflecting behaviour. For example, a Twitter user aware of their 'Klout score' in relation to their peers' may modify their behaviour in an attempt to improve their score by increasing indicators such as their numbers of 'followers', 'mentions', and 'retweets'.

This performative potential of both commercial tools such as Klout and tools for academic data collection (ranging from scientific instruments to social surveys) has been well documented (e.g. Callon 1998; Barad 2003; Law 2004; Latour 2005; Burawoy 2005). John Law, whose recent work has focused on the performativity of method in the social sciences, argues that research methods should be understood as living a 'double social life' (2010). First, they are shaped by the social: they have purposes, sponsors, and they draw upon or are adaptations of existing methodological, cultural, and/or social resources. This is important when considering the impact of the commercial context (the ownership and accessibility of data and the way it is framed by digital resources) on the development of academic research (see Williams, this volume). But second, methods also shape or *enact* the social. As well as reflecting or making discoveries about social reality, methods also make more or less self-fulfilling assumptions about the nature of the social world and in so doing tend to shape it by producing what Law (2009a) refers to as 'collateral realities'.

Returning to the example of the commercial Twitter analysis tool 'Klout', collateral realities might include assumptions about the 'influence' of individuals in relation to a broader network. Indicators for influence include: 'number of tweets' signifying level of activity; 'number of followers' signifying popularity; 'number of mentions' signifying active engagement with followers; and 'number of retweets' signifying impact. While such indicators may be appropriate proxies for influence, it is important to bear in mind what they exclude as well as include. For example, a user who invests considerable time in reading colleagues' tweets but does not write her own would not be considered – at least by Klout – as an active Twitter user.

In order to explain such mechanics of inclusion/exclusion in a research tool, Law expands Deleuze and Guattari's notion of the 'assemblage' (1987) into the concept of 'method assemblage' in which certain elements are included and certain elements excluded or 'Othered' (Law 2004: 55). A composite Klout score for influence will make manifest *writing* practices but not *reading* practices. It will also only reflect interactions occurring within the medium of Twitter. For instance, if a user decides to respond to a follower's tweet through an alternative channel such as an email, text, or face-to-face conversation, this activity will be Othered. Another assumption is that users are autonomous individuals rather than relational social actors. Tweets which are the product of collaborative interaction (e.g. postings from a project) are recorded as the activity of the account from which they originate. In this way, both non-tweeting participants and the social context of the tweet are also Othered by the Klout score.

In questioning why certain things are Othered, Law (2004: 117–120) suggests that Otherness tends to take three key forms. First, what is 'routine' might be Othered. For example, indicators such as 'number of characters in a tweet' are excluded on the assumption that the length of most tweets will be close to the 140 character limit. Second, what is 'insignificant' may also be Othered. For example, though data is available about the device on which a tweet has been composed (e.g. smartphone, tablet, or computer), this is not deemed significant to an assessment of influence and is therefore excluded from the score. Third, Othering can also serve to 'repress' certain things which might risk compromising existing phenomena. For example, an indicator which measures the level of heterogeneity in a user's network (in terms of nationalities, languages, ages, genders, etc.) may risk undermining the authority of the primary indicator for influence: 'number of followers' and must therefore also be excluded. To Law's three forms of Otherness, I have also proposed the addition of a fourth (see Fransman 2012): Things are excluded simply because they don't 'fit' with the (social or material) form of the text, artefact, or device that accommodates them. Or conversely, things are included – in part – because of the ease with which they can be transported or *recontextualized* from one text, artefact, or device to another. So, for example, the quantitative indicators which make up the Klout score for influence (numbers of 'tweets', 'followers', 'mentions', 'retweets', etc.) are clearly better suited to the purpose of summarizing large bodies of comparable, standardized data than qualitative indicators would be. They are also easily transportable across at least three artefactual domains: Twitter itself, which quantifies some of the indicators automatically and records the others chronologically; Klout as an intermediary tool, which recontextualizes some of the data and interprets the rest; and other commercial, personal, or academic tools which recontextualize the Klout score either as a representation of a single user (on a personal blog, for example) or as a composite indicator for 'influence' to be used in broader data analysis processes (in a statistical analysis package, for example). So the necessary Othering of aspects of Twitter use (such as reading rather than writing tweets or responding to tweets through an alternative medium to Twitter) is partly to do with the material *affordances* (van Leeuwen 2005) of the tools which frame the data collection. Since Twitter can't capture the act of reading a text and has no access to interactions which extend beyond the boundaries of the platform, these aspects must be excluded. This of course has implications both for the validity of the data generated through these tools and for the ontological effects of these tools or the 'collateral realities' they enact.

As shown through the examples above, perhaps the most fundamental 'collateral reality' produced by Klout is the notion of the Twitter user as an autonomous (and standardized) individual rather than as a socially relational actor. Such a conception is not surprising. Klout is a commercial service and draws on the principle of competition to entice users into comparing themselves to others in their network. This ideological principle (which enables the quantification and subsequent ranking of 'followers', 'friends', 'contacts', etc. across a whole host of social networking sites) also exists in Twitter and the quantitative artefacts it generates are therefore easily transportable across the two resources.

Both commercial analysis tools and academic research tools maintain that their purpose is to reflect rather than affect reality. However, as shown through the assumptions, affordances, and agendas of Klout, any method reproduces existing realities and may also generate new ones. And since any act of making presences also involves making absences (Derrida 1982) some realities are undermined just as others are enacted. In this way any method 'unavoidably produces not only truths and non-truths, realities and non-realities, presences and absences, but also arrangements with political implications' (Law 2004: 143). Such claims release the floodgates of an ethics of social enquiry and as Donna Haraway (1997) reminds us, *there is no innocence* in the work of a researcher. The question of what might be brought into being in the relations of research and, indeed, what *should* be brought into being constitutes 'ontological politics' (Mol 1999; Law 2004).

In the following section, I draw on data collected through a recent academic study on the use of Twitter by academics at a British university to explore how the ontological politics inherent within three very different methods gave rise to different findings and different enactments of 'the digital'.

Academics' use of Twitter at a British university

In 2011 the Open University (OU) launched an internally funded study into the use of digital technologies by academics for the purpose of research and teaching. Guided by the Institute of Educational Technology, the dual aims of the research programme were first, to develop a digital tool for measuring the 'digital footprint' of individual academics (in order to prompt personal reflection on use of digital resources and as a result promote greater use of resources) and second, to use the data generated by the tool to better understand the digital practices of academics across the university (why certain resources were or weren't being used and how they were being used in different disciplines). To pilot the study the decision was made to focus on Twitter. This would enable in-depth insight into the specific use of one resource as well as an understanding of how Twitter use linked to the use of other digital resources.

The aims of the digital footprint tool were not dissimilar to those of the commercial Twitter analysis tool Klout; that is, to identify the digital influence of academics using Twitter (and later across platforms including Facebook, YouTube, Slideshare and Academia.edu). In this way, indicators such as number of 'followers', 'tweets', 'retweets', etc. provided key measures of the size of an academic's digital footprint in a similar way to the Klout score for influence. Though the nature of Klout (as a commercial tool) differs significantly from the OU's digital footprint tool (as a tool for academic learning and career development), the two resources nevertheless shared an interest in 'influence'. In Klout, this is consistent with the broader commercial agenda of enhancing use by promoting competition between individual users, while at the OU this was consistent with the broader institutional agenda of demonstrating academic impact (and measuring the value of individual academics according to impact indicators set out by the Research Excellence Framework). Consequently, the types of indicators employed by both tools were remarkably similar.

The second aim of the OU research programme (to better understand the digital practices of academics across the university – and specifically, the Twitter practices of academics in the pilot) was originally designed to draw on the data collected through the digital footprint tool. A methodology based on metric analysis was developed to establish the nature of the Twitter networks of OU academics as well as the extent to which individual academics used Twitter and the nature of their use. However, due to delays in the development of the tool as well as challenges in obtaining private data from individuals and the inability of the tool to account for reasons why Twitter *wasn't* being used, a decision was taken to broaden out the research methodology in order to capture data on the use (and non-use) of Twitter by academics across the university. To this end, a survey was developed and administered to academics in the Sciences and Arts/Humanities faculties and an ethnographic case study was undertaken to explore digital practices in a digital humanities project.

In the following sections I draw on Law's (2004) framework outlined in the previous section to unpack the method assemblages inherent within the three approaches, highlighting what is made present or Othered by each.

Metric analysis

In the first approach, an interactive visualization tool (lDSVis) was developed to generate data on Twitter use across the university and to allow academics to explore their own usage as well as that of their colleagues. The tool accessed and displayed data in four different panels: a chart ranking users based on statistics about their use of Twitter as well as a selection of other digital platforms, a graph showing the number of tweets over time, pie charts showing the most used phrases and most mentioned users for each individual user, and a list of all tweets, ordered from the most to the least 'retweeted' (see Figure 2.1).

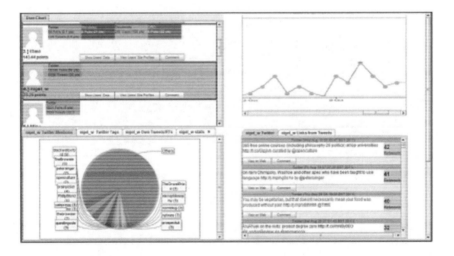

Figure 2.1 Visualization of individual Twitter use by academics at the OU

Network diagrams were then created to visualize the links between academics, illustrating the relationship between Twitter users and their followers. The data was displayed such that the size of an academic's name represented the total number of tweets they had made, and the size of a circle on their name represented the total number of followers they had. Positioning in the diagram was also significant, with proximity between users demonstrating academics with similar networks and centrality demonstrating a broad range of connections across diverse groups within the university (see Figure 2.2).

The data generated through lDSVis resulted in a number of key findings: first, that certain individuals act as 'hubs', connecting and mediating others; second, that influence in a network is based on a large number of tweets, followers, mentions, and retweets; and third, that influential users tend to make greater use of a range of digital resources (beyond Twitter). The primary conclusion emerging from these findings was therefore that developing a strong 'digital footprint' will enhance an individual's influence in academic networks: a conclusion consistent with the institutional agenda that fuelled the study.

Embedded in these findings (and the data collection and representation that informs them) are a number of assumptions that might be presented as manifest presences and Otherings. The most explicit of these is the Othering of non-Twitter-using academics who are considered, according to Law's typology, as 'insignificant' to the issue of academic Twitter practices and are consequently excluded from the visualizations. Another expression of significance is the manifestation

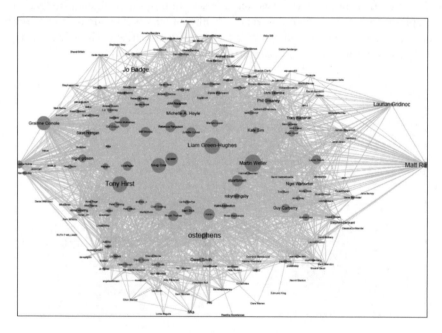

Figure 2.2 Network diagram of Twitter use amongst academics at the OU

of 'tweets over time' (represented in the graph in Figure 2.1) and simultaneous Othering of 'tweets across space', which could easily have been represented by a map – a common feature in other examples of user analytics – but this was not deemed relevant to the analysis of influence. Elements are also Othered in order to repress what may undermine the present indicators. For example, a key indicator of individual influence is the 'total number of followers' (represented in Figure 2.2 by the size of the individual's name). However, the total number of academics that an individual follows is excluded from the data, implying that influence is unidirectional. This Othering of 'number of academics followed' (as opposed to 'number of academic followers') is also determined by the material affordances of the representational tool. In order to appear uncluttered, the visualization in Figure 2.2 includes just two measures of influence (numbers of followers and tweets) represented by size (of *written* name and *graphic* circle). The visualization in Figure 2.1 also includes a measure based on 'number of retweets' which is expressed more implicitly through the ordering of the users' tweets in the bottom right-hand corner of the screen. Finally, the focus on the number of tweets *written* as opposed to the number of tweets *read* is also linked to the material affordances of the data collection and visualization tools in their inability to capture the act of reading tweets.

Survey

In order to sample a more representative population of academics and explore in more depth the nature of Twitter use by academics, a survey was developed with a follow-up focus group to probe deeper into responses. Generating both quantitative and qualitative data, the survey and focus group questions concentrated on the following issues:

- Numbers and proportions of academics using Twitter
- Reasons for joining Twitter
- Reasons for sustained use/non-use of Twitter
- Perceived functions of Twitter
- Perceived skills required to use Twitter
- Links between Twitter use and the use of other digital resources

The survey was administered to academics in the Arts and Humanities faculty and the Sciences faculty at the OU. Once the data had been processed and analysed a focus group was organized with respondents to the survey. The focus group consisted of a physical group discussion and a simultaneous virtual discussion structured around the same questions and visible to the physical participants on a central screen.

While the survey generated some substantial data, the primary finding was that very few respondents (just 29 per cent) claimed they used Twitter (see Figure 2.3). This was due to reasons ranging from perceptions about the social and material affordances of Twitter (for example, that it was a social rather than professional tool and that the 140 character limit was an inadequate vehicle for scholarly work); to perceptions about the skills and resources required to use Twitter (including technological proficiency and access to an iPhone); personal preferences (around privacy, for example); and established use of other resources to serve similar functions (including social and academic networking platforms). The respondents who did use Twitter tended to utilize other digital resources to a greater extent than the non-Twitter users and also tended to have more colleagues using Twitter. Again, the conclusions emerging from these findings were broadly in line with the institutional agenda behind the research: that Twitter use was positively linked to strong 'digital scholarship' practices and better networking across the university and that non-use was largely due to ignorance about the nature of the resource and lack of confidence about proficiency in using the resource. The development of training programmes to address these issues was recommended.

As with the metric analysis approach discussed above, the survey tool also generated presences and Otherings through its assumptions. The most notable of these was that academics were defined first by their use of Twitter (either as 'users' or 'non-users') and second by their discipline (either as Arts and Humanities scholars or Science scholars). Both dichotomies served to Other identities that fell between or beyond these categories. Examples of these included academics without their own Twitter accounts who occasionally read other people's tweets, and academics who might belong to a particular faculty but consider their academic identity to be, for instance, interdisciplinary. In both cases, the material affordances of the survey tool reinforced such types of Othering. Respondents were forced to describe themselves as either users or non-users of Twitter and were

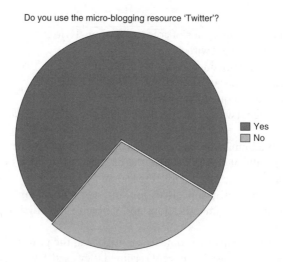

Do you use the micro-blogging resource 'Twitter'?

■ Yes
□ No

Figure 2.3 Who uses Twitter at the OU?

redirected to specific follow-up questions based on their selection. The variables of 'Twitter use' and 'discipline' were also employed for the purpose of analysis and in order to select participants for the focus group discussion. These two primary variables (as aggregates of the individual respondents and focus group participants) also concealed another type of Othering. As with the metric analysis, Twitter use was portrayed as an individual (as opposed to social) practice. Though the focus group generated qualitative anecdotes about experiences with Twitter in the social context of the faculty, university, and beyond, these were used primarily to illustrate the quantitative findings. Once again, the material affordances of the data collection tool (designed through the software 'SurveyMonkey') and the modes of data representation (as charts and graphs which might be easily recontextualized in publications and presentations) contributed to such Othering. Finally, the primary function of the survey approach – to generate a snap-shot of a cross-section of a particular population at a particular point in time – served to Other any changes in Twitter use by individuals over time or indeed any changes in the social-material affordances of Twitter as a device over time.

Ethnographic case study

To provide insight into the use of Twitter by a particular research community in the university, a qualitative case study was conducted of a project based within the faculty of Arts and Humanities. The aims of the 'Pelagios project' were to introduce linked open data into online resources that refer to places in the Ancient World. Over a three-month period, ethnographic fieldwork was conducted including observations of the project's team meetings and conference as well as interviews with key members of the project team. The data generated from this fieldwork consisted of four datasets: field notes; a record of the Pegalios 'hashtag' on Twitter; the project blog and other online resources; and interview transcripts. Initial analysis of these datasets identified central questions (such as 'How useful is Twitter for different types of academic practice?'; 'How do digital resources such as Twitter help to construct/challenge the boundaries of academic communities?'; and 'How does (non)participation in Twitter contribute to the definition of identities/roles in a research project?').

Unsurprisingly for a study of this nature, the ethnographic findings were more complex and problematized than those of the metric analysis and survey. Twitter use was found to be distinctly social, with non-Twitter-using team members often having a direct impact on the content of tweets (translated from conversations or emails by Twitter-using colleagues). Materially, Twitter use could not be segregated from other digital and non-digital literacy practices since ideas and information crossed multiple channels of communication over the course of their development. And the use of Twitter was not consistent even within an individual user but rather evolved over time as users experimented, learned from their peers, and used Twitter on new devices against an evolving backdrop of social etiquette in the broader 'Twittosphere'.

Such findings lead to a number of conclusions: that academic use of Twitter must be evaluated in context; that distinguishing users from non-users is problematic since use evolves over time and a tweet is not necessarily composed by an individual alone; and that Twitter should not be perceived as a static resource since (materially) it is constantly evolving in response to user feedback and competition from other resources, and (socially) it is constantly evolving in response to shifts in etiquette and conventions. Unlike those stemming from the metric analysis and survey approaches, these rather polemical conclusions sat in tension to the institutional agenda which fuelled the research. Rather, they reflected the personal and professional agendas of the ethnographic researcher whose own research design had been partly informed by a somewhat sceptical response to the findings emerging from the metric analysis and survey.

However, the ethnographic approach also generated presences and Otherings due to its assumptions and the affordances of its method assemblage. These ranged from the substantial amount of data which slipped through the cracks in the processes of sorting, analysing, and representing the different datasets (hashtag archives which had expired before the tweets had been consolidated and extensive video footage which was simply too lengthy to reflect in its entirety, for example) to the data which remained hidden throughout (for instance, direct Twitter messages between team members which are not publically accessible.) The focus of the observation on social interactions amongst the project team also Othered detailed insight into individualized social-material Twitter practices, which might have been captured by tools designed for studies in Human–Computer Interaction. Similarly, Twitter-based networks which extended beyond the context of the project team were also Othered. Finally, the focus on the social, human make-up of the project team Othered to some extent the materiality of Twitter as a platform and the devices on which it was used. Such types of Othering are partly due to the social-material affordances of ethnography as a (social) genre which tends to be represented as lengthy (material) written descriptions rather than the visual or graphic representations of other methodological approaches.

Locating (and enacting) 'the Digital'

As the researchers attempted to consolidate the findings from the three approaches described above, it was clear that significant tensions existed between them. From these tensions a number of conceptual and methodological questions emerged: can academics be described as either users or non-users of particular digital resources? Are digital and professional identities fixed or contextually determined? Is 'influence' a useful measure of digital proficiency and if so, how can it measured? Can digital literacy practices be invisible and if so, how might one capture activities such as reading and thinking as well as writing? And how can analysis account for changes in users and resources over time while producing generalizable data?

Any response to such questions will depend on the particular methodological and theoretical approach adopted and the conceptual level at which 'the Digital' is located. The locations of these levels might be categorized as follows: within the individual (with conceptualizations taking the form of *digital identities* and *digital skills*); in groups (with a focus on *digital networks* of individual academics; or *digital practices* in *digital communities*); in institutions (conceptualized as the *digital university*); and in the material resources themselves (concentrating on *digital devices*). Since these conceptualizations have methodological implications, they warrant some further discussion.

Locating 'the Digital' at the level of the individual: identities and skills

The first conceptual approach situated at the level of the individual centres on 'digital identities'. Emerging from the psycho-social literature, this approach involves conceptualizations of digital literacy which tend to be based on academic personality/character/identity profiling, often resulting in typologies or dichotomies such as Prensky's (2001) widely critiqued distinction between digital natives and digital immigrants. Accordingly, the focus here is on the individual academic and their digital identity which might be fixed (as with Prensky's dichotomization) or might be reformulated to suit particular needs in different contexts (see White's distinction between digital residents and visitors.) More recently, Weller (2011) has tentatively defined a 'digital scholar' as 'someone who employs digital, networked and open approaches to demonstrate specialism in a field'. Research located at this level tends to explore the ways in which different digital identities are determined by variables such as age, gender, socio-economic status, academic discipline, etc. and distributed across different digital sites and platforms. To address such issues, this approach lends itself towards a methodological design based on surveys (where patterns and trends in the aggregated digital identities of a particular population might be identified). Through such methodologies, old typologies might be confirmed, rejected, or adapted and new typologies might be designed.

A related approach conceptualized at the level of the individual focuses on the digital skills or competencies of the individual scholar (see Eshet-Alkalai 2004; Kenton and Blummer 2010). This approach tends to emerge from the literature on 'information literacy' (from information and library studies) and educational psychology where literacy is used as a metaphor for autonomous skills. In this approach, decontextualized digital skills can be acquired through formal or non-formal means and once learnt, can be transferred for use in different domains for different purposes. Methodologies such as surveys sampling particular populations might be used to capture attitudes and behaviour in relation to digital skills. Experiments based on direct assessment of digital skills might provide a more accurate measure and longitudinal experiments might be used to track changes in skills over time in line with evolving use of technologies.

Locating 'the Digital' at the level of the group: networks/communities

In the second set of approaches the focus shifts to groups. The first of these focuses on aggregated networks of individuals, the skills they require to effectively function within these networks, and the digital resources that might facilitate participation in networks. While the vast majority of studies framed by this approach are extremely positive about the effects of digital interaction (see Steinfield *et al.* 2009; Haythornthwaite and Kendal 2010 and Wang and Wellman 2010 who identify social networking as a 'social lubricant'), others have argued that much of digital communication is based on socially void interaction with non-human technologies (Nie 2001; Cummings *et al.* 2002). Studies emerging from this approach are likely to question the ways in which groups of people are configured through different digital technologies. An apt methodological design to address this type of question is likely to employ mass observation or metric analysis to collate statistics about different digital networks. As with the metric analysis of Twitter use described above, such quantitative analysis might, for example, focus on networks of users of social networking sites, determining levels of 'connectedness' or 'influence' by comparing selected indicators.

In contrast to the 'networks' approach, a more qualitative and contextualized analysis of interactions between individuals focuses on *digital communities*. In this approach, the primary focus is on the role of 'the Digital' in mediating interaction between scholars and between scholars and artefacts within a particular academic community. This might be a university or a smaller community within the university (such as the Pelagios project team described above) or even a community which extends beyond the university (linking with the public, private or non-profit sector, for example). This approach has evolved through the pre-digital work of academics such as Holland *et al.* (1998) on 'figured worlds'; and Lave and Wenger (1991) and Wenger (1998) on 'communities of practice' (CoP). Initially focusing on educational management, the notion of CoPs has been extended to account for power relations and the significance of the social context (see Barton and Tusting 2005). Scholars have also started to apply the model to online or virtual contexts (see Dubé *et al.* 2006). Though this approach tends to emphasize 'social' interactions between humans which are mediated by 'material' digital resources, it also includes studies on Human–Computer Interaction and Computer Supported Cooperative Work. While this approach then encompasses many different (and often conflicting) conceptual strands, it is generally concerned with the ways in which 'the Digital' interacts with social practices and institutional processes to contribute to the formation/operation of academic communities. In response, apt methodological designs might integrate ethnography with discourse analysis or employ action research in collaboration with a particular digital community.

Locating 'the Digital' at the level of the institution: digital universities

A third set of conceptualizations tackle 'the Digital' through the lens of the university as an institution. In these approaches, the analytical focus is on the relationship between digital technologies and institutional structures and processes (such as those surrounding management, publication, tenure, teaching and learning systems, etc.). As scholars from a diverse range of disciplines have argued, digital practices might either reproduce the institutional structures already in place or challenge them (see for example Hazemi and Hailes 2002 on networked management; Cope and Kalantzis 2009 on digital publishing; and Weller 2010 on Open Educational Resources). There is therefore a need to consider not only the internal structures within the remit of university policy but also the external structures, policy domains, and economies (such as publishing) with which it engages. An institutional perspective to the study of 'the Digital' might lend itself to methodological designs based on case studies using institutional ethnography or discourse analysis of university policy and practice.

Locating 'the Digital' at the level of the technology: the device

In contrast to the conceptual orientations discussed above which all tend to focus (to varying degrees) on human actors – either as individuals in their own right, as aggregates of individuals, as groups, or in interaction with social systems and material objects – this fourth approach focuses on the material device. Emerging from the field of Science and Technology Studies (and employing toolkits such as Actor-Network Theory – see Callon 2006; Latour 2005; Law 1991, 2004) this approach adopts a resolutely non-humanist perspective which disrupts the human–technology dichotomy by positioning artefacts (such as digital technologies, media, sites, or texts) as assemblages of heterogeneous socio-material relations (see also Lea, this volume). Due to the relational nature of each actor (which is always also an actor network), a device might be ascribed the same type of agency as a human. Accordingly, a central research question for this type of approach would be: how are digital devices materially implicated in academic practice? Or in other words, how are digital devices assembled, and once assembled, how do they configure people, other devices, institutions, and concepts? Methodologically, such questions might be addressed through analysis of the socio-material make-up of devices and the ways in which they mediate scholarship. Methods such as multimodal analysis of digital artefacts or virtual ethnography charting academic practices across devices might facilitate this.

Table 2.1 presents these four conceptual orientations, summarizing the implications for research design.

Table 2.1 Conceptual approaches for understanding digital scholarship

Level at which 'the Digital' is located	Conceptual frame	Main unit of analysis	Implications for research design
Individual	*Digital identities*	Individual identities	Explores the psycho-social profile of a digital scholar. Methodologies include: • Surveys • Interviews (multiple case studies)
	Digital skills	Skills/ competencies	Explore the type of skills/ competences that a digital scholar has or needs. Methodologies include: • Assessment of digital competences • Longitudinal studies
Group	*Digital networks*	Aggregations of and/or connections between individuals	Explores how groups of people are configured by the digital. Methodologies include: • Mass observation • Metric analysis (i.e. measures of participation in different digital spaces)
	Digital communities	Interaction between scholars and artefacts in a specific social context	Explores how 'the Digital' interacts with institutional processes to contribute to the formation/ operation of scholarly communities. Methodologies include: • Visual ethnography • Discourse analysis • Action research • Observation of interaction between people/digital artefacts
Institution	*Digital universities*	University as organisation	Explores how 'the Digital' interacts with institutional processes. Methodologies include: • Institutional ethnography • Policy/discourse analysis • Case studies
Technology	*Digital devices*	Devices (digital media, sites, technology, or texts)	Explores how digital devices are assembled and how they configure other devices, institutions, people, concepts. Methodologies include: • Virtual/visual ethnography • Multimodal analysis of design and affordances of devices

Lessons for research into literacy in the digital university

In reality, most studies into academic 'digital literacy' practices position 'the Digital' at a number of levels simultaneously. The metric analysis discussed above incorporated 'digital identities' (represented by an academic's 'digital footprint') and 'digital networks' (illustrating relationships between individual footprints). The survey also incorporated 'digital identities' (categorized as users/non-users and academics of one or another faculty) but also reflected the 'digital university' by exploring how academic identities interact with institutional processes, mediated by digital artefacts. The ethnographic approach focused on one particular 'digital community' (the Pelagios project) but included an element of the material 'digital device' by incorporating analysis of the project's Twitter hashtag. And as a whole, the mixed-method study on the use of Twitter by academics at the OU incorporated all four framings. However, as the previous discussion has demonstrated, attempts to merge method assemblages without acknowledging the different framings of the 'the Digital' inherent within inevitably results in tensions and inconsistencies in the data.

Moreover, the different enactments of 'the Digital' through method have different implications for the 'collateral realities' produced by research studies. As with the commercial tool Klout, the 'digital footprint' tool and corresponding metric analysis reproduces a particular notion of 'influence' based on certain quantitative indicators. Such a conceptualization – and one which serves the competitive purpose of standardized comparison – has the ontological potential to nudge Twitter use towards activities which will increase the size of an individual's footprint (for example, strategically amassing followers and writing as many tweets as possible). Conversely, a survey-based method assemblage reproduces particular identities (such as Twitter user or non-user or discipline-based academics) and casts digital academic practice as an individualized rather than social practice. Finally, an ethnographic approach has a tendency to prioritize the community over the individual and the social over the material (though attention to the materiality of Twitter through analysis of the 'hashtag' can to some extent mitigate this.)

In all cases then, methodological approaches to researching 'digital literacy' embed particular framings of 'the Digital' and have, in Barad's (2003) terms, 'ethico-onto-epistem-ological' implications. Acknowledging how 'the Digital' is framed by different methodological tools might ensure that data is more consistent and reliable. Acknowledging the 'collateral realities' embedded in these framings might contribute to a more explicit recognition of the ethics of the research and the ideological agendas it responds to.

Chapter 3

Crossing boundaries

Digital and non-digital literacy practices in formal and informal contexts in further and higher education

Candice Satchwell, David Barton, and Mary Hamilton

Introduction

Picture two people on a street corner, poring over a map. One is pointing in the direction she feels they should be heading; the other is twisting his head round to align the map with the physical landscape it represents. After turning the book around, and more talking and pointing, the pair set off with the map under an arm, ready to be consulted at the next junction. These people are engaging in a well-established literacy practice – reading a map with the sole aim of arriving at a destination. Later that evening, in their living room in London, this same couple might get out a map of Italy along with a guide to Florence, to plan a holiday – real or imagined. This is another recognized literacy practice – perusing visual and written literature at leisure, with a less specific objective of organizing a trip sometime in the future. Now let's imagine one of these people has a business trip the next day which involves driving to a town 50 miles away. In order to get directions, she turns to the computer and types the details into a website which then provides a route with written instructions. She prints this out and leaves it on the table to read through at breakfast and then to have on the passenger seat as she negotiates her journey. In the car, she might also have a satellite navigation device to provide spoken instructions, or a mobile phone displaying a digital map and directions.

Each of these uses of reading and writing is an example of a literacy event, which can be seen as an instantiation of a literacy practice – essentially a social practice whereby people make meaning and accomplish social goals through reading and/or writing. This approach to literacy encourages us to look beyond texts themselves to what people *do* with literacy, with whom, where, when, how, and why. Therefore, each example of map-reading has its own characteristics: using paper or digital media, spoken and/or written modes, with or without pictures; carried out collaboratively or individually; at home, in the car, or in the street; for leisure, work, or other purposes. The individuals in question apparently move seamlessly from one literacy event to another, with subtle changes in the practices and associated identities – as tourist or as business worker – being taken in their stride. However, ask one of them out of the blue to engage in an orienteering competition, and reading a map takes on a different complexion. This might be unfamiliar territory in terms of identity, purpose, relationships, equipment, aspects of time and space, values, and so on. Panic may even set in as they contemplate 'failing' or letting down team members; and the practice of 'reading a map' is superseded by feelings relating to identity and self-preservation. We suggest that recognizing these differences in the complexions, power relations, feelings, and associated identities of literacy practices is crucial to understanding the ways in which boundaries are construed as existing – or dissolving – between work and home, academic life and everyday life, in the use of literacy, digital or non-digital. We would suggest that the boundary between literacy practices is stronger, and less easily negotiated, if there are elements of those practices which are particularly dissonant. For the individual above, who is threatened by the notion of engaging in an orienteering competition, but is completely at ease with map-reading as a tourist, the boundary separating the two uses of literacy might seem insurmountable. However, a change in the feelings associated with the practice of orienteering might occur if the individual then becomes accustomed to the social rules which accompany it, leading to a change in her sense of identity as a potential orienteering competitor. This in turn would reduce the perceived boundary between the two practices and enable the participant to move more easily between them.

This chapter explores notions of boundaries and identity in the context of literacies and technologies. It uses the interpretative framework from literacy studies theory outlined below, together with examples from two research projects, one based in further education (FE) and the other in higher education (HE). Juxtaposing these two projects enables us to examine the issues of boundaries and identities from the perspective of two different contexts within the post-school landscape of education. One focuses on student practices, the second on staff practices. Together the two contexts enable us to consider ways in which both students and staff negotiate different communications technologies as part of the same learning ecosystem (Barton 2007) even if they are differently positioned within it. Significant differences between these two contexts include the characteristics and motivations of the students, organizational features of the institution and the expectations placed on staff members in relation to research, administration, and teaching.

We explore the concept of boundaries between different areas of life, for staff who see the academic institution as a workplace, and for students for whom the institution might be viewed in a variety of ways – for example, as a place of study, or a means to a vocational end. Our research has found that boundaries between domains of life can be construed both negatively and positively. While the Literacies for Learning in Further Education (LfLFE) project envisaged boundaries between domains as in need of breaching, to enable students to access literacy practices traditionally situated within particular domains, the Academics Writing project revealed ways in which academics sought to build their own boundaries. Indeed, revisiting the LfLFE data with this notion in mind recasts the 'problem' as students attempting to maintain boundaries around different areas of their lives, albeit with detrimental effects on their college education.

Both projects start from a literacy studies approach which views academic writing as practices embedded in social contexts, rather than sets of disembodied skills possessed by individuals (Lea and Street 1998; Lillis 2001; Barton 2007). These practices can be analysed according to elements of participants' everyday experience, including: social networks and identities, values and motivations, physical settings and activities, sponsors, mediators, and resources. The ways in which people mix the old and new technologies provides one significant dimension of the practices we have documented in our empirical research studies. These include the ways in which uses of technologies are rearranging the way people work in educational institutions, both students and academic staff. This 'rearrangement' is not happening evenly across all groups and activities. It may result in disjunctures, misperceptions, new learning needs, and communicative challenges. Furthermore, whether or not the literacy practices involve new technologies may be less significant than individual or group identification with other aspects of literacy practices. Identities can also change according to imagined futures and experienced presents (see Barton *et al.* 2007); hence students can adopt institutional literacies to the extent that they identify themselves as members of that institution. For example, a student in our study identified herself as a potential social worker more clearly as her course progressed – 'I'm starting to think that maybe I possibly could [be a social worker]' – and as a result she engaged more successfully with the academic literacies required to achieve that goal.

Literacies for Learning in Further Education project

The LfLFE project was funded by the UK Economic and Social Research Council (ESRC) and ran from 2004 to 2007. It was led by two universities and included four FE colleges, two in England and two in Scotland. The project combined qualitative and quantitative methods to research literacy practices in different domains of students' lives: college, work, and home. One hundred students were followed over time both in and beyond college. We examined the reading and writing demands of 16 modules of study in a wide range of curriculum subjects and worked with lecturers to develop approaches which resonated more with students' preferences and existing practices. (For details of the research design see Ivanič *et al.* 2009, pp. 191–6). The students we worked with were often perceived as having difficulties with literacy in college, and it was thought that recognizing and understanding literacy practices in different areas of their lives could help address these difficulties. As reported elsewhere (Ivanič *et al.* 2009; Ivanič *et al.* 2007), our research uncovered an abundance of literacy in students' lives.

Students were accomplished communicators in their everyday lives, using a variety of modes and media for reading and writing, yet staff in colleges perceived students as underachieving in terms of literacy. In order to understand this disjunction, we analysed the reading and writing practices engaged in by students in their everyday lives, and compared them with those demanded of them in college. Many of the students we researched were taking vocational courses; most also had part-time jobs. This meant that it was also relevant to compare the literacy practices required in the present or future workplace. Figure 3.1 illustrates these different domains of life where different literacy practices might reside, with the intersecting sections indicating regions where boundaries between domains might be breached. Originally we searched for 'border literacy practices' which could be positioned here; later we considered it more useful to identify ways in which literacy practices might be subtly altered to enable them to cross a boundary from one domain to another.

Our analysis of students' literacy practices found that the practices had different characteristics in different domains. Most notably, students' 'preferred literacy practices' – and those associated with everyday life were:

- Mostly multimodal, e.g. involving speech, music, gesture, movement, colour, pictures, symbols, in combination with written text
- Mostly multimedia, e.g. including sound, electronic, and paper media in various combinations
- Shared, interactive, participatory – virtual and/or face to face
- Non-linear, i.e. involving complex, varied reading paths
- Agentic, i.e. with the student being in charge
- Purposeful to the student
- Clear audience perceived by the student
- Generative, i.e. involving sense-making and creativity
- Self-determined in terms of activity, time, and place

One of the most obvious differences that emerged from our data was the prevalence of *digital* literacy practices in students' everyday lives, and the prevalence of

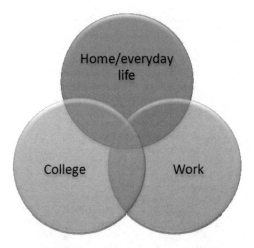

Figure 3.1 Different domains of life in which different literacy practices reside

paper-based practices on their courses. However, this was not the only difference, and we came to realize that we needed to analyse the whole range of aspects of any literacy practice in order to identify particular elements that could travel across boundaries.

Our analysis led to the development of a list of aspects of literacy practices presented in the left-hand column of Table 3.1. The right-hand column maps the characteristics of literacy practices that students prefer onto these aspects. We reasoned that a change in one or more aspects of this list could change a literacy practice.

In attempting to soften the borders between literacy practices in college and in everyday life, the project aimed to incorporate some characteristics of the students' 'preferred' literacy practices within the curriculum, by changing some of these aspects. As Williams (2009) has noted, importing popular culture texts into the classroom is not a solution in itself, since the texts are no longer under the students' control and take on new institutional meanings. However, he also suggests the importance of allowing students to draw on 'the playful, collaborative, intertextual, and multimodal qualities of participatory popular culture – and allow students to have some control of the nature and direction of their projects' (p. 197).

Based on this principle, as a 'change in practice' in Phase 3 of the project, students on a catering course module about food hygiene were given the choice of creating a kitchen layout diagram, using colour and symbols to refer to aspects of food hygiene. In previous years they were given no choice but to write an essay. They could choose whether to create their diagrams individually or with others, on a computer, on paper, as a poster, a leaflet, etc., and the products were displayed on the wall (see Table 3.2). These changes meant that, in comparison with writing an essay: the audience and the purpose were clearer, and they could

Table 3.1 Aspects of a literacy practice and students' 'preferred' literacy practices

Aspects of a literacy practice	Characteristics of students' 'preferred' literacy practices
Participants and relationships	Collaborative
Audience(s)	Clear audience(s)
Purpose(s)	Clear purpose(s)
Media	Multimedia
Modes	Multimodal
Artefacts: tools and resources	New technologies, but also pen and paper; sometimes new and old in combination
Activity/processes	Non-linear
Content/topic(s)	Chosen by/of interest to student
Text type(s)/genre(s)	Varied
Place/space	Designated by student
Time/duration	Designated by student
Values associated with the practice	Shared by student
Identities inscribed in the practice	Shared/aspired to by student

work collaboratively, using media and artefacts with which they felt comfortable. A generalized finding with the catering students participating in the project was their disenchantment with 'writing', and a leaning towards design and presentation. One student, asked why he was willing to spend hours on a PowerPoint presentation for the restaurant, while he was unhappy about writing essays, said:

> I see it as more like a publishing exercise, like, the graphics, and the way it looks . . . I prefer, like, things that look nice rather than if it just had text.

Crucially, the production of a presentation involved at least as much written text as an essay. However, the technological affordances of choosing fonts, sizes, and colours, as well as the combinations with images and sounds, transformed the students' experience of engaging with the task. Overall then, these changes in the mode of presenting information meant that the students felt they *valued and identified* more with the practice itself, which in turn meant that for many students a half-hearted essay was replaced by a meticulous diagram with detailed annotations.

The notions of values and identities are crucial to the level of engagement with a literacy practice. We found that many FE students did not 'identify' with the

Table 3.2 Comparison of modes of assessment, as experienced by students

Aspects of a literacy practice	Essay	Kitchen layout diagram
Participants and relationships	Individual	Individual or collaborative
Audience(s)	Tutor	Tutors and peers (displayed on wall)
Purpose(s)	To demonstrate (in writing) knowledge of food hygiene	To demonstrate (visually) knowledge of food hygiene
Media	Paper	Multimedia – as chosen by student
Modes	Written	Multimodal, including spoken and written language – as chosen by student
Artefacts: tools and resources on computer	Pen or word-processing	Computer or coloured pens, card, etc.
Activity/processes	Essay writing	Designing
Content/topic(s)	Food hygiene	Food hygiene
Text type(s)/genre(s)	Essay	Poster, leaflet
Place/space	College or home	College or home
Time/duration	Designated by tutor/student	Designated by tutor/student
Values associated with the practice	Academic writing – not necessarily shared	Aesthetic – likely to be shared
Identities inscribed in the practice	Student	Restaurant worker; designer

values and practices of academic literacies, in that they did not relate to the importance attached to characteristics of academic writing. For some, this changed over time: at the beginning of their college career they could not see the point of, for example, including bibliographies and references, but over time as they began to identify as 'students' and to see themselves as engaging in academic life, their attitudes to the literacies of assessment changed.

Others began to see a relationship between their course of study and their imagined future, identifying with the role for which they would qualify. Sam, a level 3 catering student, although disillusioned with school and finding the written aspects of the course a challenge, was successfully completing his course. The reason he rose to the challenge, it seems, was his clear focus on a future in the industry, inspired by observing the chef in his job in catering: 'I want to be a chef, definitely.' Asked why he had come to college to study, rather than remaining working in the industry, he explained: 'Because I wanted the qualifications. I wanted it written down that I was qualified to be a chef.'

Clearly, understanding and subscribing to the values associated with a particular practice is more likely to lead to its successful execution. To return to the orienteering competition example – if the participants either do not understand or resist the aspect of 'competing', i.e. subscribing to the need to be not only as accurate but also as fast as possible, then the participants in this particular map-reading practice will not assume the values and identities required to win.

FE students can be construed as being on boundaries in a variety of ways: economically, educationally, and socially. Although students like Sam were clearly focused on a goal, and were determined to do well, a significant proportion of the students in our study were not initially enrolled onto courses for which they had a lifelong passion; rather they were on courses which others had deemed appropriate for them, such as childcare, catering, or construction (Colley *et al.* 2007). This is not likely to produce the conditions for a student to value and identify with academic literacy practices. As Smith *et al.* (2008) demonstrate, a childcare course has a complex array of literacy practices associated with it, from writing up a child observation to mounting children's work for a display, many of which go unrecognized for their specificity and therefore remain untaught. Engaging effectively with these various practices requires a certain degree of personal investment: it became clear that those students who had a clear goal ahead of them were more likely to succeed in the academic as well as the practical aspects of the course.

Institutional attempts to dissolve boundaries through use of technology

Colleges and universities are changing in numerous ways which affect the interpretation of the notion of boundaries, including in terms of time and space. They have experienced shifts in the physical environments within which learning takes place; and there is more porosity between the institution and the outside world in terms of funding and governance. Students at universities and some colleges are more dispersed, often including geographically distant students at dispersed campuses both nationally and internationally, as well as students on distance learning programmes. For such reasons, there is increasing cultural diversity among both students and staff, leading to the reorganization of social and cultural boundaries. Professional networks extend increasingly beyond the physical boundaries of the university, with much academic collaboration being carried out at a distance. In our experience, while such networks are encouraged and facilitated amongst staff (for example, in the higher education institution (HEI) in the Academics Writing study), there is an ambivalent relationship with the external networks that students might choose to bring in: in some institutions there are attempts to draw boundaries around students' (and sometimes staff) use of digital technologies. For example, while the affordances of social networking sites are recognized as an effective means of communicating with students, aspects of their use may be prohibited by institutions, including some colleges in the study. So, while educators are infiltrating Facebook (Online College Courses 2011), students may not be allowed to access Facebook during lectures, nor to 'friend' lecturers, except under controlled conditions (Askam 2012). Similarly, mobile phones are often prohibited in classrooms, but students are expected to supply mobile phone numbers in their personal details; and some tutors will exploit students' ability to 'look things up' on their phones during class.

Digital technologies connect communities, but can also keep them apart. For some people, certain digital literacy practices may be inaccessible due to financial, social, or other 'membership' issues, such as health or cultural capital. Infrastructural boundaries can also be set up – sometimes inadvertently – by available technologies; for example, by differentiating between kinds of institutional membership, limiting who has access to electronic journals or academic chat rooms.

As distance learning and virtual learning environments (VLEs) become more widespread, the notion of drawing on students' everyday literacy practices to 'deliver' learning packages seems to make sense. If students are 'always online', surely they can pursue a course of study in this way? Following this line of thought, institutions are working towards providing courses in the forms of 'off-the-shelf' modules on a whole range of subjects, which can be delivered online (see Martin and McKenzie, and McKenna and Hughes, this volume). However, our work suggests a note of caution. While some people are invoking the 'borderless university', and suggesting that technologies are enabling boundaries to break down between academic and everyday domains of life, others indicate the need to 'revalue studenthood'. Students – particularly those who have become students against the expectations of their social background – frequently want validation, accreditation, and to be regarded as a student. This to some extent requires building or *re*building boundaries rather than dissolving them. Perhaps it is more helpful to consider the notion of 'the borderless learner', acknowledging that learning is ubiquitous; however, the literacy practices required by the university are likely to be prescriptive and different from those required in other aspects of life. As discussed by Lea and Jones (2011) and by Smith *et al.* (2008), being a student requires certain literacies, in particular for assessment. These literacies are not as easily negotiable as other literacy practices such as facebooking or tweeting for some people, while the reverse is true for others.

Tutors often assume that students are 'more digitally literate than they are' – with 'they' being a double referent (see Kemp and Jones 2007, and Lea and Jones 2011 for discussion of tutors' digital literacy skills. Also Jones, this volume, for comments on the 'digital native' debate). The notion of a student with multiple tabs open on a computer screen, with work, leisure, and social interactions all appearing together and interrupting one another gives the impression of constant connectivity and seamless movement between various activities. However, this image does not necessarily equate to a borderless university, nor to fluidity between literacy practices; rather it is an enactment of the different identities, values, beliefs, and so on that an individual embodies (almost) simultaneously, and with varying degrees of success. Thus, she or he might be an effective participant in Facebook, but a less effective academic essay writer. Furthermore, while there is an abundance of literacy practices within and beyond the university, institutional assessment practices pull people back to the academy in traditional ways.

In summary, our work suggests that practices situated in informal contexts do not migrate in any simple way into educational settings even when technology is in place to facilitate this. Students are notoriously ambivalent about the use of VLEs (JISC 2007), and attempts to replicate the massive success of social networking sites in an institutional environment have varying levels of success. It takes both sides to agree to boundaries being breached, including self-imposed boundaries. These notions are now explored in the context of the second of our projects.

Academics writing project

The second project is an ongoing study of academics' writing practices and how these are changing, including aspects of the acquisition and use of digital technologies. This project set out to explore how the literacy practices of academic staff are adapting to major changes in the culture and infrastructure of the university sector (see also Martin and McKenzie, this volume). Rather than focus on the texts academic writers produce in different disciplines (Kemp and Jones 2007; Hyland 2006), the intention was to research academics' actual writing practices, the range of writing activities which academics now engage in, and their shifting use of new technologies (Lea and Stierer 2011). We aim to make links with research on contemporary changes in HE more generally, while making comparisons with some conclusions from the student-focused research described earlier.

This exploratory project involved in-depth interviews with eight experienced academics drawn from the arts and social science departments in one UK university talking about their scholarly writing. They were carried out in March 2009. Each interview focused on a specific piece of writing and people talked about times and places to write, their use of different technologies, their range of writing, their experiences of collaboration, and how their practices had changed in the past five years. The data we will focus on here relates to aspects of time, space, and technologies for writing and the ways in which academics construe boundaries between work and home. Issues of identity are again foregrounded in the accounts people gave of their work.

> I sometimes I'm tempted to work at home . . . Because then I can smoke . . . But I generally resist that. I like to be work work, and home home, you know. So I come in every day and I don't stay at home.
>   There might be a very occasional kind of panic, you know, when I've got some deadline to meet or something like that. I will actually stick it on my data stick and take it home and do some work at night, but mostly it's, I do it here and if need be even I come in here on a Saturday.

For this academic, the boundary between home and work is important, and self-imposed – even against the temptation to stay at home where smoking is permitted. This individual uses the affordances of technology to cross boundaries – by physically carrying a memory stick between work and home, but only in times of 'panic'. Despite the ease with which data can be transferred from work to home, this person prefers to take himself to the university on a Saturday. The willingness to sacrifice the additional time and effort this takes is symbolic of the perceived need to separate work from home. This is clearly not just a geographical separation of the two domains, but an emotional and psychological distinction which is seen to contribute to the quality of the person's life. The use of the verb 'to be' in 'I like to be work work, and home home' implies the level of personal investment involved. In this case, space seems to be more important than time in the decisions taken, allowing encroachment on the weekend in order to maintain the same space (at work).

Another example makes some similar points:

> I now try not to check the email until 2 o'clock and so on. I find that very difficult to do but I think that it's absolutely essential, certainly if I'm to get my work done . . . this lifetime, then that kind of focusing and organization is absolutely essential. Keeping this place at bay, keeping the students at bay, I'm very committed to my students and my teaching, I take that stuff very seriously, but you know, if you aren't single-minded and have a clear kind of form of organization that gives you the space, it's really very difficult.

References to time, space, and distance here are telling, and again indicate the need to enforce a boundary to keep a separation from 'this place' (the university) and 'the students'. The reference to delaying accessing email echoes a point made by several participants, all recognizing the seductive relative 'ease' of dealing with email as opposed to engaging in scholarly writing. This also highlights the increasing number of administrative duties imposed on academic staff, which begin to erode the border around time and space for academic writing. References to being 'single-minded' and 'clear form of organization' indicate the kind of personal agency required to resist this erosion, to build boundaries for oneself, and to keep them enforced.

A third interviewee detailed his individual use of available technology:

> I have a laptop, a rather rickety old IBM . . . but one of the things I am thinking about doing is getting a new laptop.
>   . . . you know I have a separate machine at home that I run the internet on but I keep my laptop as a walled garden, never goes onto the internet, never leaves the house actually, don't know why I have a laptop frankly but there we go. It just sits there, I transfer stuff on a data stick between my computer and the one downstairs if I'm going to email it to somebody but apart from that I don't do anything else. . . .

The metaphor of a 'walled garden' is clearly a positive image, incorporating notions of growth and fertility, alongside peace, security, and privacy. It might also be said to be a privileged image: few of us actually have access to such a thing. While a student in FE may feel they are not located specifically within any one domain, straddling both academic and practical/vocational requirements, a university academic is securely placed within a domain wherein the values and identities associated with academic literacies are taken for granted. The walled garden here refers to a space immune to interference from technology in the form of the internet, where writing can be carried out in its 'purest' form. While some academics argue that all texts nowadays are posthuman insofar as they intertextually reflect interactions with technology (see Gourlay and Martin; Bayne and Ross, this volume), and many scholars would require an internet connection whenever they write, this individual indicates that his scholarly activity can take place most effectively without such intrusion.

The reference to physically 'transferring stuff' from one computer to another in order to use email indicates the importance of keeping boundaries in place, effectively opting out of the connectivity affordances of the laptop and keeping it securely within the walls of the garden.

A further example suggests additional ways of interpreting boundaries:

> . . . I don't take handwritten notes any more . . . I underline stuff in books and I tend to write a key to my annotations in the front flyleaf and the page number and what particular thing I've annotated, then I underline stuff in the margins but my handwriting isn't reliable and if I leave it, after a couple of weeks I can't read what I've written . . . if I can't remember what I've written, I generally can't read it and so I've always typed for years.

This person explains his use of 'typing' as a way of dealing with illegible handwriting – a pragmatic solution. He also refers to the 'illicit literacy practice' of writing in books, including library books. This invites consideration of other kinds of boundaries; between public and private property; between the rights of students and lecturers; between the written word and its interpretation. The construction of meaning requires bringing together the text on the page and the individual's response, in this case blurring boundaries between the two by superimposing writing in and on the text.

Issues of identity in both projects

Sam, the catering student mentioned above in the LfLFE project, later referred to his ability to cook without weighing and measuring ingredients: 'You can do things without . . . without weighing them, you know, I mean it's, it's weird.' When the interviewer doubted her own ability to do the same, Sam said, 'You're not . . . you're not a chef? Or a cook?' There is a clear sense that this identification with 'being a chef' was established within Sam, and therefore made aspects of his course – including those requiring specific uses of reading and writing – possible.

An academic from the Academics Writing study had a comparable notion of his own identity – this time as an academic. Similar to Sam, he described this identity as permeating borders, so that he was never without it – 'like a priest', as he described it, ministering to his flock of students without boundaries of time or space. Therefore, he would respond to requests from students whether or not he was 'at work'; and he could be thinking about or engaging with his academic writing regardless of his location. To extend this to the map-reading examples: for someone to identify himself or herself as an orienteer is a large step beyond someone being able to read a map. Researching and writing a successful academic essay is a large step away from reading and writing on Facebook: not because one is inherently more difficult than the other, but because there are so many aspects of those practices that are different. Our argument here is that issues of identity are crucial to the ways in which different people engage with different literacy practices. There are any number of ways in which the relationships are configured; but if the relationship is not a positive one – for whatever reason – the engagement with the literacy practice will be compromised.

Agency is intimately linked with identity: we found that if students felt that they did not have agency in the literacy practices with which they were expected to engage, ultimately they were less likely to adhere to associated conventions and the quality of the work was reduced. For the academics interviewed, although they were bound by constraints imposed by their roles within institutions, they inevitably have more cultural, economic, and social power than the students, and more agency within their own working lives. Crucially, academics have chosen a job which requires very specific and intensive forms of reading and writing, while FE students have generally chosen or been steered towards courses which lead to 'practical' jobs. Although the LfLFE project uncovered multiple 'hidden' literacy demands both in such jobs themselves and in studying to qualify for those jobs (see Ivanič *et al.* (2009); Smith *et al.* (2008)), the roles were not defined by the types of writing required. While the LfLFE project attempted to make the boundaries between work, home, and college more porous so that students could manage their college work more effectively, the Academics Writing study reveals ways in which academics install their own boundaries as a form of resistance to their institutions' burgeoning literacy demands in terms of administration, teaching, and research (see also Lea and Stierer 2011).

Conclusions

In this chapter we have shown how boundaries between or around different uses of literacy, both print-based and digital, are construed very differently by different people. We have argued that this depends in part on their institutional affiliation, their role, and their sense of identity. The college project recognized the significance of boundaries in students' lives and viewed the perceived boundaries between different kinds of literacies as hindering students' progress. The project therefore attempted to find ways of softening the borders to enable travel from everyday life to college, utilizing the different characteristics of everyday literacies, including the values and attitudes associated with them. In the other study academics report that they face similar issues to students, managing the pressures of limited time and complex lives. However, they are able to exert more control over their work. With their undisputed cultural capital, they could decide to draw their own boundaries more or less firmly to demarcate different aspects of their work and different domains of their lives.

While one of the differences between literacies in everyday life and college was the greater use of technologies in everyday life, the introduction of technology into college literacy practices was only one way of addressing the disjuncture. Notions of agency, identity, and power are fundamental to the ways in which different ways of 'doing literacy' are embraced or resisted, and our examples indicate that practices situated in informal contexts do not migrate in any simple way into educational settings even when technology is in place to facilitate this.

Students who find it difficult to use a university VLE, for instance, but are expert Facebookers are making choices about their different levels of engagement. A university lecturer who keeps an 'internet-free zone' in order to carry out scholarly writing is also making choices, possibly with more deliberation because he or she has a more established sense of identity and agency. A college or university which develops a VLE along the lines of Facebook cannot guarantee engagement from its students because the institutional literacies required are differently configured, albeit with a veneer of informality and accessibility.

The institution itself pulls people in contradictory directions. A powerful example of this is traditional assessment practices which require specific literacy practices with characteristics quite different from those of newer social and digital literacy practices.

It would seem that although technologies are enabling the dissolution of boundaries of time and space in various ways, these are sometimes welcomed, sometimes resisted by users. Resistance can take the form of refusing to partici- pate in certain literacies, by engaging in them only half-heartedly, or by creating or reworking boundaries between practices in terms of time or space. On the other hand, the ability to transfer written data from place to place, the possibili- ties of communicating and collaborating virtually through writing and reading across time and space, and the chance to access large quantities of information are exploited variously by both students and staff in different areas of their lives. The two studies reported here can be seen to reveal that, ironically, the affordances of digital literacies in education compel staff to build boundaries, while also contrib- uting positively to the breaching of boundaries for students.

Chapter 4

Emergent practices for literacy, e-learners, and the digital university

Caroline Haythornthwaite

Introduction

Learning on and through the web brings with it an array of new practices that extend, yet challenge, traditional expectations about universities and literate practice. As we increasingly work and learn with others online and through information and communication technologies (ICTs), we enact new ways of learning and communicating that become contemporary literate practices. These lead to redefinitions of who we are as learners, and how universities engage with literacy practice. The aim of this chapter is to provide a view of literacy in the digital university as built on and emergent from the context of contemporary communication, information dissemination, knowledge construction, and knowledge work practices. Literacy in this context can be viewed from the perspectives of the *learner*, as he or she becomes an e-learner, i.e. an individual comfortable and fluent with gaining and building knowledge online, and of the *university*, as an institution embedded in wider societal transformations brought on by ICTs, actively producing literate e-learners and e-learning practices. Overall, this chapter argues for a renewed appreciation of the term 'e-learning' that encompasses and embraces the emergent literacy of learning on and through the web, and the continuous evolution of literate practice that occurs with each new round of ICTs.

E-learning practice

While the focus of this book as a whole is on literacy, throughout this chapter the term 'practice' is used in preference to 'literacy' because the evolving and co-evolving nature of contemporary ICT involves a complex of 'reading' and 'writing' the texts of technologies, group behavior, and knowledge production, and the framing and reframing of their production processes (see also Jones, this volume). Indeed, it is a point of this chapter that the 'literacy' an e-learner acquires includes an active role in the continuous emergence of what it means to be literate with ICTs.

This understanding of emergence as the state-of-the-art for e-learning itself emerges from a wide literature on the shaping of home, work, and organizational practices with the introduction of technology (e.g. Kling, Rosenbaum and Sawyer 2005; Andrews and Haythornthwaite 2007), including articulation of the 'perpetual beta' state of new systems as the meanings of Web 2.0 technologies change through ongoing social construction (O'Reilly 2005; Neff and Stark 2004). New technologies also modify individual behavior through the adoption and determination of shared practices, identification with groups and their sociotechnical practices, and self-image as sociotechnical practitioners in communities of practice, activity systems, and professions (Wenger 1998; Engeström 2009; Becker, Geer, Hughes and Strauss 1961).

E-learning fluency – or literacy if we like – entails not only engagement with multiple social and technological 'texts', but also an ability, in both learners and universities, to address change in a fluent, active manner, continuously determining what literacy means in concert with current opportunities and constraints. It is hoped that this understanding of e-learning as encompassing active construction of social and technological literate practice will aid teachers, learners, and administrators as they promote literacy and university learning with and for contemporary ICTs.

Redefining e-learning

As noted, the aim is to provide a renewed view of e-learning. This suggests the need for a new articulation of what e-learning is. Thus, with full awareness that a single definition is unlikely to capture all the nuance of a changing field, a working definition for e-learning as intended here is:

> *E-learning* is the practice of gaining and building knowledge on and through networked information and communication technologies, maximizing the benefits afforded by contemporary technology to connect with informational and human resources.

The emphasis on 'knowledge' contrasts with assumptions that e-learning is defined by the use of technologies (e.g. HEFCE 2005), and supports an active, creative, 'building' dimension of the learning process. Engagement with technology is considered proactively as 'maximizing the benefits' of ICTs, with awareness that the ability to maximize benefits is exactly the kind of literacy needed for the new e-learner. Finally, this definition highlights both information and human resources since networked ICTs provide access not only to information, but also to human experts and peers for learning.

Deliberately excluded from this definition is the university because e-learning is not just a practice for the university. However, it is a practice to which the university is subject. Students come in with a certain level of e-learning literacy that the university works with and then enhances. There may be a question of why the university needs to address e-learning at all. The answer lies in the way that universities are not separate from society, but instead both shaped by and shaping contemporary technologies and literacies. Their position as arbiters of literacy requires deliberate attention to societal trends (e.g. in what is needed in the workplace, and for individual economic success), both to adjust to the incoming skills and expectations of students, and to examine and promote a literacy that serves societal needs.

E-learning practice: then and now

To illustrate the way e-learning practice has emerged from joint practice, and the way participants – learners and teachers – acquired new identities as e-learners, we start with the experiences of early pioneers in online learning. The first section takes us back to the late 1990s and early 2000s to hear the experiences of e-learners at a time when members of online communities were still at the stage of 'homesteading on the electronic frontier' (Rheingold 2000).

Then

In 2000, the digital university had barely begun, and the traditional university had barely been challenged by online information and communication. Online courses were beginning, but full online degree programs were limited (see the Sloan Consortium reports <http://sloanconsortium.org/publications/survey/index.asp>). In 2002, 1.6 million U.S. students (of 16.6 million) were taking at least one course online, with over 578,000 of these taking all of their courses online (Allen and Seaman 2003). Programs that did exist were 'different worlds', with practices developed locally, and students interacting with a known set of others within a single controlled environment. Online universities were starting, but were questioned for their academic status; failures of online ventures were common (for example the UK e-University; Garrett 2004). The use of the Internet in the everyday life of teaching and learning was yet to be a distraction: the etiquette of email between faculty and students was just emerging, and laptops were rare in physical classrooms, and, when present, unlikely to have connection to the Internet (outside computer labs). Open access online journals were beginning, but their status as venues for publication was questioned, as was the worth of other newly emerging online venues (e.g. blogs). Wikipedia was a year away, Creative Commons licensing two years away, Facebook four years away, and Twitter six years away.

Teachers, learners, and administrators were all new to the online experience, all learning to work in and support learning in this strange new environment. Every change – face-to-face to mediated communication, synchronous to asynchronous discussion, physical to electronic materials – was a conscious change, where the norms of practice had yet to be defined. Even the teaching approaches were new, with norms of how to lecture, discuss, and assess participation online in flux and in development. Experiences in this 'simpler' e-learning age remind us of the many aspects involved in learning the literacies of the online environment, aspects that are now more taken for granted and hidden from considerations of design.

To recapture the feeling of these e-learning times, we start with some comments drawn from research interviews with students and faculty in an online degree program. The program was a fully online, distributed option leading to a Master's degree, with the first cohort enrolled in 1996. Courses used real-time lecture delivery with audio, web delivery of lecture notes, text chat for student interaction, weekly use of online discussion boards, and a once a term on-campus mandatory session (Haythornthwaite and Kazmer 2004). A number of studies were conducted around this program, aimed toward understanding and improving student experience and the online program; two are discussed here. Haythornthwaite, Kazmer, Robins and Shoemaker (2000) conducted qualitative interviews with 17 students, four times over one year, about their experiences in the program, with a particular emphasis on how they coped with learning in this new environment. Lawton and Montague (2004) used an online forum (157 posts from 62 individuals) and focus groups (14, face to face) to learn about 'best practices' from faculty, adjunct instructors (professionals who teach courses), and students.

Students experienced this new learning environment as a 'different kind of world', marked by a boundary between those *in* the new world and those who 'can't really understand [this world] since they're on the outside' [Betty] (Haythornthwaite *et al.* 2000, online). Student comments highlight how visible the effort was to understand and acquire e-learning literacy, including learning how to *post*,

> 'At the beginning it was difficult for me because I felt like when I posted something it had to be perfect'
>
> [Ted]

. . .

> 'wondering if what I was posting sounded okay or if it sounded so bad'
>
> [Nancy]

how to be *present* online,

> 'You have to make more of a point to reinforce things because you're not going to bump into people, you have to make a point of nurturing friendships more so than you do in a neighborhood.'
>
> [Doris]

and how to manage with a *lack of presence*:

> 'You don't have to see the immediate gasping reactions to what you say . . . or write something that maybe you think "Oh, maybe that was too inane . . . ." You don't see those eyes rolling.'
>
> [Barbara]

For teachers, the whole practice of teaching was made visible, opening up practices for reassembly. The new learning environment led teachers to 'consider norms and confront prejudices of traditional models of education', and to 'look and share and be collaborative' (Lawton and Montague 2004, p. 211). Teachers learned and adopted a model of teaching that fitted this new space, recognizing a 'different learning', and accepting that while there is a 'need to plan and organize, provide a focus for the class . . . [subsequently] there is a need to let it go and be a part of it as it unfolds.' (Lawton and Montague 2004, p. 209). Lawton and Montague found that new practices emerged from active observation and change, changing tacit knowledge and practice, with teachers reflecting on the process of learning and recognizing that what the environment could do is change 'thinking about learning and how you learn' (Lawton and Montague 2004, p. 210)

Experiences with this program revealed the disruptiveness of the new online learning environment, and the effort that participants brought to creating new practices. Instead of knowing how *to be* in school as part of tacit knowledge, the process had to be made evident and visible to participants. This accords with what has been found for other ICT systems. As Gaver has noted,

> The unpredictability of most electronic systems has a common social consequence of forcing previously implicit behaviors to be made explicit, and of causing the unspoken to be spoken. People using such systems find they cannot easily coordinate their activities and instead have to explicitly negotiate their collaboration.'
>
> (Gaver 1996. p. 120)

This experience of e-learning shows how new behaviors were actively co-constructed in collaboration with fellow learners, between teachers and learners, and in concert with the facilities and constraints of the online environment and its technologies. Now, too, each new change in technology precipitates changes in how, where, and with whom we work and learn (Haythornthwaite and Andrews 2011). Even as this chapter is being written, the new phenomenon of Massively Open Online Courses (MOOCs) is opening up yet another option in learning (EDUCAUSE Learning Initiative 2011). Combine this with the social innovation of educational 'badges', designed to provide certification for skills learned on the web (Young 2012), and the technology of the Internet is set (again) to challenge how we accredit learning, or at least to provide another option in the educational quiver.

And now

Fast forward to 2012. Digital practices are widespread; laptops, tablet computers, mobile phones are commonly owned and present in university environments; wireless connectivity to the Internet is near-ubiquitous on university campuses as well as in many public (libraries, coffee shops) and private spaces (dormitories, homes). In 2011, 6.1 million U.S. students (of 19.6 million total) were taking a course online (Allen and Seaman 2011). University libraries spend major parts of their budgets on online journals, increasingly changing their real estate to learning study areas, adopting on-site automated storage systems over book-shelving options, and off-site remote storage for less frequently used physical collections. Reference services change to meet the needs of digital participants (digital reference, reference chat). While the impact of e-readers and e-books on library services and delivery of textbook content is just emerging, learning man-agement companies are heading quickly into providing such materials through their systems, changing both educational publishing and purchasing practices. Information seeking and communication entails connecting to online resources in libraries, through learning management systems, but also open on the web; and Facebook, Twitter, blogs, online news, and more, support information and interpersonal browsing for discovery and research purposes.

Studies by the Pew Internet and American Life Project show how highly wired and connected U.S. 18–34 year olds are. In 2012, 96 percent have cell phones (66 percent have smartphones); 70 percent have laptops; 69 percent a music player (iPod or equivalent); 63 percent a game console; and 23 percent a tablet computer (iPad or equivalent). They send an average of 109 text messages a day (median: 50); and 85 percent use social networking sites, with a mean of 318.5 social network friends (compared to 197.6 for the next age group, 35–46 years) (Rainie 2012).

Results from Project Information Literacy (<http://projectinfolit.org/>) shows well the way these statistics play out in the literacies of the university. Head and Eisenberg (2011) looked at U.S. student behaviors during 'crunch time', i.e. the two weeks before examinations. The study portrays highly connected, mul-titasking students, simultaneously maintaining social connections while working on assignments and reviewing course materials. In 560 interviews with under-graduates on ten U.S. university campuses, 81 percent of students approached in the university library reported that, in the last hour, they had checked for mes-sages: in email, Facebook, mobiles, etc. Of these, 60 percent reported they had also prepared assignments for submission and 52 percent had reviewed materials for class in the previous hour. The study also describes the new perspective on the use of university spaces. Few students in the library space were there to use library materials: only 21 percent had used the library portal in the last hour; 11 percent a scholarly research database, 9 percent library books, 5 percent the online catalog, and 3 percent the print journals from the shelves. The overwhelming reason for being in the library was to be in a place where they could get work done, free of distractions and temptations to do something else.

Then, now, and future

Two seemingly separate scenarios have been presented: the early graduate e-learner and the contemporary wired undergraduate. In 2000, the digital univer-sity was the e-learning program: intended for distance education, and perceived by many as the new way of providing low-cost education. Educational concerns were about developing and adapting pedagogical approaches, creating online learning communities, and disseminating education. In 2013, the digital university is the institution, inward looking to support the new technology of teaching and learning – from learning management systems to blended learning to learning analytics (<http://www.solaresearch.org/>) – and outward looking in acknowledging net generation learners (e.g. Jones, Ramanau, Cross and Healing 2010; see also EDUCAUSE, <http://www.educause.edu/nglc>). In 2000, the digital university experience often pertained to locally developed learning management systems; in 2013, the digital university experience is led by commonly used, university-wide systems, from a few major companies (see Williams this volume). In 2000, online resources and technologies were at a stage of early emergence, still the domain of early adopters; in 2013 these are ubiquitous, mobile, ever present. During these years, our views of what learning entails, and where we find resources of value and others to learn with has changed, being both pushed and pulled by online tools and social practices.

And we haven't arrived yet. In 2013, we are at the beginning of the next emergence. In this next wave, the digital university should not be seen as a passive actor, buffeted by technology and surprised by the social outcomes, but as a proactive actor shaping the direction and format of literacy and digital practices. To be sure, many institutions, individual units, and people within universities are proactive (for example in open courseware initiatives; open access journals; institutional repositories for faculty publications). Yet, the overall picture of what constitutes literacy in the digital university is still being shaped by new influences. A few of the growing trends include: further implementation of games and gaming into educational practice (Gee 2003); use of virtual worlds for simulation, distributed communication, etc.; integration of participatory practices in education (Jenkins *et al.* 2006); massing learning into MOOCs; and integrating and validating outside resources and credentialing into university programs (e.g. Khan Academy, YouTube videos, 'badges', etc.).

Another major area of emerging practice is in the area of learning analytics, which brings together initiatives in automated analysis of educational data to understand both learning and university progress (including academic analytics, and educational data mining; van Barneveld, Arnold and Campbell 2012; Ferguson 2012). 'Learning analytics is the use of intelligent data, learner-produced data, and analysis models to discover information and social connections, and to predict and advise on learning' (Siemens 2010, online). Some ways that learning analytics can be used include: enhancing learner experience by making discussion networks visible, reporting progress against other learners, or showing learner trajectories across degree completion (see also <http://solaresearch.org/Open-LearningAnalytics.pdf>; EDUCAUSE resources at <http://www.educause.edu/Resources/Browse/Learning Analytics/39193>).

While learning analytics most closely addresses university practice, the techniques and approaches inherent in the new analytics initiatives also speak to the kinds of literacies that future e-learners will need. These include the ability to manage data resulting from online interaction and the use of ICTs, to analyze that data using contemporary approaches such as text and data mining (Romero, Ventura, Pechenizkiy and Baker 2011), and to read and display data presented in visualizations (e.g. Lima 2011).

Emergent practices

As we consider what has been accomplished in developing e-learning, e-learners, and literacies for e-learning, what does the future literacy of an e-learner entail? What practices are emerging for operating in the new, continuously emergent, self-directed, 'perpetual beta' that is today's learning and literacy environment? Certainly knowing how to use any particular contemporary technology will be important, but a more general list helps to go beyond technological competence to address fluency with e-learning.

The first decade of e-learning and Internet use has emphasized the emergence of fluency with collaborative practices. This has, in part, emerged from pedagogical intent that recognizes the active nature of learning, and the ideas of collaborative learning and computer supported collaborative learning (Koschmann 1996). It is synergistic with online practices emerging from the interactional capabilities of Web 2.0 technologies, in what Jenkins et al. (2006) have named participatory culture. Its origins can be seen in the earlier emphasis on the development of online communities, and subsequent trends in connecting otherwise disconnected individuals through media and in mediated spaces, creating online mobs, crowds, and communities (Rheingold 2000, 2003; Howe 2006; Haythornthwaite 2009). At this point, while collaborative learning has gained much attention because of online environments, the digital university has the opportunity to try out more options for teaching, with new approaches to the design and the analysis of learning.

Emergent effects from collaborative online learning include *new roles* for teachers and learners. Educators are encouraged to develop a new kind of teacher presence (Garrison and Anderson 2003), often described as a facilitator role, and learners are encouraged to take on an active role as shapers of conversations, contributors of knowledge, and creators of new knowledge (Haythornthwaite 2006a; Swan 2006; Haythornthwaite and Andrews 2011). Students have been observed to fill a number of new e-learning niches: some become e-facilitators (Preston 2008) and learner-leaders (Montague 2006) taking on leadership roles in discussion; some act as braiders (Preston 2008) and patchworkers (Ryberg and Dirckinck-Holmfeld 2008) pulling together different threads and patches of materials for different audiences; and others become community-connectors (Kazmer 2007) bringing knowledge from the online learning community to their local geo-community and vice versa.

These changes in roles and connectivities lead to changes in the *social networks* that support learning. Inside and outside class, networks of collaboration, social support, and information underpin the learning process. Different communication technologies have been found to support different kinds of ties (Haythornthwaite 2008). Single media common to a group have been found to provide connections to weak ties (acquaintances), known for providing exposure to information new to our social circle; multiple, and more private media have been found to connect strong ties (close friends and co-workers), promoting the ability to get team work completed. Learning to teach and learn online thus also entails discovery of how technologies support different kinds of ties and knowledge exchange. Newer analytics research presents the opportunity to examine further the relationship between pedagogical approaches and the resulting effects on networks, learning trajectories, and learning outcomes.

Along with collective models, e-learning can also be viewed from the perspective of the individual situated at the center of a self-selected and *self-directed* network of resources and learners (Senge, Brown and Rheingold 2008, Luckin 2010; Rainie and Wellman 2012). The deliberative searching for resources and communities of interest that is now a major part of our learning and knowledge acquisition resonates with the practices of independent expert learners (Scardamalia and Bereiter 1996), and the pedagogical ideas of andragogy (adult learning) and heutagogy (self-directed learning; Hase and Kenyon 2000). These networked learners create their own user-generated contexts for learning (Luckin, 2010; Head and Eisenberg 2011), acting in an entrepreneurial manner to satisfy their own information and learning needs (Brown and Adler 2008; Senge, Brown and Rheingold 2008). In balancing meeting a personal but shared need, there is substantial resonance with motivations cited for contribution to open source and open access projects (Raymond 1998; Benkler 2006). As a whole, this train of development suggests that literacy for e-learning shares characteristics with literacy for self-directed learning, entrepreneurial behavior, and open source participation.

Another major attribute of literacy of the new e-learner is *agility*. Perhaps one of the earliest recognized agilities in e-learning has been the ability to take on the role of teacher *or* of learner, within the same context and with the same actors, and new roles such as e-facilitator. E-learners also manage in an agile manner as they navigate from community to community, operating from a user-centered perspective while managing full and partial engagement across multiple social worlds (Strauss 1987; Haythornthwaite and Kazmer 2002; Kazmer 2007; Rainie and Wellman 2012).

Agility is also demonstrated in the readiness to adopt and adapt new technologies to learning. For the e-learner, both systems and educational practices are in flux, driving the need for readiness to adopt new technologies and to adapt learning practices. A *reciprocal co-evolution* is in progress between the 'e' and the 'learning' of e-learning, i.e. that the electronic technologies are affecting and changing practices and presentations of learning and literacy as these are also changing the choices, uses, and designs of electronic technologies (Andrews and Haythornthwaite 2007). The outcome is that e-learners are continuously learning to enact their environments, e.g. in how to integrate first online discussion, and now blogs, social networking, virtual worlds, Twitter, etc., into learning practices; how to 'talk' through text in 'persistent conversations' (Erickson 1999), and now to present in video; how to be present in text-based environments, and then in virtual worlds; how to retrieve information from known sources and now to manage information selection and evaluation from multiple gated and non-gated repositories. When not gated within physical or virtual walls, the e-learner navigates across multiple media and platforms for their learning. Not only do learners acquire new literate practices for each new medium, they also learn ways of remixing and developing literacy in cross-platform and multimodal interaction (Cope and Kalantzis 2000; Kress 2003, 2010; Jewitt 2008). They make sense of their learning experience, and they make their learning experience make sense, through a sociotechnical ecology of devices, connections, networks, and people, and a sociomaterial engagement with learning (Gourlay and Oliver, this volume).

As individuals learn, so do the *groups* they belong to. Through practice, groups learn how *to be* their particular definition of a distributed, online learning community (Orlikowski 2002). Some may create a structure that persists even with change in members; while others may last only until key players leave (e.g. Bruckman and Jensen 2002). Some may be directed by authorities who control form and function; and others may run by consensus (Haythornthwaite 2009). As e-learners come and go in and across these environments, they become fluent with the process of online group development, the creation of personal and joint identity, co-construction of group technology use, and distributed group practices (Engeström 2009; Preston 2008; DeSanctis and Poole 1994; Haythornthwaite 2006a). One process to watch is the impact that digital habits acquired before and/or alongside engagement in higher education will have on institutional practice, as is already happening as the online, always-on digital habits of young adults enter university settings.

As well as the e-learner, the field of learning and the practice of education is also subject to reciprocal co-evolution, with impacts on learning practices and designs. Such changes are already evident in the way traces left by online participation become data for learning analytics, even as these analytics and technologies may drive attention to particular educational practices and outcomes (see Williams, this volume). Further, as cyberinfrastructure, e-science, and e-research drive analytics in general, non-text literacies are taking on new importance as attention turns to reading, writing, managing, analyzing, and visualizing data generated and made available from mediated social and learning activity.

A last point to make is that a view that adoption of these practices will happen seamlessly is overly optimistic and decidedly unrealistic, even as we see such practices emerging daily. Not all individuals, groups, and/or institutions are ready for or even aware of the extensive changes this new definition of e-learning suggests. Existing infrastructures, and attachments to places, roles, and practices form 'asset specificities' (Williamson 1981) that tie value, worth, and reputation to particular forms of operation, a consideration that also plays out in knowledge production (Haythornthwaite 2006b). Institutional choices come bound with concerns about cost, ease of implementation, continuity of relationships with vendors, matching peer institution offerings, and student throughput, concerns that have little or no relation to learning (Williams, this volume). Readiness for new practices can be choppy, with some individuals and/or parts of an institution well set and eager to change while others remain attached to existing practices (Haythornthwaite and Andrews 2011). It is not unreasonable to expect a mixing of old and new, and to find existing practices that should be retained. Indeed, in keeping with an emergent perspective, it is both appropriate and expected that our next learning practices will arise from the interplay of old practices, new technologies, and social purposes.

Conclusion

The aim of this chapter has been to put forward a renewed view of e-learning that encompasses learning on and through the Internet and its resources, connections, and technologies, and to engage with a definition of literacy for e-learning, and the university, that is the outcome of active engagement with ICTs for social purposes. While early e-learning emerged from the controlled digital environments of online programs, today's e-learning emerges from societal practices and a critical mass of online resources both informational and human. The digital university is an actor in this network, both shaping and shaped by e-learner practices. The literacy of a contemporary e-learner resides in their fluency with contributory practices in a collaborative context, self-directed learning supporting personal but shared needs, and an active construction of their own and their shared sociotechnical environment. With engagement, e-learners become fluent with an assemblage of skills that support adoption of new technologies and adaptation of social practices that in turn can drive the development of the next generation of technologies and social practices. It is an ambitious agenda to create such whole e-learners and also to keep up with their literacy in a changing world. The key may be what we heard from early e-learning teachers, i.e. to accept a 'different learning' – a different literacy – one that is predicated on active and continuously emergent construction of practice around literacy and technology.

Chapter 5

The literacies of 'digital scholarship' – truth and use values

Robin Goodfellow

A literacies perspective on digital scholarship

Literacy theorists have long argued for an understanding of the phenomenon as participation in social action (see Gourlay and Oliver, Lea, McKenna and Hughes, in this volume). Literacy in social settings implicates whole communities, 'values and beliefs' about knowledge, 'identities, subject positions, and potential for agency', as well as power relations which may constrain 'possibilities for self-hood for particular participants' (Ivanič *et al.* 2007: 706). Literacy research in higher education, which has conventionally focused on writing as the principal means of action, now addresses a landscape in which text-making involves multiple modes, and an increasingly complex interaction of social and technical phenomena (Kress 2003, 2010). There is a major challenge in trying to bring the perspectives of communities, power relations, individual subjects, and other actors to bear on the textual practices of the digital university. In this chapter I aim to take up this challenge in relation to the practices of scholarship.

A literacies perspective (Goodfellow and Lea 2007; Goodfellow 2011) on scholarship in the digital university focuses on the highly contextualized social meanings created by the producers, consumers, and communicators of the digital texts that come to be recognized as scholarship, in and around the university of the digital age. Its aim is to bring to light, and make available for critique, important and hitherto hidden or perhaps unrecognized aspects of the social relations between these actors, which contribute to the texts having the form and effects that they do. What values and beliefs underlie emerging forms of 'digital scholarship'? How are these implicated in the production of knowledge in digital scholarly environments? What are the possibilities and constraints on self-identification as 'scholar' that new forms of technical mediation construct? To address such questions fully would clearly require an entire research programme, combining ethnographic observations of practice, interpretations of participant accounts, detailed textual and rhetorical analysis (see some examples of such approaches in Gourlay and Oliver, Satchwell *et al.*, Lee, Lea, in this volume). But digital scholarship is only just emerging as an issue for research in academic practice and there are few in-depth studies to be drawn on as yet (see Fransman in this volume).

But what we do have are some key texts from research fields such as scholarly communication and social epistemology (Lievrouw 2010; Palmer and Cragin 2008; Borgman 2007), digital humanities (Spiro 2010; Flanders 2009), and technology in education (Weller 2011; Pearce *et al.* 2010; Katz 2010; Schön 2000) in which the concept is explored, and in which relevant practices are described. These texts may be amenable to analytical perspectives drawn from the fields of new literacies and rhetorical studies, in an effort to identify the values and beliefs behind the changes that are being documented and/or advocated. This I propose to explore here, as a first step in evaluating the contribution such perspectives might bring to our understanding of what it might mean to be a 'digital scholar'.

In this chapter I look in some detail at two contemporary texts by 'scholars of the digital' writing about scholarship: Christine Borgman's book *Scholarship in the Digital Age. Information, Infrastructure and the Internet* (Borgman 2007), and Martin Weller's *The Digital Scholar: How Technology Is Transforming Scholarly Practice* (Weller 2011), (see also Jones, this volume, for more discussion of these authors). These books are separated by five years in which the use of internet-based social technologies ('Web 2.0', the 'read/write web', the 'social web', etc.) has become ubiquitous, and a comparison between them demonstrates not only the impact that new digital technologies are having on the rhetoric and practice of scholars, but also the extent to which conventional academic scholarly literacy practices have remained stable in the face of this. The two authors hail from broadly cognate disciplinary areas, although from different practice communities: Borgman is principally an information science researcher engaged in academic service as well as research and teaching; Weller is a learning technology practitioner, involved in a range of policy, pedagogical, and technological activities as well as research and teaching. Different academic communities engage differently in scholarship, as Boyer established in an exploration of the 'priorities of the professoriate' (Boyer 1990), and differences in orientation to scholarly practice and the role of digital technologies in its future development are evident in Borgman's and Weller's approaches, starting with terminological differences in the titles of the two books: 'scholarship in the digital age', and 'the digital scholar'. Furthermore, as I will argue here, whilst both accounts address some of the same knowledge content – e.g. facts about the way that scholarly publishing is organized and its relation to alternative processes and procedures of scholarly communication conducted in digital domains – both authors are also engaged in rhetorical projects that have distinctive persuasive as well as informative aims.

I explore these texts from a broad discourse-analytic position, as described by Gee (1999), which seeks to reveal hidden assumptions underlying the specific ways in which texts are created, and theorizes about what is being enacted when the texts are taken into in the social world. The exploration focuses on the authors' academic backgrounds, the published forms in which the works appear, their textual structures and organization of the content, and their use of academic literacy conventions such as referencing. I also look at the works from a rhetorical perspective, following Bazerman's identification of characteristic features of writing in different academic disciplines (Bazerman 1981), focusing on the way topics and audiences are constructed, how literatures are used, and how the authors implicitly or explicitly represent themselves. I unpick some of what is behind these different persuasive projects, in particular the different implications of the overlapping terms 'digital' and 'open' in relation to scholarship. I aim to show that 'truth' and 'use' values of knowledge are differently evident in these accounts, and that the accounts themselves are correspondingly addressed to different audiences. I discuss some implications of this finding for the digital university, drawing on a hypothetical tension between the emerging principle of 'open-ness' allied to digital practices, and the traditional commitment of academic scholarship to rigour and methodological accountability.

Background – scholarship offline and on

The term 'scholarship' usually refers to a particular kind of orientation to knowledge work characteristic of, although not exclusive to, university and other academic research contexts. (Boyer 1990; Ellison and Eatman 2008). Whilst the actual processes of doing scholarly work varies between disciplines and institutions (see Palmer and Craigin 2008 for an overview of disciplinary scholarship), there is a general consensus that 'academic' scholarship involves a distinctive methodological orientation to knowledge shared by all who practise it. This orientation values critical reflection, the cumulative aggregation of knowledge and understanding, distinct modes of operation relating to evidence and the warranting of its reliability, and the ethic of enquiry as a primary motivation (Andresen 2000; Cowan et al. 2008; Courant 2008). The combination of these characteristics is what distinguishes the construction of academic scholarly knowledge from other kinds of knowledge production (factual knowledge, practical knowledge, common-sense, morality, the 'wisdom of crowds', etc.). The existence of communities dedicated to these values in a general sense also distinguishes the sites of production of academic scholarly knowledge (universities, research institutes, museums) from most other arenas of social knowledge practice. As some scholars (e.g. Boyer 1990, Andresen 2000) have observed, there is a strong normative dimension to the idea of scholarship – it has historically been highly valued by society for its ethics as well as for its outputs.

Whilst the ethic of knowledge sharing is deep-rooted in the traditional practices of scholarly communication, access to its formal outputs has come to be monopolized by journals and other publications that are typically accessed through university libraries, as are the databases that catalogue them. Thus, whilst scholarly books are available in principle to the general public through public libraries, the escalating cost of limited circulation books and journals puts many of them beyond the reach of the non-institutional scholar (MLAA 2002). Institutionalizing the outputs of scholarship creates a disjuncture between informal processes of scholarly communication and formal systems of dissemination and publication, erecting barriers to both insider and public access to knowledge (Borgman 2007; Lievrouw 2010). At the same time, scholars are being urged by national policy-makers to be more accountable to government and society, more engaged with professional and public interests, more oriented to work that can be measured by its 'relevance and effectiveness' (Barker 2004) as well as by scholarly methodological and ethical criteria. A considerable impetus towards making scholarly processes and outputs more generally accessible has therefore developed, and the affordances of digital technologies figure very largely in this.

The digital enabling of access to scholarship, as a research field in its own right, has its roots in the library studies, information systems, and social informatics research communities, which is the context of Christine Borgman's work. This research focuses on the design, development, and use of digital repositories and archives, online journals, email lists, and other digital fora for facilitating scholarly communication and extending access to, and the sharing of, data within scholarly communities via practices of open access publishing, self-archiving, and collaborative editing (Palmer and Cragin 2008; Borgman 2007). What is coming to be known as 'digital scholarship', however, is the relatively recent invention by cross-disciplinary groups of individual scholars, particularly from education and the humanities, who have begun to use technology to disseminate their own work outside the formal academic publishing system (Anderson 2012; Burton 2009; Weller 2011). These digital scholars have begun to promote the idea that every-day practices of mass open online interaction enabling large-scale exchanges of user-generated content (YouTube, Flickr, Wikipedia, Google Apps), peer-to-peer communication (email, blogging, Twitter), and online social and professional networking (Facebook, LinkedIn) impact on personal and professional practice for scholars (Jensen 2007; Katz 2010; Weller 2011). This is the context of Martin Weller's work. In this new field, emerging paradigms for the public construction of knowledge are explored for their capacity to transform conventional scholarly practices and also facilitate the intervention in academic communication of non-academic and amateur scholars, and informed members of the general public.

Scholars of the digital – Borgman and Weller compared

Christine Borgman and Martin Weller have been chosen for this study because they represent different 'traditions' of research on the digital in scholarship: one beginning with the scholarship, the other with the digital. Borgman is a scholar of a relatively traditional kind: her work is located within the broad disciplinary areas of information science and library studies – mainly published through conventional academic channels such as journals and books. Her university-based web profile shows that she sits on a number of national scientific committees and advisory boards as well as editorial panels of scholarly journals. Her work in the field of digital scholarship is well established – she has 24 entries in Web of Knowledge since 1997, and widely cited – there are 364 citations of the 2007 book listed in Google Scholar, 104 since 2011 (September 2012). She notes in her preface to the book that it was mostly written during a sabbatical year at the Oxford Internet Institute (2005–6) when she set out to develop some ideas introduced in an earlier book *From Gutenburg to the Global Information Infrastructure* (Borgman 2003). Weller characterizes himself explicitly as a 'digital scholar' and his scholarship in the field of educational technology is in the process of reflexive self-construction – he refers in his book (2011) to his personal commitment to open publishing and his preference for imaginative blog-type writing as opposed to the 'dry' academic genres he has previously tried to engage with (Chapter 11). His scholarship is practice and policy-oriented, and his public profile is very largely tied up with his blog 'The Ed Techie' (Weller 2012a), which he promotes enthusiastically, explicitly foregoing an 'official' academic profile. The blog was ranked by traffic in the top 50 of technology blogs worldwide every month between August 2009 and February 2011.[1] The book discussed here had about fifty citations in Google Scholar since 2011, but his overall 'footprint' on the academic internet is considerably more prominent than Borgman's – a search for his name combined with the keywords 'digital scholarship' produced 651 hits between 2006 and 2012 (excluding those on his own blog), as against for 280 for Borgman over the same period. Weller says in his introduction that the book was put together out of a series of posts he had written to his blog between 2006 and 2010, a process he compares favourably with earlier book-writing experiences.

Despite their authors' different research backgrounds, attitudes to academic scholarship, and processes of writing, the books that are the focus of this comparison are quite similar in form and nature – testimony to the stability of certain practices of academic publishing between 2007 and 2011. Both are single-authored books published by established academic publishers (MIT press and Bloomsbury Academic) and offered for sale to university libraries and to the public through bookshops and the internet. Borgman's book sells in hardback for £25.95, and paperback for £13.95; Weller's sells as an e-book for £17.99, and as a downloadable PDF or in hardback for £55. The one key difference in terms of academic publishing practice is the creation by Bloomsbury of an HTML version of Weller's book, available at no cost from the publisher's website. The HTML version is simply an online transposition of the printed book, with limited digital functionality and no additional media components. For example, each chapter is presented as a single scrollable screen, with links to previous and next chapters via the contents section at top and bottom. It is therefore not possible to download the whole book, or search digitally across chapters, although one can search for keywords within chapters by using a browser search function. Most of the in-text citations are hyperlinked to the references section, but are not bookmarked so it is necessary to scroll through the references to find the relevant one. However, despite its functional limitations this version of the book is entirely open (offered under a Creative Commons non-commercial licence), reflecting the author's personal commitment to 'open-ness' in the dissemination of his research, and the publisher's commitment to innovation in digital publishing. For the purposes of this comparison, I have used Borgman in the hardback version, as representative of a conventional scholarly output, and the HTML version of Weller as representative of an approach to open scholarship.

Literacies and rhetoric

Both accounts embed key literacy practices for written scholarship which would be familiar to any of the academic communities involved in these interdisciplinary areas, although there are significant differences that position the reader and the text in somewhat different relations in each case. Information and argument is presented via similar discourse structures (e.g. the use of chapters and sections), with Borgman's overall text somewhat longer – 336 pages in total, as against Weller's 256 pages – although the number of words for the actual content is close, at approximately 85,000 to 84,000. Borgman's text is divided into nine chapters, broken up into approximately 25 sections per chapter, with all sections and page numbers listed in detail in a seven-page contents section. Navigation within the text is therefore possible to quite a fine degree of topic specificity, which affords a broadly theoretical account of relationships between practices in scholarly communication, academic publishing, data curation, and the creation of a scholarly 'information infrastructure' (p. 19). A 16-page index increases the possibilities for finding specific terms and names. Weller has 14 chapters of approximately seven sections each and a list of contents that simply gives each chapter title. These are hotlinked to the chapters themselves but there is no navigation within chapters, and there is no index. Also, as noted above, it is not possible to search digitally across the whole book, only chapter by chapter. Borgman's reader thus has considerably more scope for overviewing the contents of the work, and for accessing specific aspects of the topic for close attention. Weller's reader is tied more closely to a narrative-type structure which broadly parallels the development of the author's own ideas, and is dependent for an overview on his in-text signposting of discussion to come. It thus appears that whilst Weller's book has been made 'open' in the sense of being accessible at no cost, the process has not enhanced systematic accessibility to its content – an important consideration for the work as a work of scholarship.

Evidence and support for key points in each author's argument are provided through citations from others' work, via similar in-text citation styles and bibliographical conventions. Borgman, however, uses considerably more citations and references than Weller – almost four times as many (797 against 220), and provides multiple citations for the more significant claims in her argument, as is typical in a social science field where both the framework of analysis and the argument itself may be novel to the audience (see Bazerman's discussion of Morton's work, 1981). Her references also draw historically on a specifically disciplinary literature, for example in her use of journal references in the information science field ranging from 1969 to 2006, with a broadly equal distribution of references across the decades in between. Weller uses citations and quotes going back to 1932 to support his argument, favouring literatures that are known more generally (for example, around the relation between publishing online and citation counts). In general his citations are used singly, draw eclectically on a range of subject areas and types of publication, and tend to be illustrative rather than evidential. They also include a number of blog posts, which are largely absent from Borgman's bibliography. As may be expected, both authors cite a lot of online sources; in Weller's case 62 per cent of his references contain URLs, compared to 42 per cent in Borgman's case (although she still has nearly three times as many overall). Twenty-eight per cent of Borgman's references are to journal articles (with no URL) against 19 per cent of Weller's. Both authors refer to books in 15 per cent of their citations although Borgman's use of 63 citations from book chapters (with no URL) compares to only four by Weller.[2] Borgman's reader is thus drawn into a wider web of evidence, albeit from a more defined disciplinary community, whereas Weller's is invited to make personal connections which are often broadly associative rather than directly evidential.

Perhaps the major difference between these two texts, viewed as works of scholarship, is to be found in the authorial 'voices' of the writers, linked to the nature of the overall argument, and the authors' positioning of the reader. As Jones (this volume) points out, Borgman takes a more institutional view of digital scholarship, whereas Weller focuses on the individual digital scholar. Borgman's key themes are copyright and intellectual property, the management of institutional repositories, the preservation and curation of data, and the digital practices of the library community. Her key message is that digital content demands different techniques for the preservation and replication of the 'scholarly record'. Weller is interested in the democratization of academia and the promotion of innovation and experimentation with new media in scholarly practice. His key message is that scholarly resistance to new digital practices can be overcome through an understanding of the contexts in which technological change is occurring. Borgman's argument is presented in a conventionally 'academic' voice which sets out to persuade via an apparently objective stance – she does not use personal references, apart from in the preface and acknowledgements sections. Her construction of her audience places the reader amongst the scholars who are in part the subject of the discussion – researchers, authors, and librarians who share much of the specialized knowledge about conventional scholarly publishing processes that is the basis for the discussion – but who may be relatively unfamiliar with digital developments and are newcomers to ideas about the shaping relation between technology and social change. This constructs an audience that is already engaged, perhaps professionally, in scholarly communication, and for whom digital developments are of conceptual as well as practical concern. Weller's voice is more informal and polemical, favouring a personal tone with use of the first person, references to himself and family, and anecdotes and 'parables' mixed in with more conventional academic citation and references. His overall approach might be characterized as didactic, rather than discursive, with regular use of bullet points and numbered lists to clarify concepts and the structure of his argument, and a lot of signposting of discussion to come up in later chapters, and summarizing in conclusion sections. This approach tends to position the reader as a relative newcomer to key aspects of the world of scholarship being described, for example the processes of academic publishing, and as having a less special-ized interest, and perhaps less personal investment, in the system as it is, so that they will need less persuasion of the imperative to change or replace it. The text positions the reader as accepting of the idea that online communication neces-sarily disrupts its print-based predecessors (this idea is explicated in detail early in the book). Weller's text utilizes some conventional social scientific rhetoric, but overall has a more speculative and directly persuasive character reminiscent of Bazerman's descriptions of the style characteristic of writing in the humani-ties (see Bazerman 1981 on Geoffrey Hartman's discussion of Wordsworth). He develops a more 'cultural' account of the issue of institutional control over traditional scholarship and the likelihood of its being undermined in the short term by digital practices that have already transformed other cultural industries. His points draw on metaphorical as well as evidential resources, which open the topics up to non-research-based interpretations. His construction of his audience places the reader amongst interested practitioners as well as research scholars – students, teachers, technologists, perhaps with an existing disposition to favour digital media over traditional ones. His own authority is constructed through his self-presentation as a pioneer of the practices and values he is promoting, exem-plified by his description of his own 'conversion' to creative writing in open fora, at the expense of a more formal research profile.

Discussion – open-ness versus scholarship?

As suggested in the introduction to this chapter, the surface similarities between the two texts compared here are as striking as their differences. This would not be unexpected if these accounts had been published at the same time, but they are separated by five years in which some quite dramatic changes to the technolo-gies of public communication have occurred. As far as textuality – the kind of symbolic cultural objects they are – is concerned, the only really significant dif-ference between the texts is the fact that Weller's HTML version is free. This is significant because it is still relatively unusual in scholarly publishing and signals new thinking amongst publishers and authors about the business and reputation models that underlie formal scholarly communication. But similarities in literacy practice are significant too – both texts demonstrate the dominance of the writ-ten mode, of a particular kind of organization of discourse, of the performance of academic credibility. The reasons for this may be straightforward: perhaps the 'open' text cannot be allowed to be superior to the retailed version for commer-cial reasons; perhaps the author of the open text is still concerned with attracting forms of prestige attached to conventional academic print practices. But as far as the underlying rhetorical projects of the two authors is concerned it is significant that the texts come out looking the same, as it suggests that there are 'macro' literacy practices around academic communication that may conceal quite important dissimilarities in what these scholars are doing at the 'micro' rhetorical level. Weller's blogging about being a digital scholar appears to have been pressed into conformity with conventional academic publishing norms in order to be published as an online book, but the open-ness achieved by making it free in a digital version does not justify what it loses as a work of scholarship when compared to Christine Borgman's conventional printed volume, or as a work of creativity when compared to the multimodality of the original blogs.

Differences in the two authors' orientation to scholarship and the digital thus come through explicitly in the key messages of the books and implicitly in their written rhetoric – Borgman is trying to make digital scholarship more scholarly, Weller is trying to make it more digital. They exemplify these differing aims through rhetorical practices, as we have just seen. Borgman's more extensively indexed and referenced text constructs a more traditional research-scholarship audience, sharing disciplinary assumptions and probably identifications with particular research communities, especially in library studies and information science. Weller's more personal and eclectic account speaks to a more practice-scholarship audience, sharing a belief in the innovative potential of digital media, and perhaps identifications with the social media-based communities of the learning technology and digital humanities worlds that the author himself inhabits. At some points in the texts the motivations of the authors do converge, on the importance of peer review, the efficiency of self-archiving, the need to widen access, etc., but at other points we can see real and divergent foci of concern: the responsibility of 'the digital' towards the accuracy of the scholarly record (Borgman) versus the responsibility of 'the scholarly' towards the media creativity of the digital academic (Weller). These divergences point towards a real dichotomy between the values of two assumptions about the role of the digital in scholarship, partially concealed by commonalities in 'macro' literacy practices (and not much exposed by a limited new format for open publishing), but evident at the rhetorical level through differing attitudes to audience, literatures, evidence, and authorial voice. The two assumptions are: (a) that digital scholarship is concerned with establishing new kinds of 'truth values' for academic knowledge that is currently being destabilized by practices, values, and derivatives generated in informal communication on the internet; and (b) that it is concerned with new 'use values' for academic knowledge to be created by opening up scholarly communication channels to a wider range of participants and introducing a wider range of media into its processes and outputs.[3] The dichotomy between these assumptions about scholarship in the new digital order recalls what Calhoun hypothesizes as a tension between 'excellence' and 'access' in the enlightenment premise that knowledge can be both authoritative and democratic (Calhoun 2006: 9). Digital scholarship as represented by Borgman and Weller reproduces this tension.

Summary and conclusion – the literacies of digital scholarship

This chapter has explored a literacies perspective on practices embedded in two works of scholarship by contemporary scholars of the digital, one exemplifying a focus on the 'digital' and its implications for scholarly practice, and the other concerned with 'open-ness' and the use by scholars of digital media to extend it. The focus was on the values and attitudes to scholarship that are revealed in the forms of the published texts and the details of the rhetorical practices employed by the authors in their writing, but the aim was not only to explore these values and attitudes but also to evaluate the contribution that this kind of literacies perspective can make to research and practice in the emerging fields of digital scholarship. In focusing on what I have called the 'macro-level' literacy practices that shape the texts as academic publications, the approach pointed up the contrast between the different background contexts of the two authors and the essential similarities in the texts they had produced, despite what should have been key differences in the shaping factors of medium and pricing. In addressing what I termed 'micro-level' rhetorical constructions in the writing itself, the approach identified the means by which the two authors signal different audiences, despite the commonality in much of the subject matter being discussed. One important conclusion has been that making a version of Weller's book freely accessible online has not made it any more 'open' as far as the scholarship of the digital is concerned, although it may have made it more useful to a non-scholarly audience. The literacies approach has the potential to pursue findings like this into other arenas of scholarly literacy practice, including where digital media play a more dominant role and where institutionally independent voices are active in promoting more significant kinds of open-ness (Burton 2009), for example in the online interactions around academic blogging, which was the original context of Weller's more dialogical style. Equally, the approach could cast further light on other findings, not highlighted here, such as Borgman's much greater use of references to edited books, with all the interesting implications for this practice that the digital opening up of publishing resources to ordinary academics may have.

The developing digital context for scholarship in the university is clearly creating pressures and opportunities for changing practice in both scholarly communication and public participation in scholarship. I have argued that there is a dichotomy between a 'truth value' orientation to the digital, which emphasizes its role in assuring precision and accuracy in scholarly communication, and a 'use value' orientation that emphasizes its capacity to make scholarly communication open to a wider constituency. Academic publishing practices signal a conventional commitment of a scholarly work to truth values, even where the rhetorical practices of the author are oriented to use. Making a conventionally structured academic text accessible by publishing it online for free does not, by itself, make that text more 'open' in the sense of being more usable to a different or non-scholarly readership. Moreover, if the micro-level rhetorical features of the text are working with a 'use value' orientation, that may actually make it less usable to a conventional, truth-oriented, scholarly community.

Digital technologies enable scholars to work with different kinds of audiences, and create different kinds of author–reader relationships with those audiences. However, it is not the technologies alone that construct those audiences but also the literacy practices of the communities from which they are drawn. Close-knit communities like university academic librarians, who have a commitment to the truth values of the texts they process are likely to respond to rhetoric which constructs a well-defined, historically stable literature, an explicit topic structure that separates data from argument and theory from method, and an authorial voice that is objective and monologic. Wider, less-defined communities, such as educational technology practitioners whose commitment is to the use value of their knowledge may better respond to eclectic literatures, transparent topic structures that are embedded in narrative or linear arguments, or authorial voices that are personal and dialogic. Open-ness in scholarship not only commits to a certain kind of digital transformation, it also commits the scholar-author to a decision about truth and use, and to literacy practices that express the values of the knowledge community that is the audience.

If a commitment to open-ness puts digital practices at the centre of a wider and more accessible constituency around scholarship, involving teachers, practitioners, employers, and the informed public as well as academic researchers, this brings with it a greater need for the explicit negotiation of what is claimed to be true and what is useful. New practices will take place in a wider range of social arenas as well – in formal and informal educational and occupational contexts (see Littlejohn *et al.* in this volume) as well as professional research and public sphere domains. Open scholarship practices may shade into events and genres which have traditionally been associated with other spheres of professional communication, such as journalism and 'infotainment', or informal interest-oriented communication, or (in the case of controversial areas of science such as climate science or bioscience) moral and political activism (Holliman 2011). Means of establishing trust, authority, and reputation which are prevalent in the more general sphere of online interaction, and which may involve actors from all parts of the professional–amateur–citizen spectrum of interest, may undermine conventional mechanisms of academic publication and expert peer review (Jensen 2007). The opening up of scholarship by digital means may thus threaten to disrupt the core stakeholder roles involved in producing, mediating, and consuming information within institutional scholarly networks. This has major implications for institutional academic scholars, not least for their practices of reward and professional recognition (Weller 2012b). Digital versus open scholarship may thus prove to be the defining dichotomy for the shape of the university of the future.

Notes

1 eBuzzing: http://labs.ebuzzing.co.uk/top-blogs/source/nogoodreason.typepad.co.uk/no_
   good_reason-SHgr (2 October 2012).
2 The figures for different types of references are derived from an informal count carried
   out manually. All references containing a URL were counted as a single category – although the documents themselves differed in type, between blog posts, official reports,
   online journal articles that may or may not have been refereed, etc. In almost all cases
   access to a URL was open. Journal articles refers to publications in listed journals where
   there is no URL given – most such articles are in fact accessible online through library
   electronic databases, which require subscriptions. Books, and chapters in books were
   self-evident.
3 The terms 'truth values' and 'use values' are not the authors' but my own, borrowed
   from Beetham's discussion of the same (Beetham 2009).

Chapter 6

Beyond 'the social': digital literacies as sociomaterial practice

Lesley Gourlay and Martin Oliver

Introduction

'Digital literacies' is a contested term with mismatching theoretical reference points and implicit views of practice. These range from a New Literacies Studies (NLS)-derived view of literacies as situated social practice, through to a use of the term 'literacies' more associated with generic 'skills' and capabilities (Goodfellow 2011). As this area of practice becomes increasingly mainstreamed as a focus for research and development, its theoretical bases urgently need not only to be clarified, but also extended. This chapter will discuss the theoretical gains offered by an NLS perspective, but also will explore the limitations of this approach for theorizing the materiality of digitally mediated textual engagement in particular. It will propose an alternative view of digital literacies as emergent sociomaterial (as opposed to purely social) practice. Drawing on posthuman perspectives on the embodied and the virtual (Hayles 1999, 2006) and sociomaterial approaches to educational research (e.g. Fenwick *et al.* 2011), this view sees digital literacies as jointly accomplished social practice achieved by engagements between human and nonhuman actors. This will be illustrated with initial qualitative data from an ongoing Joint Information Systems Committee (JISC)-funded project which addresses this area in the context of higher education. Focus group and multi-modal journaling data will be analysed, and the utility of Actor-Network Theory (ANT) discussed.

The chapter will focus particularly on the situated and emergent nature of students' day-to-day interaction with technologies as a key feature of digital literacies. It will report on the initial findings of a study using focus groups and multimodal journaling to investigate the practices of four groups of postgraduate students of education. The data reveal the complexities of these students' identities/orientations towards technologies and also the distributed nature of their practices in networks of material objects and devices – with texts emerging via both material (in the sense of embodied) and digitally mediated practices. Students were asked to document their engagements with technologies for study using images and video. This will be illustrated with focus group data, 'maps' of practice, excerpts from interviews, and multimodal journaling data. This chapter and the analysis presented will be of interest to practitioners, researchers in the field, and anyone undertaking change projects around technologies in higher education contexts.

Background

The term 'digital literacies' is a contested one, with differing uses of the term revealing competing and even contradictory theoretical perspectives (see, for example, Littlejohn *et al.*'s account of its use in UK higher education in this volume and Lea 2013). 'Literacy' itself is a contested term, often used as a proxy for capabilities, with an emphasis on 'know-how', implying a relatively stable, finite, and generic set of capabilities to be mastered; in higher education it is often associated with attributes demonstrating 'graduate employability'. In this perspective, literacies are positioned as measurable, discrete, and ultimately residing in the individual. The student is seen as a 'user' of technologies; suggesting a clear division between the human and machine, action and context, writer/reader and text, and the university and other domains of life. Work on 'digital literacies' in school contexts has tended to focus on a range of multimodal online formats such as videos, blogs, virtual worlds, and games (e.g. Carrington and Robinson 2009, Steinkueler 2007). However, in higher education the term tends to be applied with implicit reference to technologies required for assessment tasks, such as library catalogue systems, databases, Virtual Learning Environments (VLEs), and other interfaces. The emphasis tends to be on relatively traditional text-based formats such as essays, written through digital media (a topic explored by Williams in this volume).

As a result, there is some ambiguity surrounding the term 'digital literacies', which appears to be moving away from the NLS-inspired ethnographic conception – sensitive towards identities and pluralities. This slippage can be glimpsed in the formulation 'digital literacies skills', which serves to undermine the insights of NLS, and leads the field towards a less-than-nuanced 'skills' focus. It can be argued that the term 'literacies' has become 'domesticated', and is in danger of losing its critical edge and rootedness in ethnographic sensibilities and day-to-day practices.

The origins of the NLS perspective lie in critical language studies within applied linguistics and ethnographic work in social anthropology in the 1980s, which began to challenge the dominant model of 'literacy' which focused on the cognitive and the individual. Seminal studies such as Brice-Heath (1983) and Street (1984) uncovered the social nature of literacy as situated practice within communities. Brice-Heath coined the term 'literacy event' to describe a social event gathering around text and textual practices. Street also established a conception of literacy situated in ideological and social contexts, arguing that '. . . what the particular practices of reading and writing are for in a given society depends on the context; that they are already embedded in an ideology and cannot be isolated or treated as "neutral" or merely "technical" (1984: 1). These radical recastings of the term 'literacy' lead to the strand of work known as New Literacy Studies (e.g. Barton 1994), applied to higher education by Lea and Street's influential critique of dominant models, in particular of 'study skills' (1998). They provide a persuasive argument against the 'deficit' model and belief in 'transferable skills'. Instead, they advance an 'academic literacies' view of student writing as contested, complex, context-embedded, and implicated in identities and the exercise of power. A series of related studies have investigated the experiences of students, often those traditionally marginalized by mainstream academic discourse and writing requirements (e.g. Ivanič 1998, Lillis 2001).

NLS has provided a powerful critique of an area previously dominated by cognitivist perspectives which elided the importance of the social and the collective. It has also provided insights into the interplay between textual practice and subjectivities. However, one limitation of this perspective is that in seeking to move away from the cognitive and towards the social, it has perhaps tended to place rather less emphasis on the embodied materiality of textual engagement, in terms of what students actually do, where they do it and what resources and artefacts they work with. (In this sense, 'materiality' refers to the physical practices involved in engagements with texts and digital technologies.) Through its emphasis on individuals and the texts themselves, some micro-level focus on the objects, devices, and processes involved in textual engagement/production may have been de-emphasized, or naturalized as 'context'. However, a focus on the 'digital literacies' arguably necessitates an interrogation of the notion of 'context' and the material, which can no longer be taken for granted. This calls for a framing which can adequately theorize textual engagement as not only socially situated and constitutive of subjectivities, but crucially also as digitally mediated sociomaterial practice.

More recently, researchers have also linked an NLS perspective with technologies and 'e-learning' (e.g. Goodfellow and Lea 2007), with notable links made in the literature between NLS and sociomaterial perspectives. Mary Hamilton (2001) deploys ANT (discussed below) in an analysis of the International Adult Literacy Survey to explore how this textual artefact serves to maintain the social order. Barton and Hamilton (2005) also make this theoretical move in their critique of Wenger's (1998) model of Communities of Practice from a literacies perspective. Drawing on the work of Latour (1987), they point out how nonhuman actors may play roles in networks of practice, seeing texts as 'material literacy artefacts' (2005: 30) which exert agentive force. Clarke (2002) also explicitly makes a case for combining an ANT perspective with NLS in her analysis of government strategy surrounding adult literacy and numeracy. The relationship of these two perspectives to literacy studies is also considered by Lea in this volume.

However, it is worth noting that this strand of work has tended to focus on the agentive nature of policy texts in broad social domains, as opposed to applying a sociomaterial perspective to day-to-day engagements with texts, in particular in conjunction with digital devices. The following section will introduce some key concepts from posthuman theory, and will argue that a sociomaterial perspective offers a useful set of theoretical concepts which would be of utility in seeking to explore 'digital literacies'.

Theoretical framework

Posthuman theory (e.g. Badmington 2000, Wolfe 2010) is a loosely configured group of perspectives, as opposed to a unified theory. What unites these perspectives is their challenges to the dominant assumptions of humanism, questioning seemingly unassailable 'common-sense' binaries which form the bedrock of much social science and educational research; positioning the human as a centrally important and clearly separate category of being from other species, the environment, and technology. Posthuman theory relating to technologies in particular has been influenced by Haraway (1991) who proposes a blurring of boundaries, including between the biological and the technological. Haraway deployed the metaphor of the 'cyborg' within a feminist argument as a challenge to essentialism, but also as a metaphor for the hybrid, blurred nature of subjectivities in general, challenging dominant means of categorizing human and nonhuman: human and animal, organism and machine, physical and non-physical. However, the cyborg can also be interpreted as a metaphor for how subjectivities are also constituted by our discursive practices, indicative of a 'cyborg ontology', proposed by Gough (2004) in his analysis of posthuman pedagogies as 'becoming-cyborg'.

Hayles (1999) presents a compelling critical examination of embodiment in human engagements with technologies and meaning-making. Importantly, she cautions that the posthuman should not be associated with a literal cyborg – a combination of the biological with mechanical implants – but instead used as a means of understanding social practices and subjectivities involving an interweaving of the biological and the technological. As she points out, '. . . the defining characteristics of the posthuman involve the construction of subjectivity, not the presence of nonbiological components' (4).

Hayles' posthumanism may be used to elucidate the interplay between the author, text, and reader (and therefore digital literacies) in the contemporary university. If we accept her notion of the interpenetration of the technological, biological, and material, then arguably the notion of the stable and singular human author is brought into radical doubt. Authorship becomes distributed, interwoven between machine and human, as opposed to being associated with a singular, embodied human subject. In this conception, texts are produced by multiple, hybrid biological-informational entities meshed with wider online networks throughout the writing process, as illustrated by Bayne and Ross' discussion of the 'lifestream' assessment process in this volume.

A closely related perspective, ANT, also grew out science and technology studies (e.g. Callon 1986, Law and Hassard 1999, Latour 2005), and has recently begun to be applied to educational contexts (e.g. Fenwick and Edwards 2010, Tummons 2010, Lea in this volume). Like posthuman theory, it is an associated grouping of ideas as opposed to a unified position, but arguably three main features can be identified. First, there is a strong emphasis on the importance of nonhuman actors (such as objects or animals) as members of networks. As Latour puts it:

If you can, with a straight face, maintain that hitting a nail with and without a hammer, boiling water with and without a kettle . . . are exactly the same activities, that the introduction of these mundane implements change 'nothing important' to the realisation of tasks, then you are ready to transmigrate to the Far Land of the Social and disappear from this lowly one.

(Latour 2005: 71)

Second, ANT rejects essentialist a priori categories (such as social class and gender) associated with conventional sociology, preferring to see social action as constantly enacted moment-to-moment by social actors through detailed, networked practices. In this respect, it is related to ethnomethodology (e.g. Garfinkel 1967) with its emphasis on the everyday and 'micro' as the key site of social process.

Third, ANT does not seek to uncover causes for the emergence of networks of social practice, but is focused on *how* networks are created from the point of view of social actors. In these three respects, ANT becomes of utility in an investigation of student digital literacies by placing more emphasis on the fine-grained practices around texts and technologies, in order to analyse the technological and the human as interwoven in networks associated with textual engagement.

ANT's rejection of conventional categories may allow for a minimizing of questionable assumptions, such as the discredited binary of 'digital native' and 'digital immigrant', and may instead provide a research space for multiple, hybrid, or even seemingly contradictory practices and identities to be theorized. Clarke explicitly proposes ANT to address what she feels NLS has not:

. . . work in New Literacy Studies has tended to reply on pre-defined categories, which assume some of the things we want to explain. It then becomes difficult to show how literacy itself acquires attributes that set it above other forms of cognition, expression and communication. In conceptualising the relationship between local events and the special order 'out there', actor-network theory gets rid of 'out there' altogether . . . instead of assuming that we are observing traces of a macro-social system in a local context, the ANT ethnographer starts from the assumption that the local is all there is.

(Clarke 2002: 111)

As Fenwick and Edwards argue, '. . . ANT's key contribution is to suggest analytic methods that honour the mess, disorder and ambivalences that order phenomena, including education' (2010: 1).

Methodology

A JISC-funded study was undertaken in order to investigate student engagement with digital technologies, based at the Institute of Education, University of London (JISC 2012). First, accounts of practices were generated through focus groups with four main groups of students at the institution. This was followed by a six-month longitudinal study involving students assembling multimodal journal records of their practices using iPod Touch handheld devices. This chapter focuses on the early stages of this work.

Context

The Institute of Education (IOE) is the largest university centre of educational research in the UK. The student body is predominantly mature and postgraduate, with many students combining study with work and family responsibilities. Most have been out of formal education for several years, and may never have used digital technologies currently regarded as mainstream in UK higher education. However, they may be users of technologies common in other contexts, including in their personal lives, and are likely to have well-established repertoires of digital practices separate from the IOE.

A proportion of the student body is international, from a large number of countries, with a broad range of educational cultures.

Methods

The project commenced with focus groups to establish salient themes, working with four groups of students: Postgraduate Certificate in Education (PGCE), taught Master's, distance, and doctoral. Participants were recruited to ensure diversity of gender; age; home/EU or international; and full-time/part-time status. The discussions were transcribed and a thematic analysis was undertaken. The themes were then used to inform the next phase of work. In this, a dozen students from the focus groups were chosen to participate in a six-month journaling study, selecting a sample that ensured diversity against the criteria above. Three students from each group were asked to use iPod Touch devices to document their day-to-day practices and interactions with texts and technologies in a range of settings, producing images, videos and textual notes, and then assembling and discussing these in a series of interviews.

An initial meeting was held with biographical focus on uses of technology to support study, followed by guidance about how to approach the journaling.

Table 6.1 IOE student demographics (percentages)

	PGCE			*Master's*	*Distance*	*PhD*
	Primary	*Secondary*	*Post-compulsory*			
Female/Male	82/18	71/29	65/35	71/29	71/29	71/29
Home/EU and International	98/2	98/2	99/1	78/22	76/24	65/35
Full-time/Part-time	88/12	100/0	35/65	32/68	2/98	49/51

Participants were encouraged to focus on the 'messy' micro-level day-to-day lived activities, networks, and the material/spatial aspects of practice – elements of digital literacies which may be 'tidied up' by more conventional forms of data collection such as stand-alone interviews, which rely on self-report and may lead to abstraction (Gourlay 2010). The multimodal nature of the data was also designed to maximize rootedness in the practice, through a focus on images or recordings of everyday objects and processes. Students were then given a month to undertake initial work, creating different kinds of multimodal data. A subsequent interview allowed students to report and explore initial data collected, with a further two interviews scheduled. These images and artefacts serve not only as objects of analysis, but also as stimulus for in-depth exploration of subjectivities, challenges, and issues in the interviews – providing a rich set of participant accounts of technological engagement. Rather than use the project to engineer a technical 'fix', the purpose is to deepen understanding of student engagement with technologies in day-to-day practice, providing valuable insights for the institution in order to create conditions for students to thrive.

This creation of assemblages by students was an important aspect of the methodology. As Clarke points out, ANT research may be criticized for a lack of reflexivity, while NLS research has often utilized collaborative approaches in which participants contribute to interpretation and analysis. She suggests combining elements of both approaches, in order that '. . . the lessons we can draw from each would underpin a research agenda which combines the detachment and symmetry of ANT ethnography with a commitment to reflectivity and collaboration' (Clarke 2002: 120).

The study received institutional ethical clearance and followed approved procedures for informed consent, including guarantees of anonymity and confidentiality, and the right to opt out at any point. Details of the participants are given in Table 6.2:

Table 6.2 Overview of journaling participants

Category	Pseudonym	Details
MA	Nahid	M, 26 Bangladeshi
MA	Juan	M, 30s British
MA	Yuki	F, 42 Japanese
PhD	Django	F, 39 British
PhD	Sally	F, 41 British
PhD	Frederick	M, 25 German
PGCE	Louise	F, 22 British
PGCE	Faith	F, 30 Taiwanese
PGCE	Polly	F, 40 British
Distance	Bokeh	M, 30s British
Distance	Darren	M, 40s American
Distance	Lara	F, 40s Chilean

Findings

The focus groups suggested several differences between the four groups. This was seen in the way that members of the groups discovered and accessed texts. For example, PGCE tutors tended to upload resources in the course Virtual Learning Environment (VLE). The PGCE students still had to develop strategies for finding resources, as a result of confusion about the way they were categorized. ('Sometimes it's a bit time-consuming trying to find where they've actually put something . . . Yes, if another student has already found it, then it gets easier and I think that's how it works, mostly'). For distance students access to the physical library was impractical, so they discovered texts partly through the VLE but also through the online library database, which linked to electronic resources. They described the strategies they had developed to deal with 'information overload', working across a range of platforms and settings. For the Masters' students, the situation was different again: for them, library space was crucial. Participants talked about the need for quiet, with some also contrasting difficulties accessing electronic resources in this space ('before you get on the internet or on the computer, you have to wait, like, ten minutes before it's starting up') with the ease and even pleasures of the way that they accessed and read printed texts here. By contrast, the PhD students discussed text discovery in social or purposeful ways: texts were described at various times as means of engagement with others (for example, as a way of 'following people') and of gauging understanding of an area (and the consequent 'constant paranoia that there's something you've missed'). Some students suggested that the practices of incorporating texts into their own work were markedly different depending on whether they were first discovered in hard copy, from a database (which could then be exported via EndNote into writing), or from other electronic searches such as Google Scholar.

These initial findings are significant as they serve to reinforce the highly situated nature of student engagement with technologies; undermining a monolithic, convergent, or taxonomic understanding of student digital literacies, even at a relatively small, specialist, and predominantly postgraduate institution such as the IOE. These are informing an institutional move away from a generic conception of digital literacies towards a more nuanced and socially situated stance.

However, in spite of these variations in practices, there were points of consistency. Three themes were identified that are of direct relevance to this chapter; data for these could be found with all four groups, both in the focus groups and also in the interviews and journaling data. They are:

- The complexity of students' spatial domains for engagement with technologies
- The central role of networked devices in student engagement
- The locally negotiated nature of engagements with texts and devices

The next section will describe how these were identified in the initial analysis of the first set of data, with some brief illustrative examples.

Multiple spatial domains

In the focus groups (and first interviews), students were asked to draw 'maps' of their digital practices. It was apparent that all students engaged with technologies across a wide range of physical domains, as can be seen in this representative example taken from the Master's focus group (Figure 6.1).

These included prototypical 'university' spaces, such as lecture/tutorial rooms, the library, and open access computer suites. However, it also included schools, specialist libraries, offices, virtual spaces, shared research rooms, home, public transport, public spaces, and the outdoors. Not all spaces were used by all students; nor did all use them in the same way. Some students actively avoided studying at home, preferring to find, read, and write texts in the library; professional settings were only relevant to some students; some were happy to read on trains and buses, while others were not.

Even within these spaces, there were differences. Students interacted with the spatiality of the library differently, for example one student explained how 'advice from my supervisor is pick a section and then I'll walk through that section for a good half an hour and look at the other books'. Another described how 'there's certain corners that I like to work in', but that other areas were too noisy or hot.

Spaces were also sites of other activities, which raised interesting issues about the negotiation of digital literacy practices. Faith (a PGCE student) described working in a staff common room at the school placement and having to negotiate both with other trainees but also with school staff about when she could access the only computer with a printer (shown in Figure 6.2) – she chose to foreground

Figure 6.1 Sally's 'map' of her practices around technologies

Figure 6.2 Faith's image of the printer at her school placement

this in the image she created and presented for discussion in an interview, as can be seen in Figure 6.2.

Such discussions raised questions about the relative priorities of study, deadlines, and creating resources for classroom practice.

The centrality of networked devices

All the students reported interaction with a range of networked devices in order to access and produce texts. Some used several, both fixed (such as desktop PCs at home or in the library) and portable (including smartphones, iPads, and e-readers). Levels of usage varied, but for some, such devices were a fundamental part of their textual practice – and everything else. An example of this was Frederick, who when asked about the frequency of his engagement with technology, responded: 'When don't I use it? When I'm asleep'.

Yuki (a Master's student) offered the following image (Figure 6.3), which provides a further illustration of the interpenetration of mobile devices with literacy practices. This was one of several she produced depicting a range of portable and handheld devices she uses for her studies. Her interviews have revealed a very close relationship between her engagements with texts and mobile networked devices in particular.

She reported that she almost exclusively engages with digital texts for study, and regularly scans texts into her iPad in order to read and then annotate them

Figure 6.3 Yuki's depiction of her devices

digitally. She also uses her iPad to record all her lectures, as opposed to taking notes in the lecture. The centrality of devices to her practices is further illustrated by the image shown in Figure 6.4.

She explained that she puts her iPad in a ziplock bag to allow her to use it when in the bath. Although reading in the bath is nothing new, this innovation seems to be an example of an innovative practice focused on textual engagement using a networked device, constituted by an amalgam of human, text, and machine, and only made possible by the light weight and compact shape of the iPad compared to a laptop.

Devices and applications were also multi-purpose for many students. Again, this meant that some students felt they had to create boundaries in order to keep spaces and practices separate; for example, by using separate email accounts for study, professional practice, and personal purposes (which echoes the findings of Jones and Lea 2008, in their study of personal and curricular spheres of practice in undergraduate digital literacies). Maintaining this separation was not always easy, which some students found unsettling.

> I'm a little bit uncomfortable with the idea that my work email knows what shopping I do and, you know what I mean? I just find the whole thing is starting to get a little bit scary.
>
> (Sally, PhD Focus Group)

Figure 6.4 Yuki's image of her iPad on the bath

Locally negotiated engagement with texts and devices

Throughout the data, there was evidence of a complex interplay between spaces, devices, and purposes. Sometimes, students struggled to access or create texts; there were many accounts of spaces, devices, or applications being modified, reconfigured, or recombined in order to undertake particular textual practices. In this sense, digital literacy became a sociomaterial *achievement*, brought about by a constant reconfiguration of the human, technological, and text.

For example, Juan reported a preference for printed texts but cannot afford to print everything he wants to. He resolves this problem with his girlfriend, who has access to other facilities:

> I've specifically put another area which is [a nearby university]. Now they also have a large room full of computers, but they're better computers so they're faster. And then specifically what I'm going to put over here as well is there . . . they have then an area for printers and they do double-sided which this one doesn't. [. . .] So if I actually print stuff off I invariably go to [the other university] and print it off and using my girlfriend's access code and then do that because it's much . . . because it costs me half as much.

Rather than re-engineering his own material surroundings, he negotiated access to a different configuration that suited him better. At home, however, he creates spaces for study by bringing together texts and devices; however these configurations were temporary and contained, so that he could prevent study from 'colonizing' private space.

> This is my very small flat that has a bedroom, bathroom; kitchen's over here. And then this is the TV which is obviously technological but distinct, it's not really connected at all. And there's a laptop here which is on the little table and that's kind of it. There is a sort of a line from which work doesn't, university work doesn't breach really.

He focused on this theme of separation in the 'map' of practice he produced, as can be seen in Figure 6.5:

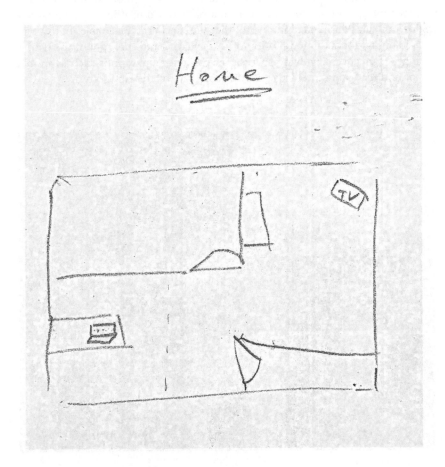

Figure 6.5 Juan's 'map' of practice

Juan also depicted the temporary and shifting nature of his use of personal space in the image shown in Figure 6.6.

Yuki's manipulation of texts also provides an example of reconstitution of texts, artefacts, and devices for emergent purposes. Her practices show a strong emphasis on active assemblage and mediation of texts in conjunction with devices, allowing her to render the texts maximally portable in terms of space, for example by manipulating texts and sound files of lectures to make them come into being or disappear digitally at any time. Her intensive use of PDF annotating software also allows her to create palimpsest-like texts digitally, written over and reconstituted in any spatial or temporal domain she chooses. She gave an account of how she had bought a book, heated it in the microwave to melt the binding, separated all the pages and scanned the whole book, so she could have a digital copy, as can be seen in Figure 6.7.

This provided a striking example of a practice which combined human agency and technology to transform a text from a print-based medium to a digital one in order to suit the situated purpose of the student. Further examples of this type of reconfiguration and modification of texts were found throughout the data in a range of practices involving spaces, devices, and applications such as mobile phone and iPad apps, interactive whiteboards, and referencing software.

Figure 6.6 Juan's image of a temporary configuration of devices in his flat

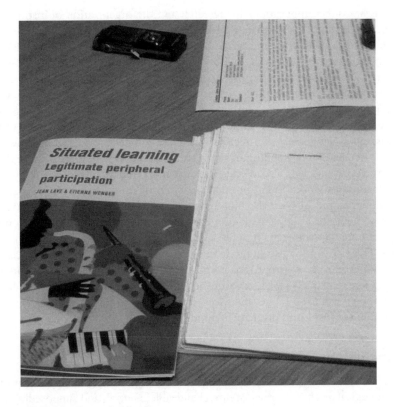

Figure 6.7 Yuki's dismantled book

Discussion

The data described above provides initial findings about engagement with technologies on the part of these students. These can be characterized by multiple spaces and domains of engagement, the centrality of networked devices, and the highly contingent, negotiated nature of practices; which were adapted and co-constituted through small, everyday engagements with technologies. In this regard, the practices seem to generate texts which instantiate Hayles's '. . . unexpected metamorphoses, attenuations, and dispersions' (1999: 30), as they are continually distributed, mediated, and transformed from one format to another both materially and digitally across networks composed of the human, the material, and the digital. These features suggest the potential of a sociomaterial approach for this dataset in particular, and for our understanding of 'digital literacies' more generally. This perspective can shed light on practices at a fine-grained and situated level, providing an account of how these practices and networks are generated, modified, and maintained.

This has direct implications for research and the organization of institutional services. Through a sociomaterial lens, 'digital literacy' involves the ability to reate spaces in which to engage in academic, professional, or personal tasks by coordinating material objects, digital objects, and other human actors. A socio-material analysis, paying attention to the detail of 'lived practice', can identify areas of struggle or breakdown, such as the problems caused by library computers taking 10–20 minutes to log into. Addressing such issues will result in networks of material and digital objects that students can co-opt more easily to meet their needs, by revealing areas of unhelpful challenge and delay, and also by providing a more detailed understanding of actual student practices and sites of struggle.

A sociomaterial lens also reveals the resilience, initiative, and ingenuity with which students work around problems – by enrolling other people, places, and things in their practices – it also highlights areas of institutional provision that need improvement, for example making it easier for students to reconfigure resources – for example, to connect a mobile device to a network via Wi-Fi to engage with texts. This perspective also suggests the limitations of a 'tidy', generic concept of digital literacies. It is inappropriate and unrealistic to assume that students will simply access texts via a VLE or institutional portal; whether they are intended to or not, they will use a range of devices. Institutional strategies and services need to be designed with this diversity in mind.

Conclusions

Conventional conceptions of educational technologies have tended to position technological artefacts as a set of interchangeable, neutral, and supposedly trans-parent 'tools' to be manipulated by 'the user'. In this view, agency is placed with the student, with the implication that the technology is there to serve the user's demands. Alternatively – and equally problematically – a deterministic view of the technology in terms of 'affordances' can be overplayed; in extreme cases placing the student in the role of a hapless pawn of the digital environment at hand. As the data suggest, the reality of student practice around texts is a complex hybrid involving a combination of agency on both sides – which a sociomaterial perspec-tive is well-suited to theorize. This perspective offers us a lens on student mean-ing-making practices which reconnects us to ethnographic observations and par-ticipant accounts in digitally mediated contexts which are simultaneously material and virtual, synchronous and asynchronous, present and distant. In this regard, it may represent a theoretical and methodological advance, allowing us to retain the key insights into the social and affective dimensions of textual engagement provided by New Literacies Studies, while also accounting for the complex and intertwined nature of textual practices in 'the digital university'.

Chapter 7

Posthuman literacy in heterotopic space

A pedagogical proposal

Siân Bayne and Jen Ross

Introduction

This chapter uses two complementary perspectives from which to theorize and understand a particular example of online course design and its associated literacies. First, it describes an experimental, multimodal, fragmented online course in 'E-learning and digital cultures', designed to be taught on the open web. It then uses Foucault's notion of heterotopia to consider how we might conceptualize this kind of usage of web 'space' within education. Next, it draws on theories of critical posthumanism to explore what happens to our notion of the learning 'subject' when we work within such a heterotopic space. Finally, having troubled the notions both of 'subject' and 'space', and reconceived them as an educational 'assemblage' or 'gathering' (Edwards 2010), we extend the discussion into the kinds of literacies which emerge within such a territory. We consider first the notion of the 'lifestream' as an assessment form, and then move on to discuss examples of multimodal digital assignments as locations which challenge academic writing as representational.

A pedagogical proposal

'E-learning and Digital Cultures' (EDC) is a fully online, 12-week course that is part of the MSc in E-learning at the University of Edinburgh. It first ran in 2009, and has been offered each year since then,[1] to groups of about 16 students at a time. The course is experimental in its form: throughout the course students and teachers work primarily in the open web, with images and with explicitly digital forms of meaning-making.[2] The assessment for the course includes submission of a digital essay, and the production over the period of the course of a 'lifestream' – we return to these in some detail later in the chapter.

The EDC course is open to the web in ways that few students will have experienced before. Even the most digitally immersed are unlikely, before EDC, to have participated in an open course (the course predates by some years the current trend for mass open online courses – see Lewin 2012). An awareness of audience – even a potential or silent one – has profound effects on the subjectivity of

Figure 7.1 A page from the 2011 EDC course site

(http://edc11.education.ed.ac.uk/)

students (Ross 2012). Almost everything that happens on the course happens in public, with hyperlinks that would take the curious casual visitor to the blogs, the assessed lifestreams, the chat archives, the tweets, the visual and ethnographic arte-facts produced during the course, and the tutor instructions, encouragement, and comments that structure it. Nothing (except for the copyright-restricted readings and student grades) seems hidden from view.[3] The course therefore draws and redraws the line between a loss of privacy and an invitation to ever-greater partici-pation. We would like to suggest that this course contains many opportunities for what Williams (this volume, citing Sheridan and Rowsell 2010) has referred to as 'creative and flexible literacy practices that emphasize collaboration, publishing, multimodality, and remix'.

Along with experimenting with form, the course is challenging in its content: it asks students to explore themes of community, literacy, and learning, and simul-taneously to question the humanist assumptions that tend to inform understand-ings of these concepts (Biesta 1998; Edwards 2010). Early in the course, a core reading discusses the very course in which students find themselves as an uncanny space, one which 'works with the idea of the learning process as volatile, disori-entating and invigorating' (Bayne 2010: 10). Debates about what it means to be human, as expressed through cinematic representations of cyberculture, give way to a discussion of multimodality and digital literacy, foregrounding human meaning-making practices and then destabilizing them through the creation of digital visual artefacts (see Figure 7.2) intended to represent students' understanding of the topics in question.

This in turn leads to a troubling of the notion of community, as students engage in some light-touch virtual ethnographic work, involving questioning what it means to have, and be part of, a digital community. Students go on to consider posthumanism (Haraway 1991; Hayles 1999) and its implications for education (Edwards 2010; Pedersen 2010). Finally, they use their blogs to propose a 'posthuman pedagogy', and grapple with all the potential contradictions this implies.

A tension around the notion of the 'classroom' as a bounded space, and the status of the autonomous, human subject of education, is expressed and worked through by the course design of EDC. The rest of the chapter explores these tensions, first by looking to the notion of heterotopia as a way of understanding the course space, and then by turning to critical posthumanism as a way of reconceiving its subjects.

Understanding the course space as a heterotopia

As Jones and Dirckinck-Holmfeld (2009) put it, computer networks have a tendency to 'disrupt and disturb traditional boundaries in education' (13), including the boundaries of public and private. Online learning contexts, however much teachers and developers work to provide safe and stable educational environments, allow 'a mixing of genres and literacy practices that does not respect conventional categories, divisions, or dichotomies, including the border that separates . . . the popular from the academic.' (Carpenter 2009: 144)

This is because, as Castells (1999) has argued, organizations (including educational institutions) may trigger, but ultimately cannot control, flows of information and communication in digital space characterized as 'an unseen, uncharted space of flows' (59). Online education requires us to think newly about

Figure 7.2 Examples of students' visual artefacts produced in the early weeks of the course

institutional space, and the various ways in which students and teachers are mobilized within it. In engaging with online education, we move beyond the 'spatial securities' (642) of the on-campus, toward an understanding of the institution as characterized by 'flux and flows rather than simple bounded space' (Fenwick *et al.* 2011: 153).

The EDC course space is different from many virtual learning environments because it makes its absence of boundaries, its 'flows', visible and attempts to work with them. The course 'space' can be thought of both as a place, and a non-place. The web site is in some senses a 'home' for the course, but it is not sealed, closed, or homogenous. Instead, it is open, 'leaky', and each student's own blog space is individualized (through their use of themes and imagery, and through their choice of lifestream feeds). Foucault's notion of heterotopia is useful, here, in framing spaces of 'Otherness', which are not *places*, but rather relationships between elements (Foucault 1984). In the case of EDC, the elements are students, teachers, the course site, and the many and varied technologies we use (including Twitter and the lifestream). Piñuelas (2008) compares the heterotopia to cyberspace 'in its juxtaposition of the real and the virtual, its overlapping, ever-vanishing and reappearing presence of real and imagined subjectivities and relations, and its paradoxical establishment and erasure of lines of territorial demarcation' (154–5).

Importantly, heterotopias are always multiple (Milojevic 2003: 445). Poster (2001), describing digital writing practices, invokes the heterotopia when he explains that:

> Digital writing in many of its forms separates the author from the text, as does print, but also mobilizes the text so that the reader transforms it, not simply in his or her mind or in his or her marginalia, but in the text itself so that it may be redistributed as another text. (68)

Digital textuality is open to being duplicated, changed, and reworked. Are online *courses* (if we view these as something other than texts) any less open to reworking? What this means for us as teachers on EDC is that we must maintain a critical perspective on our own attempts at place-making, acknowledging that reworking will take place not only through *our* choices and desires, but through the assemblages of students, teachers, content, and technologies that the course foregrounds.

Peters and Humes (2003) make an explicit link between heterotopic educational spaces and the open systems 'characterised by the distance mode and e-learning' (435), emphasizing that openness does not equal freedom, and that the spatialization of learning (Edwards and Usher 2000) and associated boundary collapses produce 'new dangers and new problems' for educational theory to grapple with (Peters and Humes 2003: 435; see also Satchwell in this volume). Warschauer (1995) describes this as a tension between heterotopia and panopticism:

the highly socialized nature of the Internet seems to suggest that forms of panopticism will continually emerge within its structures. On the other hand, the heterotopic nature of the Internet – pluralistic, chaotic, continually changing, linked by centerless flows of information – poses a challenge to the formation of stable discourse communities.' (no page)

For students and teachers on the EDC course, this is a challenge in practice as well as in theory. Students spend a two-week period in the middle of the course undertaking a 'micro-ethnographic' project, attempting to determine what (if anything) constitutes a virtual community. They are also in the midst of generating such a 'community' themselves. As students pass through the site of the course, they are both *somewhere* (expressed by an emergent sense of 'community' alongside reminders of institutional legitimacy in the form of assessment practices, course structures, and environments) and in a contested, inverted version of that institutional community space, where permeable and mobile boundaries between subjects, texts, and representations are the norm. Evolving literacy practices performed by liminal learning subjects, observed by a mostly silent and ghostly public, characterize the space of the course.

In this way, the digital spaces of EDC are fragmented, networked, and ever-changing, constituting a course home which is decidedly 'unhomely' (*unheimliche*) (Freud 2003). hooks' description of home echoes what the materialities of the EDC space can mean for students:

> Home is that place which enables and promotes varied and everchanging perspectives, a place where one discovers new ways of seeing reality, frontiers of difference.
>
> (hooks 2004: 155)

In this sense, EDC perhaps constitutes the kind of home that Lewis and Kahn (2010) have conceived as a location for a pedagogy of the outside, of the open – an 'exopedagogical classroom' or 'monstrous home' that is never a '"safe" or "comforting" retreat' (13). The 'home' spaces of EDC are both risky and generative, turning their back on the 'comforting retreat' of the contained and authenticated spaces of the conventional, closed virtual learning environment, which Williams (in this volume) describes as 'uniform, orderly, safe, predictable, enclosed, nostalgic' and containing elements of 'control, simulation, conservatism, branding, and surveillance'.

These qualities of safety and control are abandoned in favour of an openness to 'contamination' – best understood here as the unexpected interventions and interruptions from agents beyond the course. This kind of 'contamination' can take multiple forms: some are unwelcome (spamming), some are hoped for (external commentary on students' blogs), some are inevitable (for example, tagged tweets pulled into the course from those not formally enrolled on it), and others are more or less planned (the automated lifestream feeds, for example:

see below). The distinction between who is formally 'on' the course and who is not becomes blurred, while the distinction between absence and presence is troubled by interventions which are often not directly attributable to a purely 'human' agency.

This point leads us to move beyond consideration of the EDC course space as heterotopic, toward the rethinking of the learning subjects at play within it. In making such a move, we draw on critical posthumanism to recast the notion of 'subjects' within a 'class' in terms rather of assemblage of the human and non-human, what Edwards might call a posthuman 'gathering' (Edwards 2010).

Understanding the course as a posthuman gathering

Critical posthumanist thought is constituted by a diverse body of theory which is concerned with anti-anthropocentrism and the questioning of 'common-sense' notions of what it means to be human, doing so via a critique of liberal humanism – challenged as deeply reactionary by twentieth century continental philosophy – which claims the following:

> that the figure of 'Man' [sic] naturally stands at the centre of things; is entirely distinct from animals, machines, and other nonhuman entities; is absolutely known and knowable to 'himself'; is the origin of meaning and history; and shares with all other human beings a universal essence.
>
> (Badmington 2004: 1345)

Such humanism is dependent on a series of binary oppositions to enable the identity-work necessary for constructing the 'human':

> human/inhuman, self/other, natural/cultural, inside/outside, subject/object, us/them, here/there, active/passive, and wild/tame.
>
> (ibid.)

Much of posthumanism is concerned with the deconstruction of the oppositional terms outlined here. It suggests, like poststructuralism before it, that we are in the position of no longer being able to see the human subject as existing outside history or outside discourse. Instead, we can only see it as being produced within and through discursive practices.

Further, the human subject can no longer be seen as taking the position of dominant observer of the ecologies and networks within which it is embedded – posthumanism sees the human not as an observer of systems, but as constituted by those systems, as thoroughly networked to the extent that the boundary distinction between the (human) subject and the external object becomes blurred. Much of posthumanism is what Haraway calls a 'border war' – an extended 'argument for pleasure in the confusion of boundaries and responsibility in their construction' (Haraway 1991).

If we accept a posthumanist view, we can no longer think in terms of education as a 'bringing out' of an essential human potential, as the nurturing of the ideal of pure reason and autonomy; we need to rethink its purpose. For Lewis and Khan, as we have seen, a posthuman pedagogy is one which takes account of 'contamination', of the creative and generative possibilities involved in allowing humanistic boundary categories to become blurred. For Biesta, a 'pedagogy without humanism' is oriented to the notion of 'intersubjectivity' rather than to the 'bringing out' of the potential of the individual subject' (Biesta 1998), and it has to do its work without the need for 'a deep truth of what it is to be human' (13). For Edwards, also writing against educational hegemony which privileges the 'knowing human subject' (Edwards 2010), posthumanism inclines us to think towards education as an assemblage, an 'entanglement' in which the purpose of education becomes not one of 'learning' but one of the creative 'gathering' of the human and non-human.

To an extent, any distance learning course in a traditional university is engaging in a mode of education which is partly 'boundary war', partly driven by a posthumanist impulse. Technological confusions of the boundary of the 'conventional' university are increasingly in evidence in the rise and growth of distance education, online courses, and 'open education' (Parker *et al.* 2011), asking us to think anew about the 'student body' and how its material absence or presence inflects pedagogy, power, and institutional formation.

It is in these terms, perhaps, that we can most usefully view the kinds of subjects which emerge within the heterotopic, 'contaminated' spaces of EDC (see also Gourlay and Oliver, this volume). In the next section, we suggest that it is the lifestream which most clearly articulates this vision of the course as a 'gathering'.

A posthuman gathering in practice: the lifestream

The lifestream – an artefact which constitutes 50 per cent of the final mark for this course – is a collection of each student's public web content, including tweets, blog posts, blog commentary on other students' postings, Delicious bookmarks, Flickr images, tumblr posts, last.fm feeds, and any other source they choose to use. It is a little like the Facebook timeline – a chronologically organized feed of key events and interactions – though our use of the lifestream predates the Facebook timeline by some years. Students set up the feeds and accounts they wish to include in the lifestream at the beginning of semester (see Figure 7.3).

After this, the lifestream software automatically generates a stream of this content, organized chronologically, and updated every time a new object or item of content is added to any of these feeds, anywhere on the web (see Figure 7.4). Each week students are required to write a short summary of the week's lifestream content, and this analysis also becomes part of the lifestream. The lifestream is constructed/constructs itself over the period of the course (12 weeks), and is assessed at the end of this period.

By the end of their 12 weeks on the course, students have a map of their pathway through the semester which offers a dynamic, complex picture of their

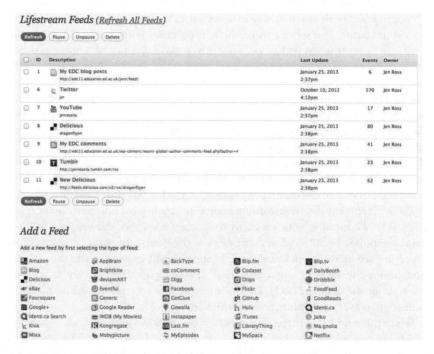

Figure 7.3 The set-up of lifestream feeds

engagement with course themes and materials. Such a piece of work emerges through the joint 'authorship' of the student and the network – the lifestream is constructed automatically, once the student has set up his or her feeds. This is a method which works at the boundary of agency and authorship – it is created through a messy partnership between the student and his or her digital networks. It is in a real sense anti-anthropocentric, removing the human subject as a secure centre to the assessed artefact, and allowing boundaries between the human-as-subject and the internet-as-object to become blurred in the process of its construction. As an assessment strategy, it disturbs the notion of 'literacy' either as an attribute of the individual or as a socioculturally informed set of practices (Goodfellow 2011). It rather proposes a literacy of the sociomaterial, a gathering of the human and the machinic which allows the 'anthropological machine [of education] to idle' (Lewis and Khan 2010: 68).

Beyond representation: multimodal digital assignments

To further relate the pedagogies of EDC to the question of literacy, we will end by providing a series of readings of student work which has been produced as part of the assessed content of the course. Where the lifestream constitutes 50 per cent

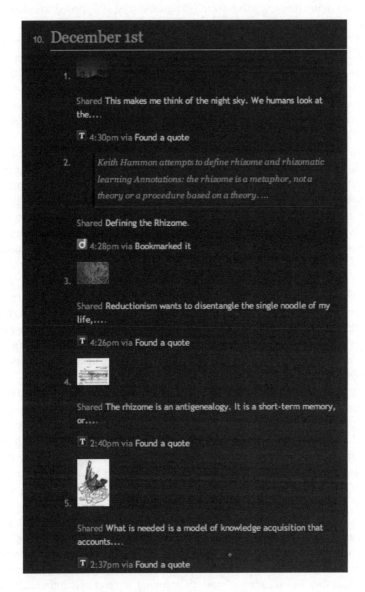

Figure 7.4 A short excerpt from a student's lifestream, showing content from two different sites (tumblr and diigo)

of the final mark, the remaining 50 per cent is given for the submission of a digital essay: students are able to choose the topic and media form freely, and are also invited to nominate their own assessment criteria for these, to complement the core criteria defined by the tutors.[4]

The aim in inviting the submission of digital essays, as opposed to conventional textual, written assignments, is to encourage students to take a critical stance toward 'the embeddedness of cultural assumptions and values associated with print literacies' (Goodfellow and Lea 2007: 68), and to engage in a hands-on way with the challenge of defining an academic discourse beyond the orthodoxies of the written essay (see also McKenna's chapter in the current volume). In a sense, it is an attempt to counter the more common erasure within formal assessment rubrics of the complex practices surrounding the use of digital texts for assessment which Lea (this volume) foregrounds.

In this, we attempt to problematize the representationalism implicit in much educational discourse (Biesta 1999) – the notion that the human subject can be seen as separate from the objects of knowledge with which it is concerned. Knowledge in the humanistic view is a question of representing accurately these objects over which we have dominance as autonomous observers; some notions of what constitutes 'literacy' might be seen as being linked with such epistemological objectivism (Turner 1999: 151–2). For posthumanism, however, this separation of subject and object is no longer tenable – the observer is inextricably involved in the system which is observed, the human is irrevocably extended into the networks within which it is entangled, and as it is no longer possible to isolate human consciousness from its 'social and technological environment' (Hayles 2006), it is no longer possible to represent knowledge of this environment from a position of externality. As Edwards puts it, 'education has focused on the learning subject as a result of an a priori assumption of a separation of matter from meaning, the object from the subject.' (Edwards 2010).

While there is no reason why representationalism could not be critiqued through the conventional written essay form, shifting the mode of academic writing to the digital (and in this way explicitly authorizing the visual, the hypertextual, the aural, the fragmented, the networked, and the playful) foregrounds alternative modes through which such critique might be approached, and possibly makes it more straightforward to achieve. It requires students to allow the network to co-author their assessed work, to draw themselves into an assessed, digital gathering 'around a matter of concern' (Latour 2004; Edwards 2010).

Here, textuality becomes more complex, more diverse, and more visual, as the image, and the logic of the screen (Kress 2005) topples the dominance of the written word and the logic of the printed page. When students engage with new forms of textuality in their academic meaning-making practices, academic discourse becomes newly strange, and the familiar is rendered unfamiliar (Bayne 2010).

Students on EDC meet the topic of posthumanism late in the semester, but its coming is prefigured in the previous eight weeks, and by the time it is introduced as a distinct body of thought, they have been surrounded by images and films of the cyborg, challenges to notions of community, of literacy, and of the dominance of text. They are practiced in reading and generating images. They are ready, in other words, to represent their understandings of the course content in ways that deviate, both subtly and radically, from traditional academic writing. Students in this way are placed in a strong position to attempt a final piece of work which materializes certain critiques of the humanist subject and its link with conventional academic literacy practices. As well as understanding these pieces of work in terms of the notion of 'gathering' already discussed (Edwards 2010), we can see the most successful examples of student work as taking a stance against representationalism, and as consciously and critically repositioning the academic writing subject.

To illustrate this, we end the chapter with an analysis of three examples.[5]

Interpretation and intentionality: the Imaginarium

The Imaginarium is a building made in the virtual world Second Life, constructed by Eneas McNulty, a student on EDC in 2009. The building was Eneas' final assignment for the course, built to investigate Haraway's figure of the cyborg and to explore popular cultural and feminist takes on this figure. Figure 7.5 shows one of the tutors' avatars standing in the middle of the reference list for the assignment – images of pages from books and articles consulted in creating the piece are scattered on the floor, as if in reference to the inadequacy of conventional academic citation norms to take account of the volatility of digital texts. To the left (off screen) is a teleporter which leads to an IMAX-type theatre, on which is displayed a looped video of cyborg imagery in films. Downstairs is a Second Life 'chatbot' called Unheimliche ('unhomely') who welcomes visitors and engages them in automated chat, delegating the speaking 'voice' of the essay to a

Figure 7.5 A screenshot from the Imaginarium: view at http://maps.secondlife. com/secondlife/Vue/78/64/24

non-human agent in a way which explicitly engages with the notion of the post-human and its 'literacies'.

There is some minimal text in the assignment – short notecards exploring, in a non-linear way, some of the key arguments in Haraway's 'Cyborg manifesto' (Haraway, 1991). However, this assignment cannot be assessed according to the expository and critical norms of the conventional text-based essay. Most of its critical significance is in its digital form, and in the assembled artefacts and spaces that the student-maker-author has drawn together.

Also present throughout the essay are a series of decomposing, decapitated, and otherwise broken cyborg figures (Figure 7.6).

These evocative figures are never mentioned in the brief texts of the assignment – the building is a museum with no labels. The visitor-assessor is left with no explanation of the author-student's intentions. The assessor's responsibility for interpretation is therefore made highly apparent within this type of assignment, and the assumed intentionality of the author which characterizes essayist literacy (Farr 1993) is rendered problematic. As assessor, what are we to take from the broken cyborgs? Is this a sophisticated statement on the part of the author, prob-lematizing the fantasy of disembodiment that accompanies much technological and pre-critical posthumanism? Did the author find these in a Second Life virtual shopping mall and think they looked cool? And if we do not know, how do we assign a mark (as we must do) to the knowledge and understanding demonstrated by the work? The act of interpretation – of assessment itself – emerges here as dependent on the intersubjectivity of the assessor and the assessed. This is true,

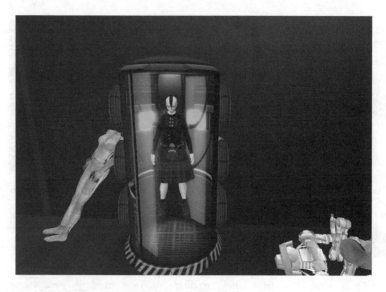

Figure 7.6 The broken cyborgs of the Imaginarium

of course, in conventional written assessment also, however here the medium and form foreground the challenge and make it newly strange.

Positioning the writing subject: the digital flâneur

Michael Gallagher's digital essay from 2010 was presented in the form of a video which overlaid a flyover of Lower Manhattan constructed using Google Earth with the narration of a more or less conventional essay (Figure 7.7). The essay argued that the figure of the flâneur (Baudelaire 1964) is a useful metaphor for understanding the learning potential of augmented reality applications for use in urban cultural heritage education:

Figures 7.7 and 7.8 Screenshots from 'The digital flâneur' (http://michaelseangallagher. org/flaneur-analysis)

The flâneur embraces the 'ambivalence of destination' enacted in augmented reality by not seeing knowledge as linear, by constantly seeking novel ways of seeing and knowing. This ambivalence of destination is well served by the flâneur in their exploration of urban cultural heritage; this exploration is enhanced by augmented reality as a means of knowing anew, a novel comprehension. Augmented reality affords the flâneur the tools necessary to recast the familiar in a new light, to recast the composition of the urban cultural heritage.

(Gallagher 2010)

The narration, on its own, bears every resemblance to conventional academic prose (as the quote above demonstrates), complete with citations and complex lines of argument. Combined with the use of Google Earth, however, the viewing of the essay becomes itself an act of flânerie. The reader travels through Manhattan (Figure 7.8) and observes the landmarks being described, as the ghostly narrator wanders through the mapped material and intellectual landscape of the essay, a disembodied, speaking student voice which is both everywhere and nowhere. The way the student positions himself as the writing subject is deeply critical – he juxtaposes his position as the 'assessed' (and the assignment as a 'submission') with his omnipresence and control as a digital narrator with whole geographical territories at his disposal. He is an embodied absence and a disembodied presence (Hook 2005), an uncanny, more-than-human (Whatmore 2006) commentator on what it means to 'write' as a student, or to 'speak' as a learner.

The textual gathering: pedagogies of deferral and difference

Our final example is an essay created by Jeremy Knox, again from the 2010 instance of the course, in which he explores 'the coming about of knowledge in the contemporary era of digital networks and Internet technologies' (Knox 2010). The form of this essay looks, on first glance, to be a straightforward and rather unadventurous piece of conventional text placed on a web page (see Figure 7.9).

However on engaging with the assignment, we realize that the student has made *every single word* of it – beyond the Prelude – a separate, individual hyperlink to an external web site chosen for its associative value with the linked word. Such a move is more than a virtuoso act of time-investment and meaningless linkage. It is used here as a critical manoeuvre designed to play out in material form the core theme of the assignment, which is itself an investigation and problematization of the notion of 'connection':

The potential for extreme, perhaps chaotic connection in such a structure is intended to highlight an excessive pursuit of knowledge through association. . . . the subject matter of the writing intentionally conveys an

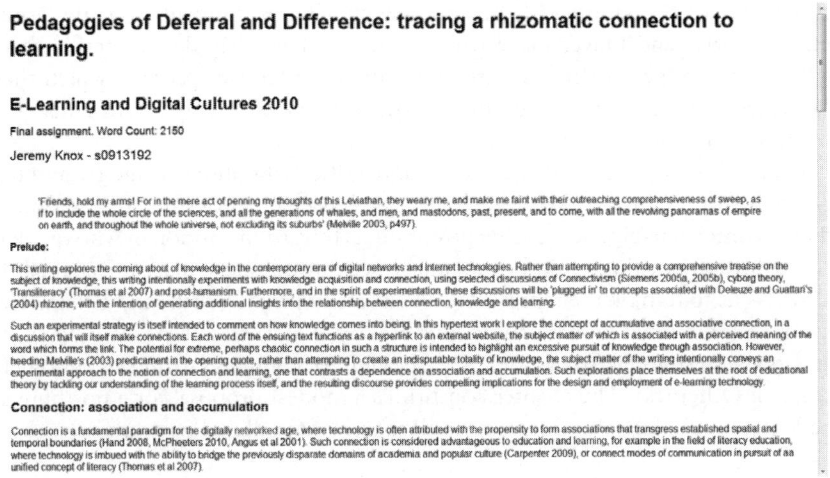

Pedagogies of Deferral and Difference: tracing a rhizomatic connection to learning.

E-Learning and Digital Cultures 2010

Final assignment. Word Count: 2150

Jeremy Knox - s0913192

'Friends, hold my arms! For in the mere act of penning my thoughts of this Leviathan, they weary me, and make me faint with their outreaching comprehensiveness of sweep, as if to include the whole circle of the sciences, and all the generations of whales, and men, and mastodons, past, present, and to come, with all the revolving panoramas of empire on earth, and throughout the whole universe, not excluding its suburbs' (Melville 2003, p497).

Prelude:

This writing explores the coming about of knowledge in the contemporary era of digital networks and Internet technologies. Rather than attempting to provide a comprehensive treatise on the subject of knowledge, this writing intentionally experiments with knowledge acquisition and connection, using selected discussions of Connectivism (Siemens 2005a, 2005b), cyborg theory, Transliteracy (Thomas et al 2007) and post-humanism. Furthermore, and in the spirit of experimentation, these discussions will be 'plugged in' to concepts associated with Deleuze and Guattari's (2004) rhizome, with the intention of generating additional insights into the relationship between connection, knowledge and learning.

Such an experimental strategy is itself intended to comment on how knowledge comes into being. In this hypertext work I explore the concept of accumulative and associative connection, in a discussion that will itself make connections. Each word of the ensuing text functions as a hyperlink to an external website, the subject matter of which is associated with a perceived meaning of the word which forms the link. The potential for extreme, perhaps chaotic connection in such a structure is intended to highlight an excessive pursuit of knowledge through association. However, heeding Melville's (2003) predicament in the opening quote, rather than attempting to create an indisputable totality of knowledge, the subject matter of the writing intentionally conveys an experimental approach to the notion of connection and learning, one that contrasts a dependence on association and accumulation. Such explorations place themselves at the root of educational theory by tackling our understanding of the learning process itself, and the resulting discourse provides compelling implications for the design and employment of e-learning technology.

Connection: association and accumulation

Connection is a fundamental paradigm for the digitally networked age, where technology is often attributed with the propensity to form associations that transgress established spatial and temporal boundaries (Hand 2008, McPheeters 2010, Angus et al 2001). Such connection is considered advantageous to education and learning, for example in the field of literacy education, where technology is imbued with the ability to bridge the previously disparate domains of academia and popular culture (Carpenter 2009), or connect modes of communication in pursuit of an unified concept of literacy (Thomas et al 2007).

Figure 7.9 A hypertext essay as textual gathering

experimental approach to the notion of connection and learning, one that contrasts a dependence on association and accumulation.

(Knox 2010)

In pursuing this strategy of hyper-connection, the student has created a text which is full of 'holes', of material routes out of the formal academic essay and into the vast network which functions here as materially co-authoring the final piece of work. It is an apparently simple, but in fact again deeply critical piece of work which challenges academic literacy norms by using the conventional essay form as merely a façade, a permeable front and interface to the digital network which is both its theme and its object of critique. The essay gathers, assembles, links, connects, and pushes well beyond the tight association of the stable authoring subject with the stable print text; it equally discusses and enacts a posthuman moment.

Conclusion

This chapter has attempted to theorize a concrete instance of course design in terms of a view of space as heterotopic, and of the student 'subject' as a posthuman assemblage. These are theoretical frameworks which have not been applied post-hoc but which have rather informed and structured the project of course design, and our understanding of the kinds of assessment practices that might be appropriate to a 'learning event' designed around the notion of posthuman pedagogy.

To discuss literacy within such a context is to work within a trajectory similar to that defined by Lea in the current volume; to open the term to its sociomaterial ecologies, to attempt to work with the notion of a literacy which has a complex and only partial relation with human agency. This is different from the argument Gourlay and Oliver make (this volume), where they define literacy from a sociomaterial perspective as a student's ability to 'create spaces in which they can engage in academic, professional, or personal tasks by coordinating material objects, digital objects, and other human actors.'

Instead, our argument has been one more critical of notions of agency and the possibility of the subject. We argue that taking assessment of student work into a digital context enables new critical positionings toward the notion of who or what constitutes the writing subject or if, in fact, we can still speak of a subject at all. It also asks us to rethink the representationalist assumptions which might characterize more established modes of academic literacy, conceiving of the learning event and its assessed artefacts as a series of 'gatherings' or couplings within an unhomely space of Otherness. The chapter constitutes a modest proposal for a posthuman pedagogy crafted for the 'contaminated' spaces of the digital network.

Notes

1 The course was last offered in 2012.
2 The most recent instance of the course can be seen at http://edc13.education.ed.ac.uk/
3 Despite appearances, not everything is visible. Students speak to teachers, and teachers to students, off-screen by email. Teachers speak to one another, informally and often face to face. Teacher input to students comes in the form of public comments, but also private assignment feedback, and a mid-point lifestream review. Also, the relationships that participants may have built up on other courses are expressed obliquely, if at all, in the archive of the course.
4 These core criteria are: Knowledge and understanding of concepts; Knowledge and use of the literature; Construction of academic discourse. (http://edc11.education.ed.ac.uk/wp-content/uploads/2011/09/edc_1112_final1.pdf)
5 We are grateful to our students, Eneas McNulty, Michael Sean Gallagher, and Jeremy Knox, for allowing us to quote from and use their work here. More examples of digital essays produced during this course can be seen at: http://online.education.ed.ac.uk/category/e-learning-and-digital-cultures/

Chapter 8

Open Content Literacy

A new approach to content creation and collaboration?

Lindsey Martin and Alison Mackenzie

Introduction

Open Educational Resources (OER) are 'digitised materials offered freely and openly for educators, students and self-learners to use and reuse for teaching, learning and research' (OECD 2007). Several drivers are changing the way teachers develop, store, and share their learning materials, such as policy, technology, and Web 2.0 developments. To a greater or lesser extent what amounts to a values-led, global OER 'movement' is transforming the education and information landscapes (UNESCO 2012). Reuse and adaptation (or remixing) of such content has potential to support scalable and sustainable practices within and beyond organizations although McKenna and Hughes (this volume) describe the very evident tensions between these values-led initiatives and an increasingly marketized higher education sector. In practice, however, it is evident that teaching staff and students need new knowledge and skills to inform how they create, store, share, and utilize learning materials which have either been digitally created or are reused in a digital format.

For colleagues working as librarians, the potential exists to extend the scope of their expertise and apply it within the context of developing OERs. Supporting academic processes in this environment still draws on many of the traditional skills base of the profession, such as selection, description, presentation, curation, and management of materials (Morris 2009). In addition there is a growing awareness that engagement with teaching staff on issues related to copyright, Intellectual Property Rights (IPR), and the discoverability of OERs will inform decision-making of staff and students creating and using open content, either as creators or 'consumers'.

The aim of this chapter is to provide an opportunity to reflect on the information literacy practices in this emerging field, to identify new skills and practices, and assess whether the concept of open content literacy can be accommodated by the principles which underpin information literacy or whether there is a need to remodel or adapt existing models to support decision-making within the context of OERs.

The OER context

The notion of sharing and reuse of teaching and learning content is not new, nor is the availability of free digital content for use in education. It is now over a decade since the establishment of the OpenCourseware project at the Massachusetts Institute of Technology (MIT).[1] In the UK, the initial focus of the OER 'movement' was on the generation of a significant volume of free, world-class quality digital content. In recent years, the UK Joint Information Systems Committee (JISC) has attempted to shape practice through significant investment in digitizing collections of materials with the Higher Education Academy (HEA), and under broad direction from the UK government, invested £12 million through its RePRODUCE[2] and Open Educational Resources Programmes,[3] to increase access to open educational resources.

Digital teaching and learning materials and resources are widely perceived to be more shareable and reusable than traditional printed versions, and the rhetoric behind notions of an open content 'movement' with associated reputational, promotional, and efficiency benefits is persuasive and enticing. Glennie *et al.* (2012) observe, however, that an uncritical acceptance of OER as a social 'good' has resulted in an absence of critical and research-based insights, with much of the literature focusing on the technology, OER products, associated challenges of finding, sharing, reusing, and remixing, and related concerns about IPR and copyright, and limited skill sets of users. (Johnson *et al.* 2010).

The OER impact study funded under the JISC Open Educational Resources Programme: Phase 2 (White and Manton 2011) suggests that academic use of digital content on an individual level is widespread but is constrained by the following logistical factors:

> **Sufficient volume of OERs** has yet to be achieved to make an impact on practice across the board. This problem is more severe in some disciplines than others, for example, performing arts, although there is insufficient data to identify those in the greatest need.
>
> **Technical and implementation issues** are all likely to deter would-be users of OER: poorly indexed materials, inadequate search engines, the requirement to register with a site or download an application in order to retrieve or run a resource, and unreliable hardware or software on the hosting site.
>
> **Poor discoverability** stems largely from low volume, poor indexing and the low power of some search engines. It can be mitigated to some extent where teachers are part of a community and can benefit from word-of-mouth recommendations, but could prove a major stumbling block where teachers are working on their own, without the support of others.
>
> **Lack of licensing** appears to be problematic where a resource seems intended for general use, but does not carry a licence. There is a lack of awareness of Creative Commons (CC)[4] licensing aimed at making it easier for people to share and build upon the work of others.

It is worth drawing a distinction between the creation of 'Big OERs' which generally arise from externally funded initiatives, with the outputs deposited in an established repository such as Merlot[5] or Jorum Open,[6] and 'Little OERs' which are individually produced, shared locally or through third party sites such as Slideshare and Flickr. (Weller 2011: 9: 6). Much of the activity associated with the building of 'little OERs' happens under the radar and may not have been considered with reuse or repurpose in mind. It is recognized that this practice is common across all disciplines and institutions. White and Manton (2011: 5) compare reuse across an institution with an iceberg.

> Above the surface is a small amount of highly visible licensed OER that officially bears the name of the institution and below the surface, often invisible beyond a specific course, is a much greater volume of other non-OER digital resources by staff and students.

Despite significant investment to date, evidence of reuse of OERs is seemingly minimal, with limited impact on practice beyond the OER 'community' (van Wyk 2012). According to Conole (2012) this is the result of a 'naive' belief that investing in and promoting digital content would result in learners using them and teachers repurposing them. More recently, there has been a shift from a focus on the use of tools, licences, and creation of content towards:

> people who have the right know-how and skills and are provided with the appropriate institutional framework (goals, values, guiding principles) and environment (for example, technical infrastructure) to make use of these means in open educational practices that are key to innovations in teaching and learning.
>
> (Geser 2007: 38)

There is little that describes the socio-technical practices (Tuominen *et al.* 2005); the interplay between the components, capabilities, practices, and behaviours around OERs (Hilton *et al.* 2010), and the use or non-use of OERs; the prevailing culture of an institution and the perceived (and real) barriers and enablers. McGill (2011) has identified a range of stakeholder groups and has selected five of the most significant barriers for each group. For academic staff, these include a lack of awareness of the benefits of releasing or using OERs; technical skills/ competencies and associated quality, and legal issues. These can be addressed and the support and expertise available from librarians and associated teams can play a key role.

The following scenarios illustrate how working with open content impacts on the decision-making and socio-technical practices of three constituent groups within a university environment.

Scenario 1: institutional perspective

This scenario imagines a meeting of senior academic managers to discuss the outcomes of the recent review into the institution's virtual learning environment (VLE) which has made a number of recommendations regarding the additional infrastructure, strategies, and policies required to ensure that the student experience of its virtual classrooms is innovative and engaging. The review recommends assertively building on the decision for a minimum (largely administration and communication) VLE presence in all taught modules. Student feedback has been largely positive but there is evidence of inconsistent practices and staff skills gaps having a negative impact on the student experience.

The review is asking for capital funding for a repository in which digital teaching and learning content can be stored. The main benefit cited is to encourage sharing and reuse across the university as a means of increasing the amount and quality of digital content available to meet the demand for web supported and web enabled teaching and learning. The key questions driving the managers' discussion may be:

> How will having a digital content repository encourage sharing? The research repository is very under-utilized so why should this be different?

> Does sharing and reuse currently happen under the radar? We have over 65 research methods modules on the books; does this mean we are constantly reinventing the wheel?

> What are the conditions under which sharing happens? Will the university's stance on intellectual property rights support or hinder sharing and reuse? What is the view of senior managers if staff want to make content available to the world? Is there other stuff already out there that we can encourage our own staff to use? Do we need a strategy and/or a policy?

> Will a repository require additional funding for specialized hardware and software to support digital content creation? Will staff create or adapt their digitized content or will they need others to do it for them? Given the known skills gaps, what are the implications for staff development, training, and support? Should this be mandatory or will this be counter-productive? Who will provide this?

> How can senior management influence academic practices around sharing and reuse in order to sustain growth, quality, and meet student expectations? Can we introduce opportunities for reward and recognition in this area?

The senior team recognize that they are experiencing a severe knowledge gap resulting in their inability to weigh up the potential costs and benefits of this investment to the institution in order to make an informed decision. Their challenge is to ensure that the strategies, policies, and infrastructure that they implement at the organizational level enable and enhance quality practices at faculty, departmental, and individual level.

Scenario 2: academic perspective

Dr Hollister is a member of the Department of Fashion and Textiles at an institution close to London where her academic work focuses on the history of fashion. She is in the process of planning a new module specifically on the twentieth century history of fashion accessories. The library collection is currently limited so she decides to look for material that is freely available, but meets the required quality standards. *Does she know what determines whether material is freely available?*

Among the resources she finds, a selection have been deposited in a repository from another university. They appear to be free and the source gives her confidence in their trustworthiness. *Is she aware of the licences which support open content use and reuse?*

The material includes readings, a bibliography of supporting sources, assessments, and sample projects. *Is the material pitched at the right level for her students and/or is it designed for adaptation? Does she want to customize it or is it usable as it is with her own pedagogic 'wrapper' to contextualize it? Will her students mind if it has another university's logo on it?*

As she digs deeper into the materials and thinks about the specifics of the course she wants to teach, she starts to see gaps in the resources and considers her options. *How much time and technical expertise will she need to develop new content or remix what she has found? Does the content quality have to be 'highly produced' or simply 'good enough'? What training and support can she call upon when designing and building her course?*

She also starts to browse for additional resources and begins to search through collections in related disciplines using tools such as YouTube, Flickr, and Google. Dr Hollister begins to uncover more material from related disciplines: history of art, sociology, and media. *Is she aware of how to construct searches to limit results to those with the appropriate rights assigned to them? Is there anyone else that she can call upon to advise her on where to look, and how to refine her search methodologies in order to search for freely available images and multimedia content in her field?*

Dr Hollister has now mapped the structure and identified indicative content for her module. *Is she confident that her students will be able to access the material indefinitely? Will she link to it or download it? Where will it be stored? Who will manage the content? Does she require support from anyone else to create, deposit, or make the material discoverable? Will she make her new and remixed content freely available? Does her university's policy regarding the intellectual property of teaching content support her in making OERs?*

Her preliminary investigations have led her to feel very positive about the potential use of open content. It is clear that she would not have the time available to construct most of this content from scratch, even though some will have to be adapted to meet her students' specific requirements. She feels that this investment on her part will be rewarded in positive feedback.

Scenario 3: A library perspective

Richard Evans is an academic liaison librarian at a large metropolitan university in the north of England where he supports the Faculty of Arts and Humanities. He is responsible for administering the institutional teaching and learning content repository and is working with academic staff to deposit content to support the university's marketing drive to attract global attention and potential recruitment opportunities from a wider international audience. The aim is to showcase high quality nuggets of curriculum content; the challenge is that these have to meet the criteria of being OERs.

On arrival in his office he checks the repository for new 'open' content that he can promote using the library Twitter account and in his weekly 'What's new' blog post. *What else can he do to encourage staff to upload their content into the repository?* He notices one new item is a scanned chapter from a book with no record of any copyright permission so he removes it from public view in accordance with the repository take-down policy. He then phones the person who uploaded the item to let them know what he has done, to find out whether a legally digitized copy of the chapter is required and explain the process. *How can he turn this around and use it as an opportunity to promote his forthcoming staff development workshop on finding open content for teaching and learning?*

Later that morning he attends a meeting with a tutor who is keen to start creating or tailoring existing curriculum content for the university's international drive. Richard will work with the tutor on how to find and evaluate relevant digital content, assess it for any third party copyright and consider which CC licence needs to be applied. Some of the other issues which the tutor asks him about, such as interactive quizzes and formats, he knows could be better answered by one of his colleagues from the Learning Technology team. This leads him to consider: *what are the potential benefits of working as part of a multidisciplinary team?* And based on his current experience: *how can he extend his advocacy role?*

Richard recognizes that his experience of managing the institutional repository is extending his skills base alongside raising his awareness of the blurring of boundaries across different professional groups. The challenge lies in balancing his own expertise while drawing on the expertise of others in order to build a better shared understanding of working with open content.

These scenarios are somewhat idealised, focusing on what the practices around open digital content could look like. In contrast, the case study that follows describes one university's lived experience and examines the associated information and OER skills and practices and the degree of readiness of the institution and individuals to mainstream practices around sharing and reuse of digital teaching materials.

An institutional case study

Edge Hill University, in the north-west of England, was one of 20 institutions funded by JISC under its RePRODUCE Programme, 2008, to test perceptions around reusable content in a real-world setting that involved developing, running, and quality assuring a technology-enhanced course using at least 50 per cent of learning materials sourced externally to the institution.

Edge Hill's ReFORM Project[7] ran for 12 months, aiming to redevelop an existing final year, undergraduate module: Dyslexia and Specific Learning Difficulties in Higher Education – Support Issues. A requirement of the funding was that all digital content (new and reused) created for the module would be made available to the wider sector. The project also sought to:

- Develop an improved understanding of the potential for reuse of digital content at practitioner level and an improved understanding of practitioner training and support needs
- Learn from the process what constitutes effective practice in creation, design, and use of digital content

The team also wished to develop an improved understanding at senior management level of the potential strategic implications of sharing and reuse on resources and changes to working practices.

The multi-professional project team comprised the module tutor, two learning technologists, and two academic librarians. The team adopted a 'flat', non-hierarchical, collaborative approach to the day-to-day management of the project and decisions were made through discussion and consensus. Over the duration of the project the following team roles emerged:

- Locating and evaluating external content, obtaining rights clearance for external content likely to be suitable for reuse, and taking responsibility for the assignment of rights to our own material (Tutor, Learning Technologist, Librarian)
- Repurposing content and creating the learning environment to provide the context within which the learning activities, resources, and teaching content would be embedded (Tutor, Learning Technologist)
- Resource locator and evaluator, project 'scribe' and module administrator (Librarian)

The evaluation plan required the team to capture individual and collective reflections on their experience. Personal journals and interviews provided thick descriptions of their first-hand experience of processes around content acquisition, creation, and reuse, and of participating in a multi-professional team.

Only a minimal amount of digital content was considered suitable for reuse. Our experience, supported by findings from the other RePRODUCE projects, was that the ease or otherwise of rights clearance strongly influenced our choice of external content. (McGill *et al.* 2008).

At the beginning of the project, the tutor's resource location skills were not well developed and the identification of a wide enough range of resources for reuse was a challenge. This provided the librarian with a real role in working with the tutor to locate and evaluate suitable digital content. The tutor also lacked confidence in her technical ability and therefore required considerable support and guidance from the learning technologist in order to move beyond simple digitizing of text materials, for example, converting files to PDF format.

The overarching RePRODUCE Programme found issues around the ways in which projects approached repurposing or remixing content compared to reuse with a pragmatic preference for 'good enough' and easy to use resources. As linking to websites requires no maintenance or updating on the teacher's part, many projects preferred to link to existing content rather than take apart and remix material. (McGill *et al.* 2008).

As a result of Edge Hill's engagement with the ReFORM project, the team's 'on-the job' exposure to new understandings, skills, and practices confirmed our view that reuse and remixing of digital content is dependent upon the acquisition of new skills and 'creating to share' through deliberate planning at the initial design stage. It also confirmed our view that curriculum design using digital content requires rethinking of traditional roles and a broad acceptance of new professional partnership approaches using multi-professional teams.

The experience has also informed our thinking about the longer-term strategies necessary for the mainstreaming of web supported or web enabled teaching and learning within our university. A key part of the strategy would be the mainstreaming of open educational practices around the sharing and reuse of digital teaching materials. Our initial explorations, however, revealed that many colleagues lacked the skills to identify, evaluate, acquire, and adapt existing digital content or had concerns about sharing their own work beyond a trusted few or community.

Two small-scale online surveys were carried out on teaching staff at Edge Hill University in 2009 and 2011 to ascertain academics' awareness of open educational resources and how as educators they might consider using these resources in their teaching; the survey responses provided a 'snap-shot' of practices and knowledge from across the institution. Results from the first survey in 2009 (a sample of 190 teaching staff drawn from all faculties yielded a survey response of 58, representing a return of 30 per cent) highlighted that 90 per cent of respondents reused materials within face-to-face teaching, including handouts and slides, and 67 per cent of respondents reused digital materials such as websites.

However many respondents commented that they felt very uninformed about the concept of OERs, with only 31 per cent being aware of an open content 'movement'. 2011 saw this awareness increase to 61 per cent. In 2009 only 24 per cent of respondents knew about CC licensing but by 2011 this had increased to 38 per cent. 2011 also saw the number of respondents reusing online materials (websites, guides, tutorials, etc.) in their teaching increase to 79.5 per cent from 67.2 per cent in 2009.

It is interesting to observe greater willingness in 2011 to share one's own content beyond the institution. When asked about the perceived benefits of sharing and reuse, comments could be grouped into the following themes: time-saving; not reinventing the wheel; access to high quality content; sharing learning from best practice. The survey also explored respondents' typical behaviours when searching for digital content. The most popular places to search by far were Google, YouTube, and Google Images, although explanatory comments also showed that academic sites such as Humbox[8] and other university websites were considered as suitable sources of OERs. Having explored colleagues' attitudes to and experience of finding and sharing content, we enquired about their perception of their ability to locate, evaluate, reuse, and repurpose digital content. In 2011, just over half (59 per cent) thought they had sufficient skills to locate open content, 54 per cent thought they had sufficient skills to evaluate it, 51 per cent thought they could reuse existing content in its complete form, and 44 per cent thought they could remix specific elements of open content and embed it within their own.

For 2011, we also thought it important to ask respondents where, or to whom they would look for skills development, support, and guidance in this area (Figure 8.1). Respondents were able to make more than one choice. 'Other' included online communities of practice such as Humbox, in-house training, and contacting the content 'owner'.

Whilst these findings comprise only a small snap-shot of attitudes and practices within one institution, they strongly support the findings of other studies. (Rolfe 2012; White and Manton 2011; Dickens *et al.* 2010). Academics are willing to

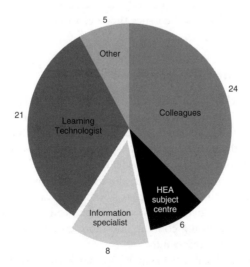

Figure 8.1 Where academic staff look to for skills, support, and guidance in using OERs

share their teaching resources through engaging with OERs although this activity is most likely to be with 'little OERs' at the local level. They are increasingly aware of the issues involved in using and remixing content, including concerns over the risks of infringing intellectual property, acquiring skills and training. Furthermore, whilst there is evidence that academics are willing to seek training, support, and guidance, there has been little consensus on where responsibility for providing these should lie and little evidence that they are being enabled at a strategic level within institutions.

These findings, which drew attention to the uncertainty many teaching staff expressed about the process of using, reusing, mixing, and remixing content, led to the development of an Open Content Literacy Framework (Mackenzie and Martin 2010) and associated development of a specific open content literacy 'lens'.

Making content open: an Open Content Literacy Framework

This framework is aimed at supporting engagement of teaching staff with open content, the acquisition of new skills and strategies, and managing the 'messiness' and iterative nature of digital content creation. It is designed to encourage a 'shared understanding' (McGill 2011) and greater depth of awareness of the socio-technical issues addressed by different professional teams. Developed in response to a perceived 'gap', it provides a structure for supporting novice open digital content creators and consumers, to inform practice by outlining components of the OER territory in order to identify necessary understandings, capabilities, and behaviours. It is organized around a number of reflective questions designed to explore different aspects of the OER creation process and is supported by links to sources of guidance and support. Its primary function is to alert creators and users of OERs to the issues they need to consider and the sources that may provide guidance.

An Open Content Literacy 'lens'

The established model of information literacy within the UK, known as the '7 Pillars of Information Literacy' by the Society of College, National and University Libraries (SCONUL), was updated and expanded in 2011.[9] One of the extensions to the model is the development of a 'lens' with a focus specifically on Open Content Literacy[10] (Appendix 1). The model provides an overview of key considerations that librarians and teaching staff, alongside other associated professional groups, for example, learning technologists, should be aware of when working in this field. It provides guidance on the issues which need to be considered when either identifying and (re)using content, and more crucially when creating content for sharing, reuse, and remixing.

Based on the principal skills, behaviours, and attributes associated with information literacy, it articulates at each of the seven stages (Identify, Scope, Plan,

Gather, Evaluate, Manage, and Present) the specific skills, knowledge, and competencies applicable to the creation, design, use, and reuse of content to develop OERs.

In drawing upon SCONUL's '7 Pillars of Information Literacy' model, which has long been championed by librarians, one concern raised was that alignment with it would present a barrier to wider adoption, for as Beetham *et al.* explain (2009, p. 69):

> One problem, though, is that where librarians have championed the digital aspects of information literacy, this is regarded as having 'solved' the problem of the digital in learning.

It is interesting to note, however, that apart from one or two tantalizing glimpses of librarians writing about their work in the area of advocacy, training, or support of the discovery, evaluation, or reuse of open digital content (Morris 2009; Dick 2010), there is little evidence to suggest that this is the norm. Indeed, anecdotal evidence suggests that librarians have almost no visibility in this field. There are tensions here, however, as the strategic challenge of mainstreaming open educational practices implicitly suggests that input from librarians is required in providing advocacy, training, and support of staff and students (White and Manton 2011). Incorporation of the current framework into professional development, training, and advocacy is therefore intended to support effective institutional practice in the deliberate planning for sharing and reuse of digital content at its initial design stage.

Conclusion

The notion of sharing, reuse, and remixing of digital teaching and learning content is not new, but in recent years, organizations such as JISC and the HEA, whose roles are to offer leadership and support UK higher education, have sought, under the broad direction of the UK Government, to achieve fundamental change through significant investment in production and dissemination of 'Big OERs'. Despite perceived reputational, promotional, and efficiency benefits, 'Big OER' production and reuse is also perceived as 'messy' and time-consuming, with constraining logistical factors such as: volume of resources; technical and implementation issues; discoverability and lack of CC licensing.

More recently, there has been a shift in focus from developing and promoting open educational content towards facilitating open educational practices that ensure practitioners have the right knowledge, skills, and access to appropriate institutional frameworks, infrastructure, and tools. The scenarios provided are indicative of the impact of open educational practices at all levels of an institution and the need for a 'joined-up', multi-professional approach to militate against the 'messiness' facing open digital content strategists, producers, and consumers.

The Open Content Literacy Framework is offered as a means to encourage a 'shared understanding' and greater depth of awareness of the issues addressed by different professional teams.

It is evident that librarians can address many of the concerns expressed, and using their expertise collaborate with teaching staff and associated professional teams, for example, learning technologists, to improve the tagging and discoverability of resources; raise awareness on issues of copyright; offer expert advice on the use of Creative Commons licences; and assist teaching staff in their choices of where to search and how to evaluate open content. Current practice suggests that librarians have not actively sought to extend their remit, either as a formal aspect to their pre-existing roles or as an opportunity to engage more proactively with the development of open content. This assertion is confirmed by the, albeit small-scale, survey of where developers of open content seek advice and guidance. Although librarians were identified as having a role to play it is clear that their expertise sits along side that of other professions, adding weight to the argument that working as a multi-professional team is perhaps the most effective approach to the development and use of content in a digital environment.

Appendix: SCONUL 7 Pillars through an Open Content 'lens'

Identify	Scope	Plan	Gather	Evaluate	Manage	Present
Understands:	*Understands:*	*Understands:*	*Understands:*	*Understands:*	*Understands:*	*Understands:*
Concept of 'openness' in relation to educational resources/practices	**What** material can and should be shared	**Where** to locate and publish suitable content	**Where** to locate content for share/reuse	**Issues of quality,** relevance, accessibility, and format	**Principles** of designing for reuse	**The needs** of the intended audience; their unique situated characteristics
That new open content is constantly being produced	**The issues** of IPR/copyright status and Creative Commons licences in relation to reuse	**How to search** for content which is available for use/reuse	**The limitations** of libraries in providing access to digital OER content	**How to assess impact** and discoverability of open content	**The content life cycle** and the passage of time on digital content	**Pedagogic approaches** to the structure, activity and context for delivery of open content
The benefits to be gained from creating, sharing, and reusing content	**The characteristics** of different types of open content and how these may affect where they are published or aggregated	**The differences** between different platforms where open content is located, recognizing advantages and limitations	**What makes** content accessible		**Interoperability** and open standards for use and reuse	**The audience** for open content is distributed and self-selecting
Impact of local policy, infrastructure, support in creating culture of sharing and openness	**Who** else must be involved in locating and/or developing content		**The importance** of folksonomies in locating open content		**The importance** of timing of availability for maximum impact	
How to assess if using open content or making your own content open will meet your needs	**Where specialist** services and support can be found		**The importance** of source files, e.g. SWF in enabling reuse/remixing of content			

Is able to:	Is able to:	Is able to:	Is able to:	Is able to:	Is able to:	Is able to:
Recognize decision to make one's content open may involve others as well as self **Recognize** a need for new skills in locating, reusing, creating, sharing content and identify the skills gap **Assess** how open content could enhance the learner experience	**Identify** material suitable for intended audience **Articulate** reasons for using and making content open **Assess** when content should not be made open **Identify** platforms and search tools for locating good quality digital content	**Use external** sources, e.g. Jorum; YouTube, etc. to extend discovery **Identify appropriate** search techniques to use as necessary **Assign** rights to any new or remixed content	**Apply** metadata tags to add value to content **Organize** content into suitable chunks for learning **Deposit content** in repository or other suitable location(s)	**Assess** the suitability of the content for the intended audience **Determine** and articulate what prior knowledge of the subject is required of the audience **Maximize** discoverability of open content by other practitioners and audiences of learners	**Identify** how text-based materials can be best transformed into digital formats **Manage** multiple versions and version control **Alter format** of content to meet audience needs **Recognize the need** to refresh or withdraw open content at the end of its life cycle	**Design** and apply open educational practices around open content in a taught context **Articulate the level of** personal engagement with a distributed, self-selected audience

Notes

1 http://ocw.mit.edu/index.htm
2 http://www.jisc.ac.uk/whatwedo/programmes/elearningcapital/reproduce.aspx
3 http://www.jisc.ac.uk/oer/
4 http://www.creativecommons.org.uk/
5 http://www.merlot.org/merlot/index.htm
6 http://www.jorum.ac.uk/
7 http://www.edgehill.ac.uk/reformproject/
8 http://humbox.ac.uk/
9 http://www.sconul.ac.uk/sites/default/files/documents/coremodel.pdf
10 http://www.eshare.edgehill.ac.uk/1425/

Chapter 9

Digital literacies as situated knowledge practices

Academics' influence on learners' behaviours

Allison Littlejohn, Helen Beetham, and Lou McGill

Changing work and learning practices

Digital literacy is a foundational capability essential for participation within society. In this sense we view digital literacies as important as read-write literacy and numeracy. Governments are recognizing the foundational nature of digital literacies and their importance in supporting new ways of working and employability (EC 2009). This acknowledgement gives rise to an entitlement agenda in further and higher education (UK Government Report 2009).

The increasing significance of digital literacy is due to socio-political, cultural, and technological changes (Jakupec and Garrick 2000), such as new work and learning practices, changing employment patterns, transformations in the nature of knowledge, alongside increasing fragmentation of knowledge across disciplinary and sectoral boundaries. As the knowledge economy develops, knowledge-based work and learning practices evolve. 'In the developed world at least, economically productive work involves – centrally or incidentally – generating immaterial products such as information, knowledge and networks' (Hardt and Negri 2004: 65). In line with these transformations, production units are becoming smaller, more flexible and dynamic, geographically distributed, and technologically mediated (Fiedler and Pata 2009). Emerging work practices include:

> *Bricolage*, or the aggregation of incongruent resources to create novel outputs. This work practice is particularly relevant to people who work with 'open source' artefacts, for example computer programmers, or people working in the creative industries. Instances of bricolage include the reuse and aggregation of software applications to create novel computer programs or the remixing of fragments of music to create an original piece. Another example is the development of novel designs. Yet another example is the sharing and reuse of design knowledge to create novel designs (Turnbull *et al.* 2011).
>
> *Localization*, or adapting knowledge and expertise to a localized problem, sometimes by transferring knowledge across boundaries. Dresdner Kleinwort, a leading investment bank, was one of the first organizations to leverage localization to encourage employees to share knowledge and expertise

across their global sites (Tapscott and Williams 2008). As employees contributed knowledge to a wiki-based global network, the network became a 'knowledge ecosystem', akin to 'Wikipedia'. Other companies, including Shell International, have introduced similar global networks to support collaboration and knowledge sharing around international centres (Hendrix and Johannsen 2008). A significant problem for these initiatives has been in encouraging experts to contribute their knowledge. However, people who contribute knowledge to a globally visible network become recognized experts over time (Margaryan *et al.* 2011).

Crowd-sourcing – posing problems or questions to a diffuse network of experts to generate a range of novel solutions. Companies including Amazon, Boeing, IBM, Procter & Gamble, Merck, and Cisco are amongst hundreds of organizations crowd-sourcing ideas to foster innovation. A large proportion of ideas are generated through open and amorphous social networks. IBM first introduced Innovation Jams in 2006 by inviting employees from more than 160 countries to join clients, business partners, and even family members in a massive, open brainstorming session. Over a three-day period, more than 100,000 people participated in a series of moderated online discussions to brainstorm ideas for industry, health, and the environment. Participation in this type of event requires specific digital literacies to source, analyse, modify, and share new knowledge. While open source research and development and precompetitive knowledge commons use Intellectual Property (IP) as open knowledge (Tapscott and Williams 2008), companies have been selective about opening their IP. However, the practice of opening IP has been advanced through *ideagoras* (Tapscott and Williams 2008), where knowledge is released publicly or semi-publicly, available at times as a solution in search of a problem to source ideas for applications of IP.

Critical to these three examples are *open knowledge practices* and *co-innovation* and *co-creation of knowledge*, with no clear boundaries between the producers and consumers of knowledge. These work practices not only depend on networked technologies, but they adopt networks as a model for organizational structures (Hardt and Negri 2004: 82). Organizational structures are becoming 'flatter', less hierarchical, and are constantly restructuring to allow for dynamic, constant change in production. Examples include production of outputs within temporary (often distributed and 'virtual') project teams and increasing numbers of people who choose to work as self-employed consultants, rather than being tied to a single employer. To work effectively in these environments, knowledge workers must develop the capability to work productively with digital knowledge, and to participate in digital networks of collaboration and co-creation as digital practices evolve with extraordinary speed (Candy 1991; Hiemstra and Brockett 1994).

The digital practices associated with networked collaboration and co-creation are central to academic work (see the chapters by Jones, Fransman, and Goodfellow in this volume). Indeed, the invention of the internet was to allow academics to collaborate, communicate, and integrate data to solve increasingly complex problems. Many areas of academic practice are, therefore, deeply inscribed with technology. Academics in almost every discipline routinely use tools of the internet age in their everyday research. Yet, even academics familiar with knowledge practices within the context of research find it difficult to integrate technology-enhanced learning into their teaching practice (Margaryan *et al.* 2011). Satchwell *et al.* (in this volume) attributes this 'struggle' to academics' wish to preserve boundaries.

In this chapter we explore the role of academics in learners' development of digital literacies. The chapter is based on findings from a national study conducted for the UK Joint Information Systems Committees (JISC) entitled Learning Literacies for a Digital Age[1] (LLiDA) (Littlejohn *et al.* 2011; Beetham *et al.* 2009; Beetham 2009) and a programme of activities funded by the JISC focusing on embedding literacy support within a number of UK higher and further educational institutions,[2] for which the authors are providing synthesis support. We begin by describing the rationale and methodologies for these studies.

The studies: the UK Joint Information Systems Committees Literacy Programme

Initial mapping of the landscape of literacy provision across the UK

The Learning Literacies for a Digital Age study was commissioned in 2009 to investigate how universities were developing students' capacities to learn deeply in technology-rich domains. The premise of this study was that learners have little opportunity to attain digital literacies as situated knowledge practices, influenced by their teachers. While university initiatives are in place to support development of learners' ICT and information skills – or at least bring these up to a minimum standard of competence – these initiatives are seldom followed through the learning experience in any coherent way, or integrated with the development of other capabilities critical to higher learning. We wanted to map the landscape of literacy provision.

During this study we mapped the ways in which learning literacies and digital literacies are supported across post-compulsory education, drawing our sample from across the UK further and higher education sector. We then identified areas of promising practice and carried out more in-depth studies of specific cases. Data was collected in four phases: a literature review; a review of relevant competence frameworks; analysis of institutional digital literacy support; an audit of digital literacy practice at 16 institutions.

In *phase 1* we carried out a literature review, starting with a number of review papers by Kahn and Kellner (2005), LearnHigher (2006), Martin and Grudziecki (2006), Goodfellow and Lea (2007), Lankshear and Knobel (2008), Futurelab (2009), and Newman (2009). We drew on and augmented these reviews with searches using the terms: digital literacy, information literacy, ICT literacy, critical thinking, academic literacy, media literacy, e-learning, e-literacy, digital participation and digital inclusion.

In *phase 2* we scoped and reviewed 34 competence frameworks, and included theoretical statements that accompanied these frameworks in our literature review.[3]

Phase 3 was an institutional audit that identified over 40 examples of digital literacy support and provision from UK higher and further education institutions. An audit of literacy provision was undertaken in 15 institutions, 13 universities, and two further education colleges (or community colleges). The sample of universities included a mix of different types of institutions, established and new organizations, representative of the national sector.

In *phase 4* we captured exemplars of 'best practice' in learning and digital literacies support through requests distributed via a variety of UK-national mailing lists for technology-enhanced learning associations and special interest groups.

The JISC Developing Digital Literacies Programme

In 2011, following on from the initial LLiDA study, JISC established a two-year programme of activity to encourage institutions to embed the development of digital literacies of students and staff within the curriculum. The authors are abstracting key messages and threads from this programme, by leading the programme synthesis. This chapter incorporates early findings of this work through baselining activities of 12 funded projects. Ten projects are based at UK institutions of higher education (universities) and two at institutions of further education. Of the latter, one project collected data from five partner colleges. In total, then, these activities present a snap-shot of the situation in 10 higher education and 6 further education institutions.

Modelling lifelong knowledge practices

Our review of digital literacy support surfaces the problems associated with the transfer of digital knowledge practices across the research–teaching boundary. From our literature review we understand literacies as knowledge practices situated in specific social and cultural contexts, from which they derive their meaning and on which they are significantly dependent for their performance (Street 1996). However, the ways in which learners access support (at least in UK universities and colleges) is usually via centralized support for generic study skills. This support structure is based around an implicit model of competence and deficit, partly because of the recognition of the foundational nature of these capabilities which leads to a discourse of entitlement; since digital literacy is foundational, learners are entitled to digital literacy training during their studies. There is a tendency to reify the support offered in the form of standardized curricula such as the European Computer Driving Licence (ECDL). While standardized curricula help to embed the relevant capabilities into institutional provision, competence frameworks can act against two requirements for effective development and embedding of knowledge practices within academic communities: to rethink knowledge practices in light of changing social and technological environments, and to embed that rethinking in specific disciplinary and professional contexts of practice. Digital literacy support should be situated within specific disciplinary and cultural contexts.

Yet, from the LLiDA study we understand that current mechanisms for supporting digital capability tend to be informed by 'competency frameworks' that set out and define each individual competency (digital knowledge practice) required by learners. Competence frameworks are rarely developmental for the following reasons:

First, they are missing the crucial notion of a situated and critical technology use modelled by subject experts (academics). It is precisely these aspects of technology use which elevate it from a – rapidly obsolescent – set of technical skills to a lifelong knowledge practice.

Second, competence frameworks do not provide a blueprint for the kind of authentic tasks that enable learners to develop and refine their practice: rather they are normative, acting as a checklist against which a designed curriculum might be assessed.

Third, the evidence from our review is that competence-based provision is unpopular with students. Therefore, a generic, competence-based curriculum would not be the answer.

Whilst the Quality Assurance Agency (QAA) subject benchmarks[4] are used to define curriculum and teaching practices in UK higher education, there is some variety in how far they address or accommodate digital literacies. In the UK, digital literacies support which is informed by specific competence frameworks is often offered as a, sometimes optional, adjunct to the subject curricula, by support services which may be perceived to have a lower status. This approach works counter to our understanding that students are motivated to transform their capabilities or identities within their subject area studies. Digital literacies need to be embedded within subject curricula to ensure that at post-compulsory level we stimulate the conscious, critical, creative use of digital technology for academic, and professional, purposes, rather than acquisition of a particular repertoire of tools and skills.

Students should not be expected to be able to adopt digital knowledge practices through competence-based approaches. However, support based around individual competence tends to be segregated both from other areas of competence development and from the work of subject curricula. This means that students' digital and learning literacies may not be addressed as they engage in meaningful academic tasks, and there is none of the extended practice necessary to develop situated knowledge practices or to negotiate new stances and identities in relation to knowledge.

'Employability' is often the stated rationale for embedding competences into the curriculum, and is assumed to define learners' ultimate goals and aspirations.

However, we found 'employability' to be very poorly articulated. Clearer focus could support subject teachers in identifying how graduate professions and employment pathways are changing with the impact of digital technologies, and in modelling how academic practices such as criticality, peer review, and innovation are becoming central to knowledge practice in many employment contexts. Similarly, the employability agenda could refocus literacy provision around authentic tasks in complex social situations. Clearly there is also a need to discuss in a broad sense what graduates can bring to their communities and workplaces. We would argue that notions of digital citizenship and participation, as well as digital scholarship and professionalism, have their place here. But we are concerned that there is little collective understanding of how learners progress towards digital literacy, and where in the learning experience this progression is best recognized and supported.

Baselining activities of projects involved in the JISC-funded Developing Digital Literacies Programme have made some attempts to further our understanding both of how students are using technologies to support their learning activities and how they are enhancing their learning practices around information behaviours, critical thinking and analysis, understandings of professional practices, digital identity and reputation management, and their academic practices.

The frameworks review of the LLiDA study uncovered a few promising areas of work. For example, UN '2000+' offers a vision of multiple and critical literacies of technology, rather than a single standard of competence (Kahn and Kellner 2005). Also, in the area of 'media literacy', theorists such as Buckingham (2007) and Kress (2003) have argued the need for learners to become proficient at creative self-expression and critical argumentation in a range of media. This presents many challenges, not least in relation to assessment, since creativity is difficult to characterize within competency frameworks. Different disciplines demand proficiency in different combinations of media, creating and sharing meaning in different ways: literate learners need to both inhabit and critique these modes. Perhaps not surprisingly, our review found very little evidence of support for critical aspects of reading different media or for creative practices of media production, except in highly specialist courses.

An important principle is that *literacies of the digital are directly related to individual identity,* in particular an individual's stance towards knowledge in digital forms. We can see anxieties about this issue in the emphasis on 'evaluation' and 'judgement' in models of digital competence. Most of these models posit judgement as a higher level skill that emerges from other skills such as finding and sorting information. From a situated practice perspective, however, judgement is not a skill so much as a stance towards knowledge that can only be occupied by a person who has had experiences of a particular kind. These include the experience that her judgement is legitimate, and the recognition of alternative standpoints which allow a critical relationship with knowledge to be exercised.

Despite these issues, there is evidence emerging of profound changes in knowledge practice; for example the ways in which people collaborate over academic writing (Cushman 2004), and the transfer of knowledge through graphical and video media (Nicholas *et al.* 2008). Yet, there is an extraordinary diversity in the competences mandated for consideration during the curriculum design and validation process. It is often difficult to see how these align with the institutional missions articulated in other strategic documents, or how learners might go about integrating them into a coherent developmental pathway.

We can draw a key principle from this evidence that *emergent digital practices could be influenced by academics as subject experts.* The transfer of digital capabilities from one domain to another – from social life to education – is difficult for learners (Cranmer 2006; Facer and Selwyn 2010). Tacit situational knowledge seems to play a vital role in competent performance. Therefore learners must engage in subject-specific tasks, with subject-specialist technologies, modelled by subject experts to be able to participate fully within specialized knowledge communities. How can academics model the identities, stances, strategies, and capabilities that learners require for effective knowledge practice?

Academics' influence on students' learning practices

The origins of the internet lie in academics' practices. Tools of the internet age were shaped by the collaborative knowledge-building needs of researchers, whose stance towards knowledge is highly specialized and attained through a fairly long apprenticeship. Transferring digital knowledge practices across the research–teaching boundary may be troublesome for academics in areas of teaching practice that are different from this apprenticeship model. What this means is that it may be relatively easy to transfer knowledge to graduate students working within active research groups, or in contexts where learning, teaching, and research practices are interwoven. Examples include project-based learning, learning through authentic tasks, or studio-based learning. Since these teaching approaches span research and teaching, and call for the co-creation of knowledge, digital knowledge practice permeates the research–teaching boundaries.

Conversely, academics are likely to encounter difficulties in transferring digital knowledge practices in situations where learning and teaching is removed from research. Examples include didactic approaches to teaching – typically lectures, particularly in situations where learners appear more comfortable with technology-enhanced learning that mirrors conventional learning approaches (Bennet *et al.* 2008; Jones and Healing 2010; Ebner *et al.* 2008). Benchmarking activities in the JISC Literacies Programme includes scoping academics' digital literacies in relation to teaching, curriculum design, and research practices. These activities provide evidence of early career researchers being more likely to use mobile and social technologies and being innovative in the areas of data capture, virtual collaboration, and building contacts. In the area of learning and teaching it is evident that academics predominantly acquire personal, social technologies and associated skills through self-directed exploration, supplemented by online materials where necessary, and informal peer support. Most appeared to be proactive in adopting and learning to use these technologies which included blogging, Twitter, audio/ lecture capture technologies, and visualization/presentation technologies such as Prezi. This offers strong indications that digital practices of academics are becoming central to their academic practice across research, teaching, learning, and communicating ideas and knowledge practices.

Other studies provide evidence that the impact of academics' approaches to teaching on learners' attitudes to learning may be reflexive. An early study of learners' use of technologies for learning (Trinder *et al.* 2008; Margaryan *et al.* 2011), found evidence that undergraduate students appear to be influenced by the ways academics model the use of technologies in their practice. Technology adoption is influenced by complex interdependencies between age, subject, the extent of technology use, and the university's support of technology adoption for learning. This finding is corroborated in a study by Sharpe (2010) which identified tutor guidance as a critical determinant of the technology-based learning practices adopted by students. Yet individual academics may or may not be enthusiasts for using specific technology tools such as wikis or social bookmarking to support exploration of disciplinary knowledge, but in the absence of that enthusiasm, learners are not acquiring these practices through informal digital participation. We are therefore left with the profound question of how learners are being supported to develop the literacies they need for life in a digital age.

With the rise in diversity of media, multiple modes of meaning-making are becoming an essential aspect of everyday life (Kress 2003; Brown and Adler 2008; Siemens 2006). As members of research and professional communities, academics understand that ways of reaching and expressing judgement are aspects of personal identity, and that managing one's identity as a knowledgeable person is different in a digital age. Identity management takes many forms; disembodiment through the use of avatars (see Bayne and Ross, Gourlay and Oliver in this volume); management of identity cross- and trans-boundary (see Satchwell *et al.* in this volume) and scholarship (see Jones, Goodfellow, and Fransman in this volume). An important principle is that *literacies continually evolve in response to changes in the technical, epistemological, and cultural order.* Students' facility with technologies has to evolve to take account of this effect.

Students' facility with technologies

Learners' reliance on tutors to transfer knowledge practices from research to teaching contexts highlights a critical weakness in the discourse of the 'digital native'. This popular concept assumes that young people – the generation born after 1980 – who have grown up with access to networks are 'digital natives' who have developed a natural predisposition to using technologies for learning (Prensky 2001; Oblinger and Oblinger 2005; Palfrey and Gasser 2008). Some theorists claim these learners have developed a broad baseline of digital literacies, 'fluency in multiple media, valuing each for the types of communication, activities, experiences, and expressions it empowers; learning based on collectively seeking, sieving, and synthesizing experiences rather than individually locating and absorbing information from a single best source; active learning based on experience representations rather than linear stories; and co-design of learning experiences personalized to individual needs and preferences' (Dede 2005). There is now considerable research evidence that learners' ICT skills are less advanced than educators tend to think (Nicholas *et al.* 2008) and that the characterization of young people as 'digital natives' hides many contradictions in their experiences (Luckin *et al.* 2009; Littlejohn *et al.* 2010; Jones this volume).

Learners can be confident about their internet use while lacking evaluative and critical capabilities, and research skills of any sophistication (Sharpe 2010). Even learners with their own laptop, smartphone, and other devices often have no idea how to use them to support their learning, and have rarely explored beyond their basic functionality (ibid.). Whilst new forms of media are clearly significant in shaping their thinking and knowledge practice, learners' engagement with digital media is complex and differentiated (Bennett *et al.* 2008; Hargittai 2009). They often face difficulties in transposing digital knowledge practices from social contexts into formal learning (Cranmer 2006; Facer and Selwyn 2010).

Some aspects of learners' everyday practices with technology are at odds with the practices valued in traditional academic teaching and assessment (Beetham 2009). For example, academics report that learners struggle particularly with tasks of judgement and evaluation, and with issues of originality in representing their ideas (ibid.). These have always been difficult issues for students, but they are now being posed in a context where identities are being constantly renegotiated online, where new ideas become instantly available in multiple fragments and copies and reinscriptions of themselves, and where 'the power of the crowd' dominates how opinion is expressed (Howe 2008). Knowledge practices depend on the learner's previous experiences (Goodyear and Ellis 2008), on dispositions such as confidence, self-efficacy, and motivation (Candy 1991), and on qualities of the environment where that practice takes place (Engeström 1999). That tools are now familiar to learners from other contexts of use does not give them access to the relevant knowledge practices.

A key principle we can derive is that *literacies are acquired through extended practice and refinement in different contexts of use*, rather than through one-off instruction (Bruner 1990; Graff 1995). Over time, learners develop personal styles of use and preferences. Luckin *et al.* (2009) and Sharpe (2010) found that styles of technology use constitute a new form of diversity among learners, and that learners qualify their preferences over time depending on their experiences of technology in the context of study. Creative knowledge building and sharing, such as the originating of blogs and wikis, tagging, meme-ing, reviewing, recommending, and repurposing, remain minority activities to which most learners are introduced by educators (Selwyn 2009), since these are digital research practices academics in some disciplines are familiar with.

Weller (2011) argues that researchers' use of digital technologies remains conservative and experimental as they do not sit comfortably with established research practice. This is also supported by the Developing Digital Literacies baselining findings reported earlier, which found that early career researchers were much more likely to utilize newer technologies to support their research practices than more experienced researchers. In relation to learning and teaching Weller describes a 'pedagogy of abundance', where content is no longer scarce and where we see a move away from a one-to-many instructionist pedagogy to more participatory, social models, supported by social networking technologies. He identifies several theoretical frameworks and approaches that support these new models such as problem-based learning, connectivism, constructivism, and communities of practice (ibid.). We would argue that for students to be able to learn effectively in connected and collaborative learning contexts they require a more sophisticated understanding of how they learn, a metacognition as described by Luckin and Hammerton (2002). They also need to understand which technologies best support their needs in a particular context, whether that is engaging with or creating content, communicating and sharing knowledge with other students or teachers, or engaging with broader social networks and communities.

Conclusions and implications for practice

Understanding literacies as situated knowledge practices has real implications for how we support learners' development. This perspective gains importance as the range of frameworks by which we might understand the world proliferate (Barnett 2000). Through the LLiDA study we have identified a tension between an 'entitlement' to basic digital literacy – which generic, learner-centred support can foster – and support for knowledge practices that are diverse and constitutive of personal identity, including subject- and profession-based identities. There is evidence to suggest that competence-based provision can undermine motivation and self-efficacy (see e.g. Zimmerman 1989). Consequently, the focus of provision in curricula should be on developing practice through authentic academic tasks, in a range of contexts in which 'digital' aspects of the working and learning environment are naturally integrated.

Rather than focusing on competency frameworks and the latest virtual environments and features, we would like to see a radical shift in the ways in which digital literacy support is viewed. The focus should be on managing digital identities, developing online communities, appropriating and repurposing technologies for personal and social goals (including learning goals), and developing a critical relationship with the technologies designed for our use and the knowledge they make available. Critically, these practices would ideally be situated and modelled by academics, to impact learners' ability and efficacy beliefs, motivations and achievement goal orientations (Wentzel and Wigfield 1998). Whilst academics are increasingly modelling digital practices, as evidenced in the baselining activities earlier, there are challenges in how transferable these are to other academics and to learners within formal educational contexts. The baseline activities of projects in the current programme also revealed fears around using digital technologies for both staff and students ranging from dehumanization, distraction, erosion of personal and professional boundaries, time management, information management, and superficiality of exchanges. There appears to be a need for staff and students to negotiate some fairly complex choices around which technologies they use and how far they incorporate them into their teaching and learning. We anticipate that this programme will reveal some interesting emerging practices as academics increasingly model digital practices within their subject contexts.

Key principles for the development of digital literacies as situated knowledge practices are as follows:

- Literacies are foundational capabilities essential for participation within society;
- Literacies are acquired through extended practice and refinement in different contexts of use, rather than through one-off instruction;
- Emergent digital practices are influenced by subject specialists (e.g. academics);
- Literacies continually evolve in response to changes in the technical, epistemological, and cultural order;
- Literacies of the digital are directly related to individual identity and reputation, in particular an individual's stance towards knowledge in digital forms and how they are perceived when interacting with others in socially networked learning and research contexts.

We see opportunities to embed these principles within education and to focus on the exploration of disciplinary knowledge and situated knowledge practices, modelled by academics, in a new digital context.

Notes

1 Learning Literacies for a Digital Age (LLiDA) http://www.academy.gcal.ac.uk/llida
2 http://www.jisc.ac.uk/developingdigitalliteracies/
3 A list of the sources reviewed is available at: http://www.caledonianacademy.net/spaces/LLiDA/
4 http://www.qaa.ac.uk/AssuringStandardsAndQuality/subject-guidance/Pages/Subject-benchmark-statements.aspx

Chapter 10

Academic literacies in the digital university

Integrating individual accounts with network practice

Mary R. Lea

This chapter raises questions about our understanding of academic literacy practices in the digital university. It reports upon some recent research in the UK, which has highlighted a potential disconnect between undergraduate online reading practices and requirements for assessed work. The chapter goes on to examine the contribution of work broadly conceptualized as actor network theory (ANT) as a complementary perspective to academic literacies approaches. It concludes that we can potentially enhance our understanding of knowledge-making practices in the university if we both interrogate our own theoretical and methodological assumptions and combine these with a network approach. Starting from a long-standing and generally accepted stance and approach in the empirical study of literacies, the chapter begins to open up questions around research and practice occasioned by the digital. This not only suggests some fundamental changes in our understanding of the ways that knowledge is enacted but should also help us towards interrogating our own practices productively.

Researching undergraduate digital practice

In the first instance, this chapter is framed by familiar research and reporting practice in the field of academic literacies, with findings from an Economic and Social Research Council UK-funded project, 'Digital Literacies in Higher Education'. The main aim of the research was to contribute to our understanding of the changing digital-rich environment with regard to the nature of literacies, learning, and technologies (Lea and Jones 2011). Its focus was on the literacy practices and associated texts that were accessed, negotiated, and produced by undergraduate students in learning environments associated with digital technologies. The case was made for drawing upon academic literacies research as a body of work with a history of paying critical attention to learning in conceptualizing literacies as social and cultural practice. The argument made was that this offered a proven theoretical and methodological framework, foregrounding issues of meaning-making around textual practice and offering a critical perspective for examining learning and technologies. It was considered particularly apposite that so much of students' digital engagement involved the reading as well as the production of texts. The findings suggest that ways of reading may be emerging which have particular relevance for understanding new knowledge-making practices across the academy (Lea and Jones 2011), not just those of students.

Language and literacy has always played a central role in higher education. Writing has been of particular significance because of its symbiotic relationship with the historical construction of academic disciplines (Bazerman 1981; Berkenkotter and Huckin 1995; Turner 2011) and the evident power of the written text in the academy. In addition, attention to writing has played an important part in understanding student learning because of the role it plays in the process of assessment. For many years, researchers in the field of student writing and learning have been concerned with the different ways in which students and academics make meaning through engaging in a range of literacy practices. This has resulted in a critical and comprehensive understanding of the written texts circulating in the university and their significance for the individuals involved, across different contexts and fields of study (Ivanič 1998; Lea and Stierer 2000; Thesen and Platzen 2006; Lea and Stierer 2011; Lillis and Curry 2010). However, there has been rather less critical attention paid – from a literacies perspective – to the practices of reading in the university, possibly because of some difficult and often insurmountable problems with capturing reading practices. A notable exception has been Mann's work (2000).

Methodologically, the research reported on here both built on an established framework and drew on familiar methods of enquiry. Undergraduate students were interviewed three or four times over a six-month period. During the meetings they talked through their use of a range of technologies in their day-to-day lives, both in and outside the curriculum (Jones and Lea 2008). The data included interview transcripts, texts from a range of web-based sites and resources, observation of student practices, departmental and other institutional documentation, and screen capture from virtual learning environments (VLEs). As with all academic literacies research, the focus was on gathering rich descriptions of student engagement and uncovering understandings of personal and institutional textual practice. Although we drew upon familiar methods of enquiry, we also foregrounded significant differences and challenges in terms of what counts as data in today's higher education learning environments and the role of the researcher. We argued that we needed to provide new ways of talking about learning, literacies, and technologies and, in particular, how best to take account of the integration of texts and technologies in terms of textual practice.

Early in the research we realized that the decisions we were making about capturing instances of textual practice were very different from those we were used to in previous academic literacies research. During our interviews, where students talked about and showed us their practices, we had to make quick decisions – *in situ* – about what data to capture from the many things that were available. This included which screen shots to save, which photographs to take of students' work in progress, and which texts to keep as digital records of practice. It was also clear that we needed an approach to understanding meaning in these contexts, which was able to take account of the integrated nature of textual and technological practice. We drew on the early work of John Law in relation to ANT and his argument that knowledge always takes on and is embodied in a material form. This material form is part of what Law terms a 'patterned network', involving a process of 'heterogeneous engineering in which bits and pieces of the social, the technical, the conceptual and the textual are fitted together' (Law 1992: 2). We saw this relationship between the social, the textual, and the technological within patterned networks as being central to the enactment of students' textual practice.

Through this conceptual lens the research pointed to two important findings. First, that a complex and largely hidden range of textual practices are being implicated in students' submitted assignments. When these are primarily web-based, they are, by their very nature, unbounded and unconstrained, with a different material quality from engagement with traditional print-based resources such as books and hard copy journal articles. Students used a wide range of sites and resources; indeed, they regularly used hard copy books and articles following guidance from reading lists. When they accessed other resources, they followed links in order to journey seamlessly from one site to another, moving on from the original source in an intertextual world. Texts had an unbounded and interconnected quality about them. The processes of meaning-making were complex as students engaged in these wide-ranging resources, making sense of them through the lens of the requirements for assessment and teacher preferences. Reading across hybrid resources and making sense of these in relation to their assessed work was a dominant practice for students, whatever discipline, subject, or vocational area they were engaged in (Lea and Jones 2011). Students talked through the detail of resources they had accessed and how they had or intended to use this in preparation for an assignment. This often involved both individual and group work. For example, some students talked around their work for a group project. This required them to create an artificial scenario and analyse economic prospects for a new biotech firm in launching a drug that would cure Type 2 diabetes. In preparation they accessed a range of resources and read across a range of contexts – what they variously referred to as getting, looking for, or finding information. However, despite the rhetorical complexity of working with a range of texts, rarely did we find examples of assignment rubrics that explicitly reflected or articulated the complexity of the processes of meaning-making and the range of textual practices which were hidden but implicated in student work.

Harnessing resources in knowledge construction

The metaphor of 'a sandwich' signifies the problem. Institutionalized assessment practices are concerned with the outer layers; at the bottom the assignment rubric and at the top the completed assignment. However, the richness of practice is in the middle, in the sandwich filling. This is where the student is primarily located in relation to the wealth of resources, which have been harnessed around an assignment. It is where the interesting work and processes of meaning-making are located and where student sense-making is happening, as they negotiate a range of textual resources. The assignment rubrics that students showed us rarely captured the complexity of the 'filling', this rich and fertile ground which offers the potential for university teachers to engage with their students explicitly about the changing status of knowledge in their discipline, what counts, and how different forms of knowledge are entering the arena and being valorized. In some subject areas, as in the group work above, students were encouraged to use resources from commercial and public media sites, often in addition to established academic sources. Clearly, different disciplines draw on and privilege digital and web-based resources in contrasting ways, as this research illustrated. University teachers are in a position to engage generatively with their students about what kinds of texts are implicated in the construction of their own area of study and the implications this has for students when using different types of resource. This means paying attention to student engagement with the processes of meaning-making as they work across hybrid texts, and explicitly integrate the reading of a range of resources into assignment rubrics. The project provided evidence that students are primarily influenced by what they believe their teachers see as valid, reliable, and authoritative knowledge (see Lea and Jones 2011 for further explanation). They recognize the role of the teachers as the final arbiter of what counts. This authoritative position offers university teachers a potentially rewarding opportunity to engage generatively but also critically with their students in examining the changing knowledge-making practices that are permeating the digital academy – specifically within their own subject areas (see Goodfellow; McKenna and Hughes, this volume).

Towards a network perspective

The literacies as social and cultural practice frame has been evidently robust in dealing with textual practice in the academy to date and taking account of particular historical manifestations of materiality, including multimodality and semiotic resource (Kress 1999). My interest here is in the potential development of the field in articulating and interrogating textual practice in the digital higher education landscape. This includes paying attention to the messiness and interconnectedness of practices. As a field we have tended to work with and taken for granted our established categories and binaries. These include: distinguishing between academics' and students' textual/technological practices; focusing on writing and assessment; articulating the relationship between individual identity and meaning-making; identifying gaps between student and tutor understandings, particularly around feedback; positioning teachers as authoritative and powerful and students as powerless.

For example, although in the research reported above we were sensitized to the digital context in relation to an actor-network perspective, there was a tendency in both the data collection and analysis to foreground familiar categories, practices, and concerns. Arguably we relied upon some unquestioned assumptions about the categories we were using, seeing digital practice through a familiar lens in order to access and understand what made this context different from those researched in earlier work. We were keeping the familiar lens of the student/teacher dyad as an organizing principle and a sense that meaning-making was located in the practices of individual students and academics. Through this approach we uncovered and made visible the dominance of reading practices but also the resistance of assignment practices to change.

The rest of this chapter is framed significantly by the work of Law around ANT. Although the language and terminology may prove difficult to access for those who are both unfamiliar with this and more used to conventional educational discourses, for more than a decade researchers interested in literacies as social practice have found value and synergy with approaches to practice which emerged from ANT and earlier related work in science and technology studies (Latour and Woolgar 1979; Latour 1987). The complementarity of the work is increasingly evident as research on literacies and technologies are elided and literacies researchers look to expand their repertoire of resources to help them make sense of changing institutional contexts (Morgan 2002 *et al.*). In short, a concern with literacy in the digital university forces us to interrogate much that we have taken for granted and integrate perspectives from other intellectual traditions – as other chapters in this volume attest – despite the challenges of engaging with new and unfamiliar discourses.

In this respect, recent work which foregrounds ANT can help us to interrogate and rethink our categories, refocus on academic literacies, and begin to take account of practices being enacted in emerging and powerful networks. This involves, for example, a consideration of staff and students as part of the same networks engaged in a myriad of knowledge-making practices. It can help us to consider the enactment of knowledge as network practice rather than foregrounding the student learner through a lens of agency, identity, and individual processes of meaning-making. It also makes visible the interplay between different networks in the digital university. In this respect I turn now to consideration of work that is broadly conceptualized within an ANT perspective, taking as my starting point Law's work.

In a recent article (Law 2009b), Law reiterates his long-standing argument that ANT is not a theory nor concerned with what he calls strong accounts but offers a 'toolkit for telling interesting stories' (p. 142) and a sensibility to messy practices. Fenwick and Edwards (2010) suggest that this makes it particularly significant in terms of challenging the overriding concern of educational research with categorizing and tying down how things work in educational settings. Law describes ANT as a 'disparate family of material-semiotic tools, sensibilities, methods of analysis that treat everything in the social and natural worlds as a continuously generated effect of the webs of relations within which they are located. It assumes nothing has reality or form outside the enactment of these relations. Its studies explore and characterize the webs and practices that carry them.' (p. 141). A central premise of Law's approach is that it is always grounded in empirical case studies and how they work in practice. Law specifically foregrounds the relationship of ANT to other intellectual traditions, including social theory and sociology but, interestingly, not to critical language or literacy studies. However, there is an implicit link to Fairclough's work on critical discourse analysis (1992) which drew extensively on Foucault and, in association with Gee (1996) was foundational in new literacy studies, whence academic literacies developed.

Law argues that 'material semiotics' – a term he uses now in preference to ANT – is a kind of toolkit that can be understood as a powerful set of 'devices for levelling divisions which are usually taken to be foundational' (p. 147). It undoes the dualisms of human/non-human; meaning and materiality (his concern is not with a linguistic view of meaning as literacies researchers would understand it); big and small; macro/micro; social/ technical; nature/culture. This kind of orientation helps those of us who are literacies researchers to think outside the box and interrogate our own categories, the things we take for granted, the ways we have understood our work and approaches, our focus on individual actors and our attention to meaning-making and identity, as exemplified in the research reported on earlier in this chapter.

Law suggests that networks always involve different kinds of actors, human and otherwise. Related to this is his concern with materiality and what he terms material semiotics; this refers not just to the social world but to how a range of things, for example, behaviours, practices, artefacts, technologies, texts may count or be disregarded within networks. At its simplest, material semiotics is a combination of things and ideas (concepts) and, arguably, closely aligned with what literacies researchers might term material practice (Brandt and Clinton 2002). Both are concerned with enactment and with the ways in which particular things (texts) and practices come into being.

Educational research tends to work with entities: classrooms, students, teachers, assignments, computers, policy documents (the same observation can of course be made of academic literacies research) but as Fenwick and Edwards (2012) argue, these are actually assemblages of myriad things which order and govern practices in particular ways. Seen through an ANT lens they are often precarious networks that take a lot of work to sustain them. Take, for example, today's dominant categorizations of digital natives and digital immigrants, discursively and empirically precarious but presented as having a material quality residing in the actions of individual students and their teachers. Fenwick and Edwards suggest that there is always the potential for counter networks, alternative forms and spaces to develop, with some networks being more powerful than others. There is always constant tension between networks and their enactment; this pull and push between networks is at the heart of how the university is constantly reinventing itself. The chapters in this volume attest to this tension in their varied articulation of literacy in the digital university.

Key to the ways in which networks maintain power is the creation and role of 'immutable mobiles'. Law (2009) suggests that immutable mobiles enable texts, ideas, images, concepts, for example, to move from place to place and be used for different purposes in different networks at different times. They are immutable because they don't change – because they have become reified – but they are also mobile because they can move from network to network. In short, they are powerful ways of ordering the world and therefore take on particular significance within networks. The term 'digital literacies' acts as an immutable mobile as it embeds a range of presuppositions and beliefs about practice which are played out in different networks (see Goodfellow 2011; Lea 2013).

Law's concern with networks is how different realities relate to one another and in exploring how such a patchwork of realities may be enacted in other ways. This seems to be a key consideration to those of us concerned with how networks work with respect to diverse textual practices within the digital university. His perspective leads us to ask questions about how we have assembled academic literacies and how, in the process, we may have failed to see other things in the web of networks, in particular the power of institutional networks over and above the activities of particular groups of people such as students and academics.

A precedent for using ANT alongside a social practices approach to literacy is offered by the work of Clarke (2002) and Hamilton (2011). Clarke argues that the value of drawing on an ANT approach is that it offers educators the possibility of challenging the 'hierarchical ordering of knowledge, skills, learners, teachers, technologies and spaces that characterize our working life' (p. 108). She is drawn to this because of 'its concern with a process in which networks combine in particular ways to produce objects, knowledge or facts through the displacement or suppression of dissenting voices' (p. 109). She offers similar conclusions to those being rehearsed here, suggesting a tendency in literacies research more generally to rely on predetermined categories, which assume some of the things we want to explain. Academic literacies research has foregrounded student writing and its products, in particular the student essay and tutor feedback practices. It has paid particular and detailed attention to aspects of texts and practices that are easily available for scrutiny, rather than aspects of practice which are less immediately visible. This may in part offer an explanation for why research into academic literacies has paid very little explicit attention to reading practices. As a field of enquiry, there has also been a tendency for academic literacies to rely significantly upon participant accounts. Digital contexts provide a visibility around some practices that were previously hidden but it could also be argued that our reliance on familiar categories around text types and practices has somewhat blinded us to other ways of seeing. That is, it is not necessarily the practices per se but our ability to both see and capture them which is changing in the shift to the digital.

Both Clarke and Hamilton focus on literacy policy in identifying moments of 'translation'. For example, Clarke explores how different actors – without distinguishing between human and non-human – are transformed into manageable entities as they are transported into reports and speeches. She illustrates how immutable mobiles move from network to network in support of her argument that some understandings of literacy hold more power than others. As she argues, 'the fact of literacy is unavoidable' (p. 119) and, in this respect, conceptualizations of literacy are always a 'material and symbolic means of ordering and classifying knowledge and social interaction' (p. 108). For Clarke, drawing on ANT in order to understand this fact of literacy, invites 'educators to challenge the hierarchical ordering of knowledge, skills, learners, teachers, technologies and spaces that characterize our working life' (pp. 107–8).

Hamilton's interest is more in ANT as a philosophical and methodological approach to policy analysis and she uses this in her exploration of the International Adult Literacy Survey (IALS). Hamilton points to story as method, what she refers to 'as back-room workings of social technologies in the making' (p. 56). She uses an ANT orientation to track and understand histories of educational policy reforms, relating this to literacy studies, and the attention paid to literacy as contingent and situated social practice. As Hamilton suggests, the ontological and epistemological assumptions behind the 'sociology of translation' (a term used in association with ANT) are particularly compatible with the social practice perspective on literacy because of the similarity of ideas, even though they may offer different emphases and language of description. Her argument is particularly pertinent to those concerned with the digital context of higher education and the concomitant colonization of terms such as literacy to promote powerful institutional and government agendas (see below). She suggests that, as a key process in translation, metaphor is a powerful move in organizing the knowledge of a field and argues that there are big naturalized metaphors around literacy. Within the context of the digital university, the adoption of the metaphors of native and immigrant in association with the digital have become key organizers for framing the relationship between students and academics. The metaphor of literacy as capability underpins this organizing frame (for further discussion see below). As Callon (1986) argues, stable mobiles are crucial to assembling any new network because they have the effect of synchronizing meanings across time and space – or at least appearing to do so.

Hamilton's position is that that ANT is a promising perspective in relation to literacies because it 'works with a dynamic view of social life which acknowledges power and contestation and assumes multiple perspectives. Its central metaphor is of an open field of competing social forces and projects that are continually shifting with alliances being formed and dissolved' (p. 69). She argues that in looking for 'better analytical languages for big problems like structure and agency, global and local relations, we need to compare theoretical approaches which might work together to develop insights into the social world' (p. 69). The concerns of this volume – captured in the notion of the digital university – can be enhanced by adopting the approach that Hamilton proposes, particularly with regard to understanding the significance for teaching and learning of changing knowledge practices.

Although both Hamilton and Clarke foreground the complementarity of ANT with a social practice view of literacy, ANT offers a very different perspective of agency – emerging through relationships that come into being through actor networks, rather than residing in individuals. Hamilton argues that the recognition that a powerful actant in one context may be rendered powerless in another is of particular significance in terms of how we view issues of identity, a key area of concern for academic literacies research and practice. She argues for exploring a theory of identity which could be viewed as a network effect rather than residing primarily in an individual (see below for further discussion).

Individual practice and actor networks

Bringing together the critical contested perspective from academic literacies with an ANT approach – in both research and practice contexts – offers a counter to, what appears to be, the relentless drive of higher education to both stabilize the digital and align it uncritically with literacy. The predominant interest of universities is a concern with entities, not as complex sets of contested processes and practices but as named things which can be defined, reified, and objectified. Examples of these include: Google/Wikipedia/VLEs/Web 2.0/Facebook/YouTube/plagiarism (Turnitin and Copycatch). This is described by Morgan *et al.* (2002) as 'black-boxed' (p. 41), and by Fenwick and Edwards (2010) as 'concealing negotiations which are brought into existence' (p. 11). Networks which cohere around learning technologies often align with a view of digital literacy as capability (Goodfellow 2011; Lea 2013) and also bring into being characterizations of both students and academics as in deficit. These are enacted through an association with devices and applications as if the digital is a set of stable and named entities.

The final section of the chapter revisits the empirical research context where the chapter began and explores how we might think differently about literacy in the digital university. It suggests that ANT approaches can help to make visible practices which literacies researchers may have historically found difficult to explore through a literacies lens – for example, disciplinary reading practices. The move being made here is towards the enactment of knowledge as practice and engagement in hybrid and diverse knowledge networks. This offers a complementary approach; one less constrained by the a priori categories which both guided but also emerged directly from our research, for example, a sensitivity to reading in contrast to writing, the relationship between students' online practices in contrast to the conventional demands of the assignment rubric, and a possibly unhelpful separation of student practice from teacher practice. The intention is not to seek to dispel the valuable insights and approaches that academic literacies research has had and still has to offer but to suggest that it may be generative to pay explicit attention to how the practices that we have identified are implicated in taking a network approach. This requires us to complement our reliance on individual accounts and to tease out issues of agency and meaning-making within a broader perspective, which takes account of configurations between different networks. It also means asking questions about how such an orientation could enhance the significance and relevance of empirical research – such as that introduced at the beginning of the chapter – in understanding teaching and learning in contexts where powerful discourses associated with other agendas, e.g. learning technologies, employability, are increasingly taking centre stage. It should help us to explore different kinds of questions in relation to the workings of other powerful networks.

Central to this move is the idea of the 'immutable mobile'. As processes become reified, their 'thing-like' quality enables them to act as entities and at the same time become very mobile. They can move from network to network and exert power through combining with each other. A pertinent example of this process is that of 'digital literacies'. The research reported on above was entitled 'Digital Literacies in Higher Education'. Its aim was to examine the lived experience of undergraduates' textual worlds and interrogate the ubiquitous notion of the 'digital native', which appeared to have gained currency on the basis of scant research-based evidence. The plural 'literacies' in the title explicitly signalled the social, cultural, and contested nature of literacy practices, as evidenced in previous academic literacies research. Simultaneously, the idea of 'digital literacy/ies' was being taken up by learning technologists and, in the UK, was particularly evident in approaches that signalled the competences or skills that young people needed to function not just as students but in the wider economic world:

> We propose defining digital literacy in as neutral a way as possible, following the lead of the European Union and the JISC-funded LLiDA project.
>
> *digital literacy defines those capabilities which fit an individual for living, learning and working in a digital society*
>
> Defining a particular set of capabilities as a 'literacy' means that:
>
> - they are a pre-requisite or foundation for other capabilities;
> - they are critical to an individual's life chances;
> - they are essential to the making and sharing of culturally significant meanings;
> - as a result, there is or should be a society-wide entitlement to these capabilities at some level.
>
> (p. 2 JISC 2011a)

The combination of digital with literacy acts as an 'immutable mobile', as an entity which appears unchanged and stable as it moves around within different network configurations, for example, networks associated with research into academic literacies, the practices of librarians, open educational resources, government-funded bodies tasked with supporting learning technology; networks reflected across this volume. In reality of course digital literacy/ies is not a thing at all – it captures a whole range of processes and practices, but once it takes on a 'thing-like' quality it can be called into action to promote and service particular agendas in more or less powerful ways (see Lea 2013).

The idea of the digital native acts in a similar way. Indeed, despite its conceptual usefulness being largely discredited in the research literature (see Jones; Gourlay and Oliver, this volume), it carries a powerful message in institutional policy, with regard to the necessity for digital immigrants (university teachers) to respond to the demands of digital natives (their students) and deliver a curriculum that aligns with students' digital worlds. In any network where delivering a technology-enhanced curriculum is central to its configuration, the digital and its association with literacy plays a powerful role in determining particular manifestations of policy and practice.

Directions

ANT offers important insights about processes and objects of education because we are always dealing with contested practices. It helps us to see how things come together, how they are held together, and what connections are created between things: in short, the assembling of networks. Taking this approach to what is going on in institutional contexts enables us to concentrate on networks of knowledge players and knowledge makers in the digital university: people, things, and processes involved in the enactment of knowledge, rather than confining our explorations to, for example, the individual practices of teachers as opposed to the practices of students. It also helps us to be more sensitive to the categories that have guided our understanding of academic literacies as both practitioners and researchers. Seeing students and teachers in the same network, rather than implicitly within diverse networks, forces us to think about practice and meaning-making in the digital university in different ways. Returning to the empirical research discussed above, an interest in reading practices as an aspect of myriad networks in an unbounded digital world – rather than the practices of individual students – immediately renders human agency and identity less significant. Indeed, it could be argued that academic literacies research has paid particular attention to aspects of individual agency but failed to engage with the broader social nature of practice and artefacts. It has tended to adopt a very human-focused perspective, grounded in identifiable human actions of individuals. As illustrated in the research project reported earlier, accounts of meaning are primarily given by what individual participants say about their own textual practice. Other institutional networks are alluded to but tend not to be central to the research. For example, although we drew on data about students' individual use of VLEs in terms of understanding more about online reading practices, we did not undertake any detailed exploration of the VLE as an aspect of network within a broader institutional context. The question this now raises is what we might have gained from complementing the approach we took with an orientation that forces us to explore simultaneous networks of knowledge and practice, not only those where individual accounts of practice are being observed and articulated. This would entail going further than detailed analysis of a range of institutional documentation – which has been one of the primary ways in which academic literacies researchers have attempted to capture institutional perspectives (Lea and Street 1998; Lea and Stierer 2011). This resonates with the argument made by Williams, this volume, with regard to the ways in which course management software is driven by material and ideological imperatives of efficiency, control, and surveillance that are central to the cultural workings of the contemporary university.

The very nature of the changing context of literacy in the digital university makes it somewhat different from previous manifestations of the academy – not least the ease with which with the digital circulation of texts enables powerful networks to colonize conceptions of practice and use them to promote and serve policy agendas which enact strong versions of the university. This is a consequence of the power of networks to bring things into being and to maintain them. The way in which organizations, such as JISC, can appear to 'own' digital literacy is an illustration, making a more contested, practice-based view of teaching and learning difficult to articulate visibly in institutional networks. Combining individual accounts from empirical research with a network approach may offer a way for researchers to make visible the messiness of literacy in the digital university and for practitioners to interrogate the part their own taken-for-granted and often hidden practices play in maintaining black-boxed approaches.

Chapter 11

Text-making practices in online writing spaces

From research to practice

Carmen Lee

Introduction

Participating in new digital media occupies much of young people's lives. In the US, for example, 94 per cent of 18–29 year olds are online (Pew Internet 2011). A similar trend is found in Asia. In Hong Kong, for example, 35.5 per cent of internet users are university students (eMarketer 2011). Most online platforms are textually mediated, involving a great deal of reading and writing activities. Producing and using digital texts thus becomes a crucial part of young people's literacy practices. It is for these reasons that this chapter focuses on university students' private writing practices online. Creative linguistic features in online writing such as abbreviations, emoticons, stylized spelling and typography, or what Crystal (2006) refers to as 'Netspeak', have been studied extensively from a linguistics perspective (e.g. Shortis 2001; Crystal 2006; Goddard and Geesin 2011). While teachers may be aware of these innovative linguistic features, they rarely have access to students' private online writing. This is also causing moral panics and much public debate about how digital media are negatively affecting students' literacy skills (Thurlow 2007). What teachers need to understand is not just what new linguistic features are available but *why* and *how* they come into being, and how informal learning takes place as students engage in private online writing activities. In view of this, research on digital literacies emerged to look into details of everyday digital practices (Ito *et al.* 2010; Sheridan and Rowsell 2010). Much of this work has *practices* as a starting point, leading to implications for pedagogy. Alongside details of practices, this chapter adopts an approach that also foregrounds the role of digital texts as *language*.

In the rest of the chapter, I first introduce my theoretical and methodological orientation in researching digital texts. I draw on the concepts of 'text-making practices' and 'discourse-centred online ethnography' to offer a linguistic dimension to digital literacies. I then present a study of instant messaging (IM) among university students in Hong Kong and discuss how this language-based research, which did not have an education agenda, incidentally informed my teaching practices. A case study of an academic Facebook group is presented to illustrate how members of the group reappropriate and remix their existing text-making resources. I argue that this group can be understood as a 'third space' (Bhabha 1994; Moje *et al.* 2004) where everyday and academic discourse practices meet.

Researching students' digital texts in non-academic settings

The New Literacy Studies framework has established the tradition of researching details of informal and everyday literacy practices. One primary aim of this approach is to inform formal education and policy (Hull and Schultz 2002; Ivanič *et al.* 2008). The *Literacies for Learning in Further Education* project (Ivanič *et al.* 2008; Satchwell, Barton, and Hamilton, this volume), for example, explores the relationship between college students' everyday and college-based literacy practices, both digital and non-digital. The project has identified characteristics of students' informal literacies such as hybridity, multimodality, and collaborative knowledge sharing, which lecturers can draw upon in pedagogy. Although originally the project did not focus primarily on technologies, its findings suggest that new media play a central role in college students' textual practices and meaning-making processes.

Empirical studies of *digital literacies* emerged as a focused area of research that examines new forms of everyday literacies. One of the few large-scale studies on youth digital literacies is Ito *et al.*'s (2010) three-year multi-sited research in the U.S. This work provides in-depth ethnographic case studies of young people's digital practices and how they shape youth identities and learning experience. On the other hand, a number of studies highlight the *textual* dimension of digital literacies. Black (2007), for instance, shows how fan fiction authors and commenters on FanFiction.net co-design a supportive English learning environment through various discourse strategies. Other digital literacy researchers have examined young people's digital texts on different platforms, e.g. chat rooms (Merchant 2001), instant messaging (Lewis and Fabos 2005; Lee 2007a), and video gaming (Gee 2008), among others. This body of work has come to the consensus that digital texts are creative, hybridized, and multimodal. For example, Merchant (2001) shows how teenagers display extensive creativity by combining features of spoken conversation and writing in chat rooms. Merchant argues that innovative linguistic strategies are indeed marketable skills that formal education often devalues. Also focusing on textual practices, Lea and Jones (2011) make a stronger link between academic and digital texts. Their data illustrate that the meaning-making process of assessed writing in higher education often involves students drawing upon a wide range of digital and non-digital genres and modes.

All of the studies reviewed here are explicitly or implicitly education-oriented. They were either conducted in formal learning contexts, or they discuss implications for formal education. Other studies, which are not covered here in detail, also aim to recommend the practical applications of technologies, such as the value of computer conferencing in university students' writing for assessment (Lea 2001; Goodfellow *et al.* 2004). While these studies provide valuable resources for understanding the possible connection between informal and formal literacies, Street (2003) warns that not all aspects of out-of-class literacies are valuable and relevant to formal education. Lea and Jones (2011) also recommend that researchers should pay more attention to 'textual practice around learning and less upon the technologies and their applications' (p. 377). Studies that have a primary focus on everyday digital texts are limited but they are beginning to emerge in applied linguistics and sociolinguistics research, some of which draw on insights from literacies. Vold Lexander (2012), for example, looks into multilingual text messaging in Senegal. The literacies dimension of the study allowed the researcher to understand texting within its social context. Also interested in multilingual literacy practices are Barton and Lee (2012) who argue how meanings of vernacular literacies change as texts online become more multilingual and multimodal. Following this line of research, this chapter also foregrounds the *texts* produced by young people in digital media. In doing so, I combine the practice-based tradition in literacies research with what is referred to as 'discourse-centred online ethnography' (Androutsopoulos 2008). This approach complements existing discourse analytic research through a literacies lens (e.g. Ivanič 2004; Moje *et al.* 2004; Lam 2009). The following section illustrates how this approach was adopted in a study of IM.

Text-making practices of private IM by university students in Hong Kong

The study reported here looks into how a group of bilingual university students in Hong Kong deployed their multiple text-making resources when participating in private and voluntary IM activities. The basic unit of analysis is what I call 'text-making practices', 'the ways in which people choose and transform resources for representing meanings in the form of texts for different purposes' (Lee 2007a: p. 289). This notion captures the situated nature of writing and focuses on the production and representational aspects of texts. In particular, I analyse IM texts in terms of *language*. Language is central to meaning-making and is essential in shaping changes in students' lived experiences. These changes also influence the ways students use language, which I broadly refer to as *discourse*. To study details of practices, I also consider IM participants' insider knowledge and thoughts associated with their text-making online. Researching text-making under these assumptions requires a method that combines discourse analysis and ethnographic insights from observing authentic writing activities online. This approach is referred to as *discourse-centred online ethnography* (DCOE) (Androutsopoulos 2008) which:

> combines the systematic observation of selected sites of online discourse with direct contact with its social actors. [. . .] DCOE uses ethnographic insights as a backdrop to the selection, analysis, and interpretation of log data, in order to illuminate relations between digital texts and their production and reception practices. (p. 3)

This approach enables researchers to strike a balance between micro-level linguistic analysis (e.g. features of grammar, stylized typography and spelling, etc.) and broader level social practices, i.e. what people do. That way, details of both language and its use are given a reasonable amount of attention.

Multiple methods were adopted to elicit a wide range of qualitative data, including chat logs, participant observation, diaries, and semi-structured interviews. Depending on how accessible the participants were, not all of them were researched with the same research procedure; also, the same participant might have been involved through different pathways of data collection. Some participants were studied through a mixture of traditional ethnography and electronic methods, including the following stages:

1. *An initial observation session*: The researcher went to the participant's home or student residence and sat behind them to take field notes as they were sitting at their computer and chatting with their friends online. This way, the researcher had access to students' private spaces of communication, of which teachers had limited knowledge. This close observation also revealed other online practices such as multitasking – some of the participants never stayed on task but often switched to other applications such as MS Word for homework, with IM in the background at the same time.
2. *Collection of chat logs*: The participant was asked to print out the chat history from (1). This ensured the authenticity of the textual data.
3. *Face-to-face interview*: Based on the researcher's field notes, a face-to-face interview was conducted with the participant on the spot.
4. *Initial analysis*: Then the researcher went away and analysed all the data collected from (1)–(3). This phase started with a discourse analysis of the chat texts collected from (2). Linguistic features identified in texts then became themes for follow-up interviews.
5. *Follow-up*: Based on the themes emerged from (4), follow-up interviews were conducted either face to face or online, depending how accessible the participants were. Keeping in touch with the informants helped track changes in their IM usage. For example, towards the end of a semester, some participants used IM for project discussion with classmates instead of just for social and interpersonal chat.

As the research progressed, an alternative procedure was developed in response to the participants' everyday digital lives. Here the participants were studied primarily through online methods.

1. *Electronic logbook*: Each participant was asked to keep a 7-day word-processed diary or logbook, in which the participant describes their daily IM and online activities. They were also asked to copy and paste their chat logs into this logbook, which was then emailed to the researcher.
2. *Initial analysis*: The logbooks were analysed and coded. Interview topics were identified.

3. *Online interview*: Follow-up interviews were mostly done through IM. This interview method was particularly suitable for researching students whom the researcher did not know well or had only met electronically, or those who were not able to meet with the researcher face to face.

The electronic methods were particularly suitable for university student partici-pants. For one thing, email, IM, and working with Word documents were inte-gral activities in university students' lives. Understanding students' online habits allowed the researcher to develop a *responsive methodology* (Stringer 1999, Barton *et al.* 2007) that revolved around these electronic tools – interviewing via IM and writing diary entries in MS Word. Fitting data collection activities in participants' everyday practices can greatly enhance student participants' interests and moti-vation when taking part in the process of data collection. Because the research involved a series of data collection stages at different points in time, these online methods could easily fit in with university students' busy schedule.

For each participant, a profile was created according to the information obtained from field notes and the various stages of data collection. Figure 11.1 below is an extract from the personal profile of one research participant.

Snow is a 22-year-old postgraduate student in linguistics. She first used ICQ when she was 15, and switched to MSN last year. Snow is also a friend of mine and has been my MSN contact for about two years. In general, she has easy access to the computer and the Internet. At home, she logs on to IM whenever her computer is switched on. As a research student, she has her own office space in the university. So in addition to chatting at home, Snow logs on to MSN whenever she is in her office (see Gourlay and Oliver, this volume). Snow uses IM for interpersonal communication. Snow has friends living in different countries. IM becomes a tool for her to keep in touch with them. She also performs many other tasks when she is using IM. For exam-ple, she studies or works on her thesis and chats with friends simultaneously. Apart from text-based chatting, she has also used multimedia features of IM such as voice messages and video conferencing.

Snow is certainly a multilingual IM user. She code-switches easily when she chats with different interlocutors. Snow speaks Cantonese, a variety of Chinese commonly spoken in Hong Kong and Southern China, as her first language. She is fluent in both spoken and written English as it is the language she uses on a daily basis at university. She studied German and took a summer course in Ger-many. So she sometimes writes in German when she chats with her friends from her German courses. She has also studied the Cantonese romanization system called Jyutping, which was developed by a group of linguists in Hong Kong. This system is mainly used for transcription in her linguistics research. Ever since she started chatting in Jyutping with the researcher for fun, she has discovered that it is indeed the most convenient and expressive way to write in IM.

Figure 11.1 Informant's profile: Snow[1]

My direct contact with Snow and in-depth understanding of her background was essential in interpreting the linguistic features identified in her IM messages. Initial text analysis of her chat logs showed that Snow, like some of the other participants, drew upon *multilingual* and *multiscriptual* resources in her IM messages. Multilingual text-making practices include ways of switching between languages in the same chat session. Multiscriptual practices are the ways in which IM participants creatively or even playfully deployed the writing systems available to them. These resources were not mutually exclusive but were often combined to form meaningful messages. Extract 1 below is an IM conversation between Snow and her friend Shu, who also grew up in Hong Kong and was a student in Germany at the time of this chat. Table 11.1 shows that Snow writes predominantly in Cantonese, with occasional English words inserted into her sentences:

A key linguistic phenomenon in this extract is code-switching – alternation between languages and the coexistence of two or more languages. Some of the mixed language messages have high resemblance to Cantonese–English code-switching in everyday speech. This means, when read aloud, they would sound exactly like what would have been heard in a face-to-face conversation. Names of places such as 'Freiburg' (turn 3) and 'London' (turn 8), and food words like 'muffin' (turn 10) do have Cantonese equivalents but it is also common for educated people to just say them in English. As shown in her profile, Snow, being a postgraduate student in linguistics and relatively fluent in English, was very used to the practice of inserting English words into both Cantonese speech and IM writing. However, a closer reading of the extract reveals some rather peculiar forms of code-switching. Turn 10 ('我果時 only 食左個 muffin . . .') is an example of an unnatural sounding sentence, if heard in offline situations. Snow and I discussed this in the interview:

Table 11.1 IM log data between Snow and Shu

		Original chat log	Translation
1	Snow:	今日去m記,好開心喎,因為好內冇食過	I'm glad that I've been to the McDonald's today, because I haven't eaten any (McDonald's food) in ages.
2	Shu:	都好耐冇食過呀~~~~~~~~~~~~~~~~~	I haven't eaten there for a while too.
3	Snow:	喂我果時o向freiburg好似冇見過m記......	Hey, I don't think I came across any McDonald's in Freiburg when I was there.
	[...]		
8	Snow:	果時見到london果d好多沙津囉......	I also remember there were many kinds of salad in the McDonald's in London.
9	Shu:	係呀~ 不過都唔跟餐	Yes, but they don't come with the set menus.
10	Snow:	係呀係呀我果時only食左個 muffin..........1euro, 已經好抵咁.....	Oh yeah, and I once had a muffin only, and it cost 1 euro, seems quite reasonable already.

Extract 1. Interview transcript (originally in Cantonese)

Interviewer: *Here [referring to turn 10 in Extract 1], you write* "我果時 *only* 食左個 *muffin"* . . . *Would you have talked like that?*

Snow: . . . *because I like it. What? You mean orally?*

Interviewer: *Yes.*

Snow: *Oh no, never! That sounds awful. How can I say that [in speech]?*

Interviewer: *Why not?*

Snow: *OK, I would say [orally] 'muffin' in English. But I wouldn't say 'only' when I talk. I wrote 'only' because it was difficult to type* 淨係' *[Chinese equivalent for 'only'] but 'only' was easy to type. That's the reason [why I wrote 'only' in that message].*

In the first place, Snow was indifferent to my question which was intended to highlight the distinction between code-switching in everyday speech and that in IM. She said 'because I like it', which somehow indicates the normality of code-switching in IM. Later, she realized that I was referring to the oral dimension of her sentence. Her strong reaction to my question (*'Never! That sounds awful. How can I say that?'*) reveals that her criteria for 'acceptable' code-switching practices in speech were different from those in IM writing. That is, in IM, she would choose to write in a language which requires the least typing effort.

Findings from this IM research are actually in line with much research on out-of-class digital literacies, that college students' writing practices in new media tend to be *creative, hybrid,* and *fluid* (Ivanič *et al.* 2008; Lea and Jones 2011). Much of existing English-based research already shows how college students creatively deploy modes and genres in meaning-making. To multilingual students like Snow, they have the additional resources of languages and scripts to draw upon. These resources often offer different affordances for meaning-making (Lee 2007a). Snow's code-switching practice is not directly carried over from face-to-face contexts, but has been readjusted to respond to the constraints of the technology caused by Chinese typing (see the explanation of processing Chinese online in Lee 2007b). Elsewhere in Snow's chat database, she would write entirely in English to speak to a different audience. All these indicate university students' text-making practices online are *purposeful* (Barton and Hamilton 1998). While text analysis of Snow's IM data offered a snap-shot of the language features that characterize her IM writing, her case reveals the social meanings of code-switching as an integrated literacy practice.

A linguistic dimension in digital literacies research: some implications

What does a focus on language and discourse have to offer to digital literacies research? First of all, it provides empirical evidence, both in the form of authentic texts and students' insider knowledge, that there are mismatches between discourse style in online and offline contexts. Different combinations of languages, scripts, alongside other text-making resources are evident in online writing by multilinguals around the world (Danet and Herring 2007). Very often, it is the affordances (including constraints) of the media that open up new meaning-making possibilities that are not normally available in offline settings, classrooms included. The language education policy in Hong Kong is one that fosters linguistic purity (see detailed discussion in Evans, 2002). For example, written assignments are expected to be in either English or Chinese but not mixed-code. As with other vernacular literacy practices (Barton and Hamilton 1998), hybrid text-making practices online are not always valued in institutional practices (Barton and Lee 2012). However, code-switching online often demonstrates students' abilities to creatively remix their existing text-making resources to respond to constraints of the media, so as to achieve different communicative purposes. As Merchant (2001) argues, creativity and being responsive to change is important in terms of cultural capitals and marketable skills that students need to draw upon in their future career.

The second implication is a methodological one. The hybrid linguistic practices identified in the IM research also shaped my discourse style when interviewing on IM. For example, like many of my participants, I would use an informal style of language, and adopt IM linguistic features that are often found in their texts such as attaching emoticons and playing with languages, as illustrated in Extract 2:

Extract 2: Code-switching in IM interview

1 Interviewer: what language do you use in school gar? lecture notes and assignments all in english?
2 Participant: yes english!
3 Interviewer: i see. but do you think the kind of English you use in ICQ is different or the same as the kind of English you use in school gar?
4 Participant: different ga, icq 唔多 注意 grammar

As can be seen, throughout the interview extract, the participant and I did not adopt a formal and standard style of writing. Code-switching is evident (e.g. turn 4). A good example is my frequent insertion of the Cantonese particle *gar* at the end of my questions in Turns 1 and 3, which is a pervasive linguistic feature in Hong Kong-based online texts (Lee 2007b). These sentence-final particles are important discourse markers in Cantonese as they help express the speaker's attitudes. Adding these to my questions allowed me to situate myself in my informants' discourse community. It also allowed me to assert an IM user identity, not just a university researcher who had power over these university students. This experience has incidentally influenced my teaching practice, as explained in the next section.

Informing practice: text-making in an academic Facebook group

As mentioned, my IM research did not have learning and education as a starting point. Nonetheless, the research findings have informed my adoption of new media in my teaching of university-level courses. In the spring semester in 2011, I formed a Facebook group for my senior undergraduate course *Language, Literacy and Technology*. While sharing most features on Facebook, a 'group' on Facebook is a membership-based area that gathers people with shared interests and purposes. A group may be public or private (called a closed group). This course group was a closed one meaning that only course members were allowed to join and access the contents. In this group, all members were encouraged to take the initiative to post. Students, tutor, and lecturer interacted through multimodal means, from text-based posts and comments to images from other sites and videos from YouTube. A feature that is exclusive to the group area on Facebook is 'Docs', which allows members to compose and share text-based documents – that is also where I shared my lecture notes with the students. Participation in the group was voluntary and no contribution in the group was formally assessed. All 33 students joined the group as they interpreted their Facebook participation as part of their general participation grade, which counted towards 10 per cent of their overall coursework. At the end of the course, a questionnaire survey of students' experience of using Facebook in the course revealed that 92 per cent of them preferred the Facebook group to other course platforms that they had used. This positive feedback was partly due to the fact that all students were already avid Facebook users. A course-based platform on Facebook would not have created extra work for them. Whenever they logged in to Facebook, the latest course information was there. In terms of frequency of posting, although most original posts were still teacher-initiated, over 350 comments (together with many 'Likes') were made by students throughout the 14-week semester.

A strong sense of community was developed through adopting hybrid text-making practices by the course participants. Although the group was lecturer-initiated and academic in nature, course members drew upon a mixture of conventional and unconventional discourse styles that did not seem to exist in the classroom situation. The following extract shows an original post by a student, Carrie, who shares her view on an internet-specific word that appears in Yahoo Dictionary, followed by a comment from me.

Extract 3: Hybrid discourse styles

Carrie Chan: This page really shocks me today! I haven't thought of having this as proper vocabulary in English! BTW using 很牛 to explain 給力 is still too vague to those non-Chinese netizens . . .
(NB: In the original post, Carrie shares a web link to the word *geilivable* Yahoo Hong Kong Dictionary. *Geilivable* is a blending of

the Chinese internet jargon *geili*, meaning to give force, and the English suffix – *able*.)

Carmen Lee: thanks for sharing, carrie! and here are more examples: http:// news.xinhuanet.com/english2010/china/2010-12/25/c_ 13663775.htm

In this post, Carrie adopts a hybrid discourse style that does not normally exist in formal academic interaction. First of all, the post employs code-switching, which is commonly found in students' informal digital communication. Second, internet-specific discourse features such as 'BTW' and trailing dots (. . .) are incorporated into the post. Third, the hyperlinks embedded in Carrie's post and the lecturer's response also demonstrate *intertextuality*, a major characteristic of young people's textual practices (Ivanič *et al.* 2008; van Meter and Firetto 2008). This student-initiated post also provides a nice example of how Facebook affords collaborative learning. It shows how Carrie exercised agency (see Satchwell, Barton and Hamilton, and Gourlay and Oliver, this volume) and shared her views on this newly discovered information with the rest of the class, including the course lecturer. Thus, the roles of teacher and student are not always clearly defined and are constantly renegotiated in this space.

Course participants had different opinions about the relationship between how they wrote in this Facebook group and how they wrote elsewhere on the internet, as two students reflected:

> *Big C:* sometimes it's more formal when i write in facebook group as it is like an academic platform. but it also depends on the nature and formality of that message. if it is not related to academic field, i would rather switch to some chinglish as it looks more friendly and funny.
>
> (online interview)

> *Tony:* I used English only in the group, and I seldom do that elsewhere on facebook. I do think this is an academic group, so I feel uncomfortable about using loose grammar, having typos and using excessive Netspeak features. However, I use emoticons all the time as in other online platforms.
>
> (online interview)

These comments interestingly take us back to the notion of text-making practices. These two students were well aware of the text-making resources available to them for meaning-making in this teacher-initiated space. While acknowledging the academic nature of the group, they also brought in their everyday, private, vernacular online text-making practices to the group interaction (See Satchwell, Barton and Hamilton, this volume). Even though Tony pointed out he was not entirely ready to adopt a non-standard linguistic style in the group, emoticons could be tolerated, which turned out to be Tony's negotiated form of online academic discourse.

As the lecturer, I also found myself constantly negotiating between my university teacher identity and my active Facebook user identity through reappropriating my text-making practices. For example, I once shared a YouTube video which introduces a new book written entirely in PowerPoint style. This is how I described the video in my post:

> Carmen Lee: hmmm writing a novel in PowerPoint format sounds fun! More thoughts for the notion of 'affordances'. hmmmmm..I wonder if that makes writing easier or more challenging.. :-)`

In this post, while attempting to bring in a course-related concept (affordances), I framed my message in a relatively informal, interpersonal discourse style that is typically found in youth online writing, such as the insertion of an emoticon :-), trailing dots (..), and hedges (hmmm) to indicate what I was thinking and I welcomed ideas from the group. This was certainly inspired by my interviewing experience in the IM research, where I actively situated myself in my participants' discourse community. This allowed me to play down my lecturer identity in the course so as to build rapport with my students.

This Facebook group can be understood as a 'third space' for teaching and learning (Lee and Lien 2011). Moje *et al.* (2004: p. 44) defines a third space as a space that 'brings the texts framed by everyday Discourses and knowledges into classrooms in ways that challenge, destabilize, and ultimately, expand the literacy practices that are typically valued in school and in the everyday world'. This is exactly the case with my course group. As shown in the examples above, the group is a space where the relatively controlled academic discourse and interpersonal, hybrid, and informal discourse styles met. While facilitating teaching and learning activities, what was particularly revealing was the ways in which students constantly negotiated and reappropriated their discourse styles and identities according to how they perceived the purposes of the group. The written texts in this group, as shown in the example posts and comments, exhibit a hybridity of languages (Chinese, English), discourse styles (academic, interpersonal, formal, playful), and voices (teacher as student and student as teacher).

Concluding remarks

This chapter has demonstrated how a linguistic perspective in digital literacies research has informed my own university teaching practice. The IM study illustrates the contribution of adopting discourse-centred online ethnography in digital literacies research. It is through paying close attention to students' online language that the study is able to reveal the level of linguistic diversity in students' everyday, non-academic text-making activities. An important text-making practice that relatively little digital literacies research covers is multilingual text-making practices (but see Lam 2009). While Snow's case serves as a local and micro-example of multilingual text-making, it implies that multilingual literacy practices have gradually become a crucial way of participating in the globalized online world (Lam 2009; Barton and Lee 2012). This also has important implication for policies related to medium of instructions in multilingual communities like Hong Kong that have focused largely on using one language at a time in academic settings. The level of dexterity and creativity that students demonstrate in online communication is an important indicator of their preference for a more linguistically diverse learning environment. In their pedagogical design and practice, university teachers ought to consider the underlying creativity and the superdiverse nature of the internet (Blommaert and Rampton 2011).

My understanding of students' text-making from the IM research has influenced my teaching practice to a large extent. First, I have been able to create a third space using a Facebook group where students and lecturer participate by combining languages and discourse styles that are not normally present in the physical classroom context. As a way of bringing together my research and teaching practice, I end this chapter by summarizing what university teachers may consider in developing a digital university. Some of these issues are also addressed in other chapters in the volume:

1. *Developing a responsive online pedagogy*: Inspired by the responsive methodology adopted in my IM research, I have come to realize that online pedagogy also needs to respond to students' everyday practices. One way of doing so is to conduct surveys at the beginning of courses to find out which online platform is most preferred by students; and at the end of the course, the lecturer can also conduct an end-of-course survey to elicit students' experience with their chosen platform. My experience suggests that students show more enthusiasm for a platform that they frequently use in their private lives (e.g. Facebook) than in one that is exclusively designed for academic purposes (e.g. WebCT), see also Williams this volume on Blackboard. However, there remain uncertainties as to whether students are all ready to recontextualize their private practices for classroom learning. A number of studies have warned that it is not always easy to transfer private literacy practices to the academic context (e.g. Kinzie, Whitaker, and Hofer 2005; Satchwell, Barton, and Hamilton, this volume). For one thing, concepts of time and space in the physical classroom context are very different from those in interpersonal digital communication. As noted in the IM research, private IM activities are often nested and multitasking is taken for granted; whereas face-to-face lectures are organized into individual sessions which do not match with the temporal and spatial flexibility of online interaction.
2. *Being reflexive*: Many teachers in contemporary society have had years of experience with technologies themselves. In making decisions about pedagogical uses of everyday technologies, they should also constantly reflect upon their own relationships with new media in and outside the classroom context (see, for example, Graham's (2008) study of how teachers' own

experience with technology impacts on their teaching practices, and Martin and MacKenzie's, and McKenna and Hughes' discussion of teachers' use of digital resources in this volume). My decision to use a Facebook group grew out of reflecting on my years of experience with both educational and informal technologies. My dual identities as a university teacher and an active Facebook user continuously shape the way I participate and use language when interacting with students online.

3. *Becoming a member of students' online discourse community.* As shown in my Facebook case study, I have been able to adopt a discourse style that university students often employ in their private online text-making practices. Even when presenting academic topics in the group, I make use of multiple linguistic resources and modes that are frequently found in private online discourse. Having seen the lecturer adopt their everyday style of online writing, students would also be happy to take on an informal and even playful voice. This constant negotiation of discourse styles certainly helps foster a friendly and pleasant learning environment.

4. *Continuous awareness of students' everyday text-making practices.* Digital literacies is a fast-changing area of research as technologies and their use change rapidly (see Haythornthwaite, this volume). However, one dimension of digital media that has remained quite constant is their *textually mediated* nature. For this reason, literacy researchers have the important task to continue to focus on *texts* and how the changing affordances of technologies possibly shape students' writing online. This cannot be achieved by carrying out occasional studies, but through ongoing and perhaps longitudinal observations of students' digital practices inside and outside the classroom.

Acknowledgements

Part of the findings reported in this paper grew out of a broader project funded by the General Research Fund of the Hong Kong Research Grants Council (Ref: 446309).

Note

1 All names of student participants in this chapter are pseudonyms.

Chapter 12

The digital university

A concept in need of definition

Chris Jones

Introduction

This chapter is about the idea of the digital university. It explores this using three lenses and addresses whether the term 'digital' can be used to identify any particular characteristic set of technologies or to a specify a particular university type. It also examines the claims that are made for the affordances of digital technologies and the implications these may have for education. The term '*digital* university' suggests a binary distinction between universities supported by new information and communication technologies, based on computing, and previous universities founded on analogue technologies up to and including television and telecommunications. Digital university is therefore a term that needs some further development, and elaboration.

The chapter is also more broadly about the relationship between technology and social forms. In educational technology there has been little recent discussion about the role of technology (Oliver 2012). This has not been true in other areas of study and there is a rich tradition in the philosophy of technology (e.g. Feenberg 2002) which has explored the relationship of the design of technologies with social and political choices founded on the hierarchies found in capitalist societies. There has also been the development of studies of science and technology and the idea of the social shaping of technology (e.g. Pinch and Bijker 1987; MacKenzie and Wajcman 1999), which showed how the process of designing and developing technologies embedded social interests, and was shaped by these competing interests. Grint and Woolgar (1997) argued that technologies could be thought of as being written (by designers) and read (by their users). These approaches had in common a concern that technology could not be understood as a force acting on society and viewed in terms of effects. Rather they explored the ways in which the design and development of technology was shaped by social concerns. This chapter argues it is time to draw attention away from how social conditions inform the design of technologies back to the influence technologies can have on society and social forms.

Technology as a term can have 'at least half-a-dozen major meanings' and perhaps just as importantly some of these meanings conflict (Arthur 2009: 5). Arthur provides three definitions of technology:

1. Technology as *a means to fulfil a human purpose*
2. Technology as an *assemblage of practices and components*
3. Technology as the entire collection of devices and engineering practices available to a culture.

(Arthur 2009: 28 emphasis in original)

These three definitions can be applied to digital technologies and to the technologies applied to education and in learning. The first definition points to the use of technology as a tool, something with a relatively clear and precise function. Learning technologists often speak about technology in this way and the term '*learning technology*' builds in a human purpose for the technology deployed. Technology in the sense of an assemblage of practices and components is less common in educational discourse but it is entailed in notions such as Technology Enhanced Learning, Computer Supported Collaborative Learning, and networked learning, all of which entail digital technologies but are intertwined with particular social practices and ethical or political choices. Technology as an assemblage cannot be reduced to a singular purpose and is always a complex system. The final sense of technology points to the wider social and cultural system and structures in which learning technology is embedded. This is the networked society (Castells 1996) or education in the digital age (Selwyn 2011). Selwyn uses digital technology to allude to 'the ongoing digitisation of culture, politics, economics and society that can be associated with such technologies – what can be termed the "digital age" for want of a better label' (Selwyn 2011: 6).

The university

The university is a changing feature of civilized life, dating its origins back to the Middle Ages in Europe (Collini 2012). The university has a particular form, related to mediaeval guild traditions and it retains aspects of the self-governing bodies of teachers and scholars that grew up in early Europe. Universities preserve the right to award credentials, in the granting of degrees, and they also maintain a key liberty, academic freedom, which protects universities from other powerful institutions. Early universities often had their roots in religious schools and were frequently established by kings, but the university remains distinct from earlier institutional forms by its ability to self-govern and its quasi-independence from secular and religious power.

This abstract and to some extent imagined continuity masks periods of rapid and significant change. The modern university emerges from periods of nation building, war and empire and from the late nineteenth century an engagement with industrial development using science and technology. Currently the university is subject to perhaps its most massive expansion and its most significant period of change. The university as an institution is extending rapidly across the globe. Student numbers have increased and there is a recurrent pressure for universities to engage in society and for the outputs of the university to have a measurable impact, ensuring an elusive value for money. The university as an institution in society is a complex mixture of imagined stability and actual rapid change, of relative academic freedom and public accountability. Within those changes, and perhaps central to them, is the rapid growth of digital and networked technologies.

The digital

The idea of encoding in a binary form has been known from at least the mid seventeenth century (Dyson 2012). However the general move to digital technology is remarkably recent, only dating back to the mid twentieth century. Prior to this time digital technologies were largely inferior to analogue technologies and, generally, inaccurate (lacking fidelity) and slow (Dyson 2012). Analogue technologies were dominant as late as the 1950s and into the 1960s. One of the difficulties of dealing with the digital as opposed to other aspects of the new technological environment is that the digital, when used as a general term, remains separable from its particular instantiations and remains difficult to pin down. Although digital university is a poorly defined term, it can be taken to apply to all university functions as they are revised to make use of digital technologies and to accommodate to their impacts. This suggests a dynamic process in which universities are actively engaged in seeking to develop new modes of working that make use of the possibilities that digital technologies make available (for a further discussion see Williams, this volume). At the same time universities are not entirely masters of their own fate and they have to accommodate to changes beyond their control which derive from the deployment of digital technologies elsewhere in society.

University education is arguably one part of a more general change affecting all levels of education and the processes and practices of learning. Säljö (2010) argues that digital technologies may be changing the nature of how learning is understood and what it means to know something. He argues that digital tools challenge institutional traditions of learning by giving rise to pressures on learning as practised within formal institutional contexts. In particular Säljö argues that it is the capacity of digital technologies to store, access, and manipulate information that can transform how learning is done and how learning is understood. Säljö argues that rather than considering computers and digital technologies primarily as instructional aids, they should be considered in relation to social memory, defined as 'the pool of insights and experiences that people are expected to know about and to make use of' (Säljö 2010: 56). Säljö identifies three significant pressures on formal education in this context:

1. the role of the technology as a tool for storing information and building up a social memory;
2. the consequences of the recent developments in our abilities to have access to social memory; and

3.   the increasing capacity of technologies to perform analytical, cognitive-like operations that were previously made by people.

(Säljö 2010: 56)

Säljö's second point was that technology does not facilitate or improve learning in any linear sense and digital technology cannot be 'introduced to boost learning and performance levels in the system as it exists' (Säljö 2010: 56). He argues that technology changes the interpretation of the nature of learning and that technology also changes expectations about what it means to know something. The introduction of digital technologies changes what we mean by learning, from reproduction of what is already known, towards being able to transform what is already known into something new, interesting, and potentially able to have impact in the world. An interesting feature of Säljö's account is the way it is framed in terms of choice and possibilities. Digital technologies are often proclaimed as revolutionary but they are then counterbalanced by the institutional requirements for the organization of learning and teaching. The approach to choice outlined by Säljö contrasts with the technological determinism applied to university reform elsewhere (see Tapscott and Williams 2010; Prensky 2010).

The approach that Säljö takes explicitly draws on the notion of affordance and he provides an account of learning that rests on the notion of technology as a tool, a means to fulfil a human purpose, the first of Arthur's definitions of technology (Säljö 1999). Säljö draws on sociocultural theory and emphasizes the cultural and historical sides of knowledge. In the next section of the chapter, the concept of affordance is developed as a way of understanding the general influences technologies can have in education.

Affordances

The idea of affordance arose out of the work of Gibson (1977) and his understanding of visual perception. He argued that the properties of technology, which are not in and of themselves determinant of the uses made of them, can present definite features which are available as affordances in use, and they can make certain kinds of practice more available and likely to be enacted than others. For example, 'replicability: Content made out of bits can be duplicated' is a feature of digital texts identified by boyd (2010: 46), which makes it possible to replicate and share at limited or no cost. This feature of the technology is related to the ease of duplication and sharing online and the reaction to that possibility by content producers using proprietary software and Digital Rights Management such as Apple (iTunes) and Amazon (AZW).

The idea of affordance was further developed, and significantly amended by Norman in relation to design (1988). Perhaps the most fundamental revision was whether a distinction should be drawn between 'real affordances' and 'perceived affordances' (Norman 1999) or between affordances and perceptions (Gaver 1991; McGrenere and Ho 2000). Gibson's view was strongly relational and differed in significant ways from the later application of affordance by Norman (1999). Hutchby has argued that affordances frame while not determining the possibilities for action in relation to an object. This approach does not return to the discourse of technological effects but it develops a perspective on the constraining as well as enabling materiality of technologies. Technologies possess different affordances, and these affordances constrain the ways that they can possibly be 'written' or 'read' (Hutchby 2001: 447).

Any technology has a limit built into its material form and while there is interpretive flexibility (Pinch and Bijker 1987), there are also material limits to what can be done with any specific instantiation of a technology. Technologies as material real-world artefacts constrain the ways in which they can be written (by designers) or read (by users). A significant problem remains in the concern that by moving from the (direct) perception of animals in their environment to human activity, with its location in a culture, the original conception of affordance misses out central human characteristics. Human activity is reflexive and social and any understanding of perceptions involves second order activity, not simply perceiving an affordance but attributing meaning to it (Jones and Dirckinck-Holmfeld 2009; Kaptelinin and Hedestig 2009). The design of technology can only have a direct effect on those features that are available to become affordances (including latent features not immediately obvious to the user) and an indirect effect on what sense and meaning users of the technology take from those features. Affordance as a relational feature of technologies remains a contentious area and this applies to education in particular, as Derry has noted: 'The leap from ideas originating in perceptual psychology linking perception and action in a non-cognitive relation of organism and environment to an educational context dependent on interactions between humans, is at the very least questionable' (Derry 2007: 504).

Nevertheless this chapter takes the view that affordance remains a useful concept to capture general and non-determinate features of a broad technological form such as the digital. An account of a broad area of technology, set out in terms of affordance, is an attempt to provide some relative and provisional stability to the term digital and not an attempt to provide a singular, fixed or determinant definition setting out the essence of digital technology. Combined with Arthur's views about the levels at which technology can be understood, the idea of affordance can provide a basis for an appreciation of the ways in which the digital can affect the university and consequent political and policy choices.

The digital university

At a time of financial crisis and significant restraints on the allocation of public funds, the university finds itself in a position of great tension. Governments are still driven by notions of a knowledge economy and the need for a large educated workforce, but they are reluctant to pay for the necessary expansion. Politics remains focused on the nation state at a time when academic life is becoming increasingly global and in some senses beyond the reach of national governments. All this is happening at the same time that digital technologies continue to develop and disrupt the normal workings of the university. The next section explores the university in relation to the digital using three lenses. The first lens is that of the changing profile of the student and the way it has fed into technological determinist accounts. The second lens is the idea of digital literacy (-ies). The focus is not on different ways of thinking about literacy but on the topic of digital literacy (-ies). In this it differs from many of the chapters in this book which seek to set out a particular view of literacies of the digital. In particular it centres on the way a focus on literacy can lead to a deficit model of both staff and students and a misreading of their capacity for change. The third lens is the idea of digital scholarship and notions of a new invisible college. Digital scholarship illustrates the nature of choice occurring at different levels in the university and how policy and politics can have an influence on the shaping of the digital university.

Digital natives

Various authors such as Tapscott (1998, 2009), Howe and Strauss (2000), Prensky (2001, 2010), Oblinger and Oblinger (2005), Palfrey and Gasser (2008) have argued that because today's generation of young people have been immersed in a world infused with networked and digital technologies, they behave differently to previous generations. It is claimed that they think differently, they learn differently, they exhibit different social characteristics and have different expectations about life and learning.

Empirical work in a variety of contexts has found these claims to be largely unfounded. There is no generational break from students in other age groups and young students entering university are a more complex group than the digital native literature would lead readers to expect (Czerniewicz *et al.* 2009; Hargittai 2010; Jones *et al.* 2010; Kennedy *et al.* 2008). There are significant differences within the digital native age group and little evidence that students from these age groups have consistent or urgent demands about the ways in which they are taught (Jones *et al.* 2010). Furthermore empirical studies showed that students' high levels of use and skill did not necessarily translate into preferences for increased use of technology in the classroom (Schulmeister 2010) and a large number of students still hold conventional attitudes towards teaching (Margaryan *et al.* 2011). Indeed the picture of digital native students, fluent with digital technologies and easily able to adapt has been disrupted by studies showing that many young students have a superficial ease with new technologies but find it hard to adapt to using digital technologies in education. For a recent literature review see Jones and Shao (2011), and for proponents of the digital native thesis and their critics debating the issues in a single edited volume see Thomas (2011).

For the purposes of this chapter, the important points are about the way technology is viewed as causative in accounts of generational change and the way the account has been broadly accepted in political and policy discourse. The digital native thesis is at the centre of debates about the future of the university reinforced with a strongly determinist rhetoric. Prensky argues that because of the technological environment in the twenty-first century 'It is inevitable . . . that change would finally come to our young people's education as well, and it has.' (Prensky 2010: 1). Prensky is not alone and Tapscott (2009) argues that education is a central location for the broad institutional changes caused by a new generation. Tapscott and Williams (2010) provide the following determinist account of the necessity for radical change:

> Change is required in two vast and interwoven domains that permeate the deep structures and operating model of the university: (1) the value created for the main customers of the university (the students); and (2) the model of production for how that value is created. First we need to toss out the old industrial model of pedagogy (how learning is accomplished) and replace it with a new model called collaborative learning. Second we need an entirely new modus operandi for how the subject matter, course materials, texts, written and spoken word, and other media (the content of higher education) are created.
>
> (Tapscott and Williams 2010: 10)

All these authors encourage the idea that education has to change because there has been a generational shift caused by a process of technological change. In this determinist view, technological change is seen as arising independently and then having an impact on other dependent domains in society. This argument suggests that the ubiquitous nature of digital technologies has affected the outlook of an entire generation. A more useful way of interpreting the relationship between digital technologies and the young is to note that these technologies make available specific features that allow certain types of social engagement. The first, determinist argument needs to be abandoned in the face of the empirical evidence. The second argument has the potential to provide stable advice on which policy can be based.

Digital literacies

The term 'digital literacy' is more fully developed, with a critical commentary in relation to some of the views presented in this chapter, elsewhere in this volume (see Gourlay and Oliver, Lea, Lee, Satchwell *et al.*). Digital literacy, especially as used in policy discourse, points to the central requirement in a digital society of being able to function by incorporating a range of practices and devices containing digital technologies (see for example Paynton 2012). However, digital literacy is often reduced to notions of individual skill and competence and in this sense involves the training of staff and students in the ways to use newer kinds of digital tools and communication systems (see for example Hargittai 2005). When viewed positively the term digital literacy points towards the historic centrality of the written word and to the new practices emerging around a variety of media related to digital technologies in education. If viewed negatively, the use of the term digital literacy can imply training in a narrow set of skills and competences.

For academics working in the field of New Literacy Studies (NLS), literacy is thought of in terms of a set of changing communication and academic practices (see Lea, this volume). Literacy practices are viewed as the constructions of specified social groups and knowledge is viewed as a social accomplishment rather than being attributed to individual cognition. The growth of NLS corresponded with a broader interest in the work of the Soviet sociocultural tradition (Vygotsky 1978) and social and situated views of learning (Brown *et al.* 1989). In education, a growing interest in cultural historical activity theory (Engeström 2001) and Communities of Practice (Lave and Wenger 1991; Wenger 1998) ran in parallel with the introduction of digital technologies and the development of NLS (see Mills 2010 and Goodfellow 2011 for extensive references).

Mills comments that NLS has recently been applied to new practices related to digital technologies:

> The most recent, significant shift in this field has been what could be called the 'digital turn'—that is, the increased attention to new literacy practices in digital environments across a variety of social contexts, such as workplaces and educational, economic, and recreational sites.
>
> (Mills 2010: 246–7)

NLS takes the discussion about literacy away from skill deficit and moves it to a focus on social practices and the contextual and specific (see Gourlay and Oliver, Lea, and Lee this volume). Säljö (2010), however, drawing on the same sociocultural frame of reference makes more general and broadly based claims. Säljö argues that meaning-making practices are contingent on how the social memory is organized. He makes an historical case linked to the rise of Protestantism and the growth of schooling in the nineteenth century and a technical-scientific literacy associated with the period after the Second World War (Säljö 2010). He then contrasts these with the practices that develop in the new media setting provided by digital technologies and the availability of new kinds of texts that organize information in different ways.

Säljö argues digital technologies provide access to information from a wide range of sources and to make meaning in this new setting requires an ability to select and to direct our attention in ways that imply disregarding much of what is available to us. The 'attention economy' means that an ability to select based on a very limited reading is an essential practical element of our day-to-day lives (Goldhaber 1997). Drawing on Kress (2003) he goes on to suggest that a move is taking place from 'reading as interpretation' to 'reading as design'. In reading as interpretation, the meaning is there in every word and the task is to be able to read the text and to interpret and transform what is clearly present. In multimodal texts, the emphasis shifts from telling to showing and the task is to impose order and select for relevance, a practice of 'reading as design'. The shift to multimodal forms places the emphasis on the practices of decoding, and in this view reading becomes an act of participation in which the reader has more flexibility to produce a version for their own purposes (see Lea, this volume). Digital literacy (-ies) illustrate the possibilities for choice and change related to features of digital technology. Multimodal texts do not necessitate reading as design, but they open up the possibility of change which depends for its realization on the capacity for change amongst students and academic staff. The nature of digital texts (multimodality) is an instance of the features of a technology being available to become an affordance, but only when taken up in terms of social practice (e.g. reading as design).

Digital scholarship

Weller has written about the way the affordance, identified earlier, of replicability enables new forms of scholarly practice (2011). Borgman (2007) also discusses scholarship in a digital age in the context of large distributed teams who make use of the affordances of new technologies: 'The internet lies at the core of an advanced scholarly information infrastructure to facilitate distributed, data and information-intensive collaborative research.' (Borgman 2007: xvii) (for a discussion of Borgman and Weller see Goodfellow, this volume). Borgman's view is in terms of large-scale infrastructure rather than individual or 'lone ranger' adoption of specific digital tools. Beyond these approaches to scholarship Wagner (2008) has written about the new invisible college, drawing on the history of the emergence of scientific disciplines and peer review procedures in the seventeenth century to suggest that digital technologies may have a similar profound effect on academic practices.

Weller advocates the revision of reward schemes and regimes of accountability in education to recognize and promote the new ways of working (Weller 2011). He argues that recognition of digital scholars indicates the value of these new ways of working to other academics and encourages institutional innovation. Weller's approach illustrates two features of the digital scholarship debate. Digital technologies open up new possibilities and they constrain older practices. However digital scholarship remains subject to choices that have to be made at a variety of levels: personal, institutional, and by the nation state or internationally. The reluctance of academics to engage fully with the open practices that digital technologies enable is seen by Weller as a barrier and social processes are enrolled to support his preferred changes in academic ways of working.

Weller is advocating that universities promote certain practices above others but such practices can be seen as a political and policy choice and possibly even as undue pressure to adopt one academic practice over and above others. Opponents may ask if there is a place in digital scholarship for an academic to cut away from current trends, to pursue paths currently out of fashion and to refuse to engage closely with the public. Some of these traits have served academic life well and are central to the idea of academic freedom. Public pressure can lead to a narrowing of intellectual debate, the downplaying of academic and scientific criteria for judgement, and the introduction of religious or political standards into academic work. The key point for the argument presented here is that social practices are subject to choices made at various levels including the university, the state, and the market.

Digital scholarship is not an automatic outcome of the introduction of digital technologies even though they allow definite social practices, such as open scholarship, to emerge. Choice has to be exercised by the academic, by academics collectively through their self-organization in conferences and associations, by universities and by government and international agencies. All of this in the context of a global market for digital technology in which education is only a fractional part.

The digital university does not currently describe any real or existing university. The university retains its imagined continuity with the past, even as new digital technologies are deployed, both in universities and in society more generally. The nature of the student intake is changing, in ways related to new technology, even if not in the dramatic and determinist way that the digital native thesis would suggest. Fundamental aspects of university practices are being affected by the deployment of digital technology; including what it means to learn, the practices of academic reading, and the way scholarship is conducted. To make sensible policy decisions in relation to these changes requires a stable conception of digital technologies.

Conclusions

This chapter provided three illustrations of how digital technologies have had a direct influence on issues and policies in higher education. The digital native debate illustrated the way a technologically determinist line of reasoning about digital technologies has had a powerful and persistent influence on policy debates despite repeated academic criticism based on empirical and theoretical work. The issue of digital literacy (ies) illustrated the role of social practice in the ways that digital technologies are adopted and adapted in academic life and the possibilities for change enabling academic and educational incorporation of the available digital technologies. The chapter also drew attention to the debates that have arisen around notions of digital scholarship and the academy. This third example illustrated the way political and policy choices are central to the way digital scholarship is viewed and for the policy measures that are advocated to enable its development.

The conclusion that I draw from these examples is that technologically determinist accounts are attractive to policy-makers because they offer simple solutions. If students are a relatively homogenous grouping with similar relationships to digital technology then policy and planning appear simplified. The problem with such accounts is that they are unsupported by the evidence and theoretically weak. They also lead to poor decision-making. Digital literacies can have a significant contribution to make in the understanding of literacies as context-dependent social practices, and the idea of reading of multimodal texts as design and the active transformation of existing resources for a purpose. Finally, the example of digital scholarship illustrates the area of policy and political choice. Digital technologies do not require digital scholarship, though they enable it, and they can constrain traditional academic practices. Digital scholarship opens up a range of policy choices that need to be carefully examined. The policy lessons drawn from the three examples point to the need to avoid simple determinist solutions, to see digital technologies as deeply imbricated with social practices and to clearly explicate the range of available choices rather than close off the discussion of alternatives.

This chapter takes the view that although simplistic accounts of digital technology are dangerous, broad, relatively stable accounts of digital technology are necessary. Although social practices are context-dependent they are also patterned and recognizable across time and space. I argue that a careful use of the idea of affordance can help in crafting provisional and relatively stable descriptions of the general character of digital technology understood in Arthur's third sense of technology as the entire collection of devices and engineering practices available to a culture. It can also be useful when thinking about digital technologies in the two other senses Arthur outlines. Affordances understood as relational but real aspects of technology can help in outlining those aspects of digital technology that enable and incline users to particular kinds of social practice and to identify those aspects that act to constrain either existing practices or the possibility of certain social actions in the future.

Chapter 13

Control and the classroom in the digital university

The effect of course management systems on pedagogy

Bronwyn T. Williams

The seduction of order and control

My brother-in-law and his wife work at Disney World. They are a devoted uncle and aunt to my sons, so it happened when my sons were young that we ended up making the trip to Florida. Inside Disney World, things are clean, orderly, safe, predictable, enclosed, and everything you need during a given day, from food to bathrooms to medical care, is available at a moment's notice. Kids like the familiarity of the rides and the characters and it's easy to begin to feel the seductive ideological pull of the 'Disney moment.' Of course, as many have noted, it only takes a short step back to realize Disney World is also a place of control, simulation, reactionary conservatism, corporate branding, and surveillance. While fine for a family visit, this was not the world I wished for my sons.

The allure of course management software is remarkably similar to that of Disney World. Purchased at the central university level and often mandated for use by teachers and students, such software is uniform, orderly, safe, predictable, enclosed, nostalgic, and supposed to contain everything you need to work in or out of the digital classroom. Yet, like Disney World, the same disturbing elements of control, simulation, conservatism, branding, and surveillance are also integral to the software. Course management software has become a pervasive part of the digital university. When we think about digital media and literacy practices and teaching, we must think about how the course management software that faculty and students are not only provided, but often required to use, shapes our pedagogy. Course management systems organize life in and out of the classroom for many students and teachers, and illustrate how the digital university as an institution has evolved. The software appeals to university central administrators because it is a centralized system that offers efficiencies of scale. The university only buys one system, can organize its technical support around that system, and once teachers and students are familiar with the system there is no need to relearn software for every course. If the vision of many educators for the digital university is one where new technologies create possibilities for participation, flexibility, networking, and multimodality that allow students more agency and creativity in their education, the vision of course management software companies is one of efficiency, enclosure, and monitoring of students and faculty.

In this article, I discuss how the adoption and promotion of course manage-ment software is driven by material and ideological imperatives of efficiency, con-trol, and surveillance that are increasingly central to how the institution of the university works in contemporary culture. The decision to purchase the software illustrates the distinct differences in how the digital university is perceived by administrators and by many teachers and researchers working with digital media and technologies. As Blackboard is the largest corporation designing and selling such systems with an international reach, I will use it as my central example, but the arguments also apply to other systems. In using Blackboard, we are complicit in reproducing institutional and cultural ideologies that are as hierarchical, rigid, and prescriptive as the software. In this way dominant ideological conceptions of knowledge and literacy – tied to notions of efficiency – find their way into class-rooms even as we may imagine a pedagogy that encourages students to resist such conceptions. It is important that we think critically and act more explicitly to resist the implementation and uses of these forms of digital media. I conclude by dis-cussing how we must teach students to approach these technologies from a more critical perspective, both in understanding the epistemological and ideological forces that shape such systems, and in engaging with alternatives that allow them to more fully explore the uses of digital media toward collaboration, multimodal-ity, and the open distribution of and access to information and texts.

Integration and efficiency

In the early days of digital media, the vision of the digital university was of new technologies creating more democratic classrooms and increasing student agency and creativity. Trent Batson, in 1988, offered an argument typical of the time, that 'networks create . . . entirely new pedagogical dynamics. One of the most important is the creation of a written social context, an online discourse com-munity, which presents totally new opportunities for effective instruction' (32). Today that promise continues in many ways as teachers and scholars, including contributors to this volume, find innovative uses for digital media. Students can collaborate with peers through social networking sites, create multimodal texts, publish and distribute their work, and draw upon the breadth of the online world for information and inspiration. What's more, many sites and software are avail-able for free – from blogs to wikis to discussion boards to content posting sites. It might seem appealing to administrators to encourage instructors and students to use these resources and lessen the load on straining university budgets.

At first glance, Blackboard would seem an important partner for the digital university. On its website you find this statement:

Around the globe, Blackboard solutions are helping to improve every aspect of the education experience. Clients are using our technology to reach more students in immediate, personalized new ways. They are helping their educators become more effective. Keeping everyone informed, involved, collaborating together, and meeting the high expectations of today's learners. And they're doing it in a cost-effective way that helps to sustain services and programs, even as outcomes are improved over time—finally, the new generation of education is here.

(Blackboard 2012)

This is followed with a statement about how Blackboard is a tool for 'Improving educator efficiency, promoting social and mobile learning, and offering integrated digital content. It's all right here with Blackboard Teaching and Learning solutions' (Blackboard 2012). While there are words and phrases in these statements such as 'collaborating,' 'involved,' 'personalized,' and 'social and mobile learning' that would be welcome to many educators, there are also other words and phrases that indicate a rather different set of priorities for Blackboard, such as 'cost-effective,' 'educator efficiency,' and the somewhat ominous connotations of 'keeping everyone informed.' It is these latter qualities, of cost-effectiveness, efficiency, centralization, and control that appeal to administrators. As Goodfellow and Lea (2007) point out, the institution of the university is interested in maintaining a particular structure of teaching and learning that is reflected in the construction and deployment of systems such as Blackboard. The rhetoric in an article written for administrators is not unlike that found on Blackboard's own site.

(Web-based education) is becoming more demand-driven and universities are starting to pursue more customer-oriented management strategies. Universities are streamlining operations, consolidating offerings, and creating strategic partnerships. Effectiveness and efficiency are becoming keys to survival. Consistency, reliability and seamless access are becoming important as universities try to incorporate continuous improvement principles to Web education to achieve these goals.

(Aggarwal, Adlakha, and Mersha 2006: 3)

Such rhetoric offers insights into what a university expects when it purchases Blackboard. I use the term 'university' in this context to represent the institutional systems and ideologies that are reproduced and enacted by upper-level administrators. The ideological positions inhabited by administrators reflect an increasing emphasis on centralized control of information and technology as well as an adaptation to the cultural shift toward treating education as commodity and students as consumers. In a cultural moment in many countries in which public funding for higher education is suffering deep cuts, forcing universities to rely increasingly on student fees and corporate funding for financial support, it's little surprise to see the evolution of a corporate mindset among university administrators where the financial bottom line is their primary concern (Harkin 2005). For many administrators, then, the digital university is a place where the value of technology is measured in revenue and efficiency, not pedagogy.

The move toward a corporate university means that systems such as Blackboard offer several appeals. First, in terms of budgetary incentives, Blackboard offers universities economies of scale. Though it may cost more to purchase Blackboard initially, universities reason that having one standardized system throughout the institution will, in the long run, be economically efficient. Blackboard's website reminds visitors time and again, through promotional slogans and customer testimonials, how having a standardized system will result in 'cost savings.' Just as assembly lines improve efficiency by standardizing parts and specialized jobs, Blackboard allows the university to provide a standardized product for instructors and students. Technical support from university information technology staff is simplified as only one system needs to be learned, and some technical support is outsourced back to the company. Once such a system is purchased, the investment of time and resources make it difficult – and expensive – to switch to another system. Standardization also means that Blackboard is bought as a package, often with little input from the faculty or students who will use the system.

There are also technological reasons that Blackboard appeals to university administrators. As Blackboard incorporates more applications into its software it allows more and more functions of the university to run through one site. Blackboard is much more than simply software for courses. It offers software for advising, student services, grades, financial aid, and other university departments. To quote the website, 'Discover how Blackboard can help you transform the educational experience within every step of the student lifecycle. Get the technology and expertise you need to meet your institution's goals' (Blackboard 2012). Again, this kind of integration is sold to administrators as simplifying the work of the university by standardizing and collecting all the functions in one place. As another quote puts it, 'From admissions to financial aid to campus life, stay ahead of evolving student demands with Blackboard. It's more than just a learning management system. It's a whole campus of solutions' (Blackboard 2012). Not only are economies of scale at work again with this push toward integration, but Blackboard promotes the efficiencies of time and training of having so many functions of the university integrated into one system. Students can access their advisors or financial aid when they log on to the same place where they see course assignments. It is the university technological equivalent of one-stop shopping. The impulse toward integration of systems and applications is not unique to course management systems, but reflects similar trends seen by sites such as Google and Facebook that try to be one-stop portals to online activities.

Finally, Blackboard appeals to the institutional functions of the university. The recent demand for quantifiable, standardized assessments by education policymakers has made such assessments key goals of schools (Newkirk 2009). The ability to amass and control information, such as grades and student papers, in a culture in which universities are increasingly called on by outside government and accreditation bodies to account for their work is deeply appealing to university administrators. With Blackboard, student papers turned in to fulfill course assignments can be kept and accessed for large-scale assessments. Faculty syllabi posted for students can be made available to accrediting agencies for review (as is the policy at my university). These same functions also make it easier for the central university to observe and track the activities of students and faculty, for the university's internal purposes. Blackboard offers a site for these institutional purposes that is private and controlled, and protects the university from potential lawsuits about infringement of privacy. All of these functions can be combined in Blackboard, with an image or logo of the university happily perched atop each webpage.

The reasons Blackboard appeals to universities are not dissimilar to the reasons that shape university decisions about bookstores, physical facilities, or food and janitorial services. In all of these instances, as with large corporations, the questions of economies of scale, integration of information, efficiencies of training, and the need to fulfill institutional mandates are the primary concerns of universities in deciding to adopt software such as Blackboard. The fact that universities increasingly adopt the strategies and discourse of large corporations, including Blackboard, is not news, but a reminder that the goals of central university administrations are to organize and balance the books of the institution, and are not necessarily about teaching, research, or the creation of knowledge.

Rhetorics of ease

As with corporations such as Walmart or Disney, universities rarely publicize concerns of economies of scale and standardization. Instead, the public rationale universities give for purchasing course management systems is much more likely to draw on rhetorics of convenience and ease. In fact the words 'ease' and 'easy' are sprinkled throughout the Blackboard site. 'You'll have the right toolkit—one that is proven and constantly evolves to meet your needs. It will be flexible and easy to use—from managing content, engaging learners to assessing outcomes. And we'll help you manage change and increase adoption' (Blackboard 2012). My university, like many others, picks up this rhetoric of ease in its messages to faculty and students. An announcement for a Blackboard training workshop at my university says, 'Take full advantage of the new and improved features in Blackboard 9.1 by attending this workshop! Enjoy easier and more accessible management of your courses, improvements to tools you already use, and several new options for adding content to your courses' (Delphi Center 2012). Of course rhetorics of ease and progress have been a common part of digital technology discourse over the years, including in education. From the early days of personal computers, the technologies have been marketed as saving time and making difficult tasks easier to accomplish in and out of the classroom. Such arguments about efficiency are often persuasive to faculty and students. Not only is the Blackboard website filled with testimonials from instructors and students attesting to the ease and convenience of the system, scholars have published work arguing for the use of Blackboard because of its uses in motivating students (Larkin and Belson 2005), its ability to integrate classroom and library resources (Lawrence 2006), its uses in uploading student papers for response (Landry *et al.* 2006), or its ability to replace lectures with podcasts (O'Bannon *et al.* 2011).

Blackboard also offers the allure of support for those not comfortable with or too busy to learn digital technologies. As Kristine Blair notes: 'Inevitably, with little training in the use of digital tools, teachers have equally little choice but to opt for what is available, free, easy to use, and technically supported, in other words, the course management system' (Blair 2007: 3). The all-in-one interface of Blackboard is attractive to non-experts in the same way that a large store that carries many different kinds of items will probably satisfy a consumer not looking for a distinctive or customized product. If you go shopping at Walmart or ASDA, you may not find the best quality item, but you might find some item that will serve without a large investment of time and money. Consumers trade higher quality and individuality for lower prices and efficiency.

None of these reasons – integration of services, cost savings, integration of technologies – have pedagogical concerns at their core, even as Blackboard maintains that purchasing it will lead to better teaching and learning. Yet there is no doubt that when Blackboard becomes the default digital course system, the easy system, the mandated system, it shapes pedagogical practices. That's where the readings are posted, that's where you can set up a discussion board, that's how you must submit your grades. It can be easier to alter pedagogies to conform to these mandates and systems, than always be working against them. Work lives are busy enough without having to struggle against this centralized conception of the digital university. The response of faculty may be to complain, but then shrug, and acquiesce to the demands of the institution.

Acceptance and adaptation on the part of teachers, however, has consequences for pedagogy and for the conceptions of digital media literacy practices. For Blackboard and its cousins are, in a number of ways, antithetical to what we might consider the best pedagogical practices in the digital university. Evolving technologies are increasing our capacity for collaboration, participation, multimodality, and distribution in ways that can enhance creative thinking by students and instructors. Innovative instructors have found that digital technologies can, for example, disrupt the idea of the traditional classroom and connect students with varied audiences (Bayne and Ross, this volume), or find and reuse a broad variety of material for learning (Martin and MacKenzie, this volume). Such approaches emphasize learning in which students have an increased latitude and power to build and shape their knowledge and literacy practices in participation with an instructor. When used well, and reflectively, digital media offer the possibility of more agency for students in how they engage with learning and texts. Yet course management systems are usually imposed on teachers and students from the top down, and like Disney World, are essentially conservative environments that offer the illusion of participation while limiting contact to the outside world and maintaining hierarchical control and surveillance at several levels.

Commodification, teacher control, and surveillance

I want to focus briefly on three concerns of course management systems in terms of pedagogy in the digital university: the emphasis on commodification of knowledge and efficiency, the emphasis on conservative conceptions of the classroom, and the emphasis on control and surveillance.

Although the traditional humanistic ideal of the university may be to facilitate the creation and transmission of ideas, as powerful an ideology in the modern corporate university is the regulation of discourse and epistemology. When the university limits admissions, charges for courses, and certifies graduates, it makes knowledge a commodity for which students, and others in the culture, are willing to pay. Blackboard is part of that system of limiting access to and commodifying education. By creating an enclosed space that is only available to those paying course fees, Blackboard emphasizes exclusivity. Like Disney World, you have to pay to get in, and be assured that others will be kept out. In fact one of the graphics on the Blackboard site that shows how the system can integrate all elements of university work portrays the university campus as a walled-in enclave. Blackboard and some administrators argue that these virtual walls are there for the protection of students, but like all walls they also serve to enclose and limit. One limit is the distribution of knowledge outside of the university. Course syllabi, articles, student writing, or any other content placed on Blackboard will not circulate outside the university. Blackboard's enclosed system contributes to the '(re)inscriptions of normalized identities and ways of knowing privileged and maintained through dominant cultural modes of production and reception' (Payne 2005: 485). In the efforts of companies such as Blackboard, and the university administrations with whom they work, we see an attempt to maintain traditional conceptions of the ownership and distribution of knowledge. Such efforts run counter, however, to the possibilities articulated by digital media scholars advocating for open scholarship (Goodfellow, Martin and MacKenzie, this volume). The tensions created by these different perspectives of scholarship and publication promise only to increase in coming years.

What's more, information posted for a particular class on Blackboard is usually limited to the temporal confines of that class. Once a class is over, students often lose access to that information, as do instructors unless they archive the material. And, as Davis and Hardy (2003) point out, discussion forums around specific assignments or readers are set up in such a way that they often encourage closure once the activity is passed. Blackboard also limits students' connections with the rest of the online world. While Blackboard emphasizes that it is an online service, in fact, once logged on a student can't connect to the rest of the Web unless an instructor has provided specific, and limited, links. Again, rather than actually providing the experience of engaging with the resources of the online world, Blackboard provides a simulation of that experience.

A second concern in the uses of Blackboard in the digital university is its conservative conception of pedagogy and teacher–student relationships. Although the rhetoric on its website argues that using Blackboard will lead to innovations in teaching, like its name, Blackboard actually encourages pedagogical practices in ways that are traditional and hierarchical. First, Blackboard is teacher-centered software. As others (Davis and Hardy 2003; Payne 2005; Blair 2007; Goodfellow and Lea 2007) have pointed out, activity on Blackboard is heavily controlled and regulated by the instructor. Most actions, such as posting assignments, documents, links, starting discussions, or enabling applications such as blogs or wikis, take place only through the action of the instructor. Even the few activities that students can initiate often must be approved by the instructor. This level of control continues the tradition of classroom teaching that has characterized university education for hundreds of years, but does not embrace the possibilities for more democratic, student-centered participation that are possible with digital media Not only that, but Blackboard employs terminology and interfaces that mimic the conventions of the traditional classroom, such as syllabi, readings, assignments, grades, and so on. While such adaptations of the face-to-face classroom to the online space may seem straightforward and obvious, such choices and representations of interfaces are never value-neutral (Selfe and Selfe 1994; Goodfellow and Lea 2007). Adopting different representations and metaphors of interfaces could alter how learning and teacher–student relationships are enacted and perceived. In adopting the language and organization of the classroom of the past, Blackboard imports the ideologies of authority and control of those classrooms as well. It uses technology to create nostalgic, unthreatening simulations of the past in the present. When I teach current or future teachers in workshops or courses, it is clear that for many instructors maintaining the level of teacher-centered control that Blackboard affords is one of its appeals. As Tyack and Cuban (1995) point out, teachers tend to adopt most readily the new technologies that work in concert with their existing pedagogical practices. Still, we must recognize that the vision of the digital university constructed by Blackboard is a profoundly conservative vision in which traditional conceptions of pedagogy and teacher authority are being transferred onto software.

Blackboard also perpetuates a conservative view of learning and pedagogy in its emphasis on print and its inability to be modified by individual users. Although there are icons on Blackboard and it is possible to upload images and video, there is no mistaking that print is its privileged medium. Not only are the menus and interfaces based in print, but the work students are asked to do, from posting on discussion forums to turning in course materials, are designed to take place in print. Again, the metaphor of Blackboard is instructive here in that, like the blackboard in a classroom, communication happens through print at the permission of the instructor. Although print remains central to teaching and research in a university, Blackboard is particularly ill-suited for the kind of academic multimodal work that is growing in fields from education to engineering. Also, Blackboard's applications for uploading video or podcasts are particularly clumsy and difficult to use. One of the great advances of digital media is the ability given individuals to compose not just in words but also video, images, and sound, and Blackboard operates as if such advances are still in the future. What's more, a student cannot modify Blackboard in any significant way, as she or he might with other open-source software, nor can an instructor, aside from turning on or off already existing applications. As Payne notes, 'The tendencies toward homogeneity built into Blackboard's space are an unmistakable result of its being designed for mass production and consumption in a market economy' (Payne 2005: 495). Mass production requires standardization and Blackboard certainly follows that model. A student could open a Blackboard system on any campus around the world and see much the same system – and be unable to do anything about it. The argument in favor of such standardization is that, like many mass-produced items, it will be familiar, unchanging, and easy to use, combining ease and convenience. Yet, as with fast-food restaurants and big-box stores, such standardized convenience means less choice and less agency. Blackboard claims to have everything you need, all in one place, without mentioning that there will be less choice. Blackboard does add new applications that mimic new digital technologies – such as adding a wiki or podcast function. Yet, like a fast-food restaurant trying to diversify its menu items, the functioning of the new applications is often distinctly inferior to other sites available, and can discourage instructor and student use.

The final concern about Blackboard's role in the digital university is its construction as an instrument of control and surveillance. Blackboard offers instructors and others in the university a system for gathering a variety of information about students, from compiling grades and assessment information to tracking whether students have opened course documents or discussion threads. Blackboard celebrates these tracking features, and some scholars have agreed that they can be helpful for projects such as identifying at-risk students (Macfadyen and Dawson 2010). Yet a less benign analysis is that Blackboard's capacity to gather and distribute information about students increases the ability of those in power in the university to watch and track student behavior. The capacity of digital technologies to collect and track user behavior is not news and has led to public debates about these practices and expectations of privacy on sites such as Facebook and Google. Blackboard further complicates these questions by creating an enclosed system in which the instructor and other administrators are in control of what information is gathered and which behaviors are observed. As Davis and Hardy (2003) point out, this kind of surveillance – or possibility of surveillance – creates parallels to Foucault's metaphor of the Panopticon. For Foucault, the power of the Panopticon is that surveillance is always possible and never certain, consequently the prisoner begins to internalize the discipline and behaviors sought by the institution. The key is that the 'surveillance is permanent in its effects, even if it is discontinuous in its action; that the perfection of power should tend to render its actual exercise unnecessary' (Foucault 1977: 201). In terms of employing Blackboard to track student activity, such as whether students have opened assigned course readings, Davis and Hardy see this parallel:

The resulting dissymmetry between seen and seer extends educational discipline beyond its traditional reach. In most classrooms, we accept that only
during class time or office hours can we observe students at work; elsewhere,
their time becomes undifferentiated and, to some extent, unreadable. When
our students work, how often they turn to our course, whether they open
their texts—these are questions that now open themselves to our inquiry and
potentially to our abuse.

(Davis and Hardy 2003)

Of course schools have always gathered information and watched students, but
digital media increase the reach of this kind of observation. Recent additions
to Blackboard, such as plagiarism detection software, have only intensified this
kind of surveillance, as well as the inevitable student resistance and resentment to
the ongoing observation (McKenna and Hughes, this volume; Williams 2007).
The level of surveillance is not always obvious to students, as it is possible with
Blackboard to hide such actions from students. When I tell students about all the
different ways I can track their actions on Blackboard they are generally surprised
at the range of activities I can observe, but not that instructors might be trying to
observe them outside the classroom. Their responses indicate how fully many of
them regard school as an institution of surveillance and regulation. In turn they
tell me of tactics they use to resist observation, such as opening discussion forum
posts so that action is noted by the software and so they receive credit – or avoid
punishment – from the teacher, but not actually reading what is written on the
posts. This game of surveillance and resistance calls to mind a guard-and-prisoner
kind of relationship that is poisonous to a healthy and respectful environment for
teaching and learning.

Critical and creative approaches

Outside the classroom our students spend their time with digital media sending
messages, creating social media pages, watching videos, writing fan fiction, participating in discussion forums, and engaging in hundreds of other digital media
practices they find vibrant and empowering. Part of what draws them to these
practices is the degree of control they have, the ability to shape and participate
with the texts, and the movement they can make across media and platforms
(Satchwell, Barton, and Hamilton, this volume; Williams 2009). They find the
digital media they engage with to be fluid, flexible, and responsive. By contrast,
Blackboard is a system that is standardized, rigid, and not just out of their control, but often used to control them. Digital media, by themselves, do not make
the contemporary university a more participatory and creative educational space.
Instead, Blackboard actually works to reinforce traditional conceptions of the university as hierarchical, controlling, print-based, and obsessed with assessment.

Although universities have their reasons for adopting Blackboard and encouraging its use, that does not mean instructors are powerless to respond. First, we

have a political role to play. Even if faculty are not consulted about the adoption of Blackboard, that does not mean we cannot continue to explain the limits of the system in terms of best teaching practices. We have expertise about pedagogy and digital media that many administrators do not and we can work to educate them about the kinds of technology that are most beneficial to creative and critical learning. It is a long education that takes patience, but we must continue to point out the limits of systems such as Blackboard and how alternatives offer more productive ways of engaging students in collaborative and multimodal digital work. Such arguments mean recognizing the uses for which universities need standardized systems, such as student records and registration, but also helping administrators to understand that the 'black-box fallacy' (Jenkins 2006: 14) of finding one system that does everything inevitably results in problems and disappointment. We can help administrators see that a system such as Blackboard does not help students understand how to read and write in a digital world as well as many of the available alternatives.

At the same time we should seek out and design what Sheridan and Rowsell (2010) call 'architectures of participation' in digital environments. Architectures of participation are those digital technologies that, rather than restrict student attempts at design or make it difficult to use modes other than print, instead encourage flexible literacy practices that emphasize collaboration, publishing, multimodality, and remix. Wikis, blogs, discussion forums, editing and webwriting software that are not restricted like Blackboard also provide frameworks for conversations about how and why we can use digital media in effective pedagogy. Also, such technologies allow the possibility of creating genuinely collaborative and participatory spaces that move students toward working as independent scholars. Such an approach helps us try to differentiate between digital media that can enhance student learning, and technologies that may only be a passing fad. Online spaces such as Wikispaces or Wordpress, for two current examples, offer free, flexible spaces for everything from online discussions, to posting of course materials, to collaborative work, and multimodal composing. What's more, these spaces, and many others, offer the option of creating password-protected sites for course work that allay concerns about student privacy. Finally, by not trying to do too many things, these digital spaces are easier to use, more rewarding, and more like the kinds of digital environments and software students encounter outside the classroom. They are easy to use – in many cases easier than Blackboard – and there are countless tutorials, videos, and suggestions online for how to incorporate them into teaching.

Of course no system is perfect. Like shopping at local stores instead of a big-box store, using online sites outside of the university takes a bit longer and requires more planning. Also, university IT support will not troubleshoot such sites, though again there are many online discussion forums offering such troubleshooting that may very well be more useful and friendly than a university IT department. Like shopping at local stores, the reward is often a more tailor-made and higher quality product or experience.

Even if we use Blackboard for our courses, we should engage students in a critical conversation about how and why Blackboard is set up as it is. We should talk with them about its emphasis on teacher control, reliance on print, inability to be modified, and capacity for surveillance and the reasons why software in a university might be set up this way. We can connect conversations about Blackboard to contemporary conversations about privacy online, about information ownership and transfer, and most important, about how digital media can either facilitate – or hinder – effective communication.

As educators and scholars, it is our responsibility to articulate for instructors, administrators, and students what the digital university can look like in regard to which technologies best support our more effective pedagogies. One of the key concepts about digital media we should be teaching is how new technologies offer choices in terms of multimodality and participation and distribution, but that those choices are shaped by the software and digital spaces we use or are given to use. In this way we help students develop the kinds of critical perspectives about digital media that can change their perceptions and actions at school and in their daily lives.

Bibliography

Aggarwal, A. K., Adlakha, V. and Mersha, T. (2006) 'Continuous improvement process in web-based education at a public university', *e-Service Journal*. 4, 2: 3–26.

Allen, I. E. and Seaman, J. (2003) *Sizing the Opportunity: The Quality and Extent of Online Education in the United States, 2002 and 2003*. Needham MA: SCALE.

Allen, I. E. and Seaman, J. (2011) *Going the Distance: Online Education in the United States, 2011*. Babson Park, MA: Babson Survey Research Group.

Anderson, T. (2012) 'Technologies, pedagogies, and the next generation', *Next Generation Learning Conference*, Dalarna University, Sweden, 21–23 February, http://www.slideshare.net/terrya/sweden-keynote-2012 (accessed 14 April 2013).

Andresen, L. W. (2000) 'A useable, trans-disciplinary conception of scholarship', *Higher Education Research & Development*, 19, 2: 137–153.

Andrews, R. and Haythornthwaite, C. (2007) 'Introduction to e-learning research'. In Andrews, R. and Haythornthwaite, C. (eds) *Handbook of E-learning Research* : London: Sage: 1–52.

Androutsopoulos, J. (2008) 'Potentials and limitations of discourse-centered online ethnography', *Language@Internet*, 5, 8, http://www.languageatinternet.org/articles/2008/1610 (accessed 12 December 2012).

Arthur, W.B. (2009) *The Nature of Technology: What It Is and How It Evolves*. London: Allen Lane.

Askam, W. (2012) 'Gate-crashing the Facebook party', Blackpool & The Fylde College, unpublished report.

Badmington, N. (ed.) (2000) *Posthumanism*. Basingstoke: Palgrave.

Badmington, N. (2004) 'Mapping posthumanism: an exchange', *Environment and Planning A*, 36: 1341–1363.

Barad, K. (2003) 'Posthumanist performativity: toward an understanding of how matter comes to matter', *Signs*, 28, 3: 801–31.

Barker, D. (2004). 'The scholarship of engagement: a taxonomy of five emerging practices', *Journal of Higher Education Outreach and Engagement*, 9, 2: 123.

Barnett, R. (2000) 'University knowledge in an age of supercomplexity', *Journal of Higher Education*, 40, 4.

Barton, D. (1994 and 2007) *Literacy: An Introduction to the Ecology of Written Language*. London: Blackwell.

Barton, D. and Hamilton, M. (1998) *Local Literacies*, London: Routledge.

Barton, D. and Hamilton, M. (2005) Literacy, reification and the dynamics of social interaction. In Barton, D. and Tusting, K. (eds) *Beyond Communities of Practice: Language, Power and Social Context*. Cambridge: Cambridge University Press: 14–35.

Barton, D. and Lee, C. (2012) 'Redefining vernacular literacies in the age of Web 2.0', *Applied Linguistics*, 33, 3: 282–298.

Barton, D. and Tusting, K. (eds) (2005) *Beyond Communities of Practice: Language, Power and Social Context*. Cambridge: Cambridge University Press.

Barton, D., Hodge, R., Appleby, Y, and Tusting, K. (2007) *Adult Learners' Lives*, London: Routledge.

Batson, T. (1988) 'The ENFI project: a networked classroom approach to writing instruction', *Academic Computing*, 2, 5: 32–33.

Baudelaire, C. (1964) *The Painter of Modern Life, and Other Essays*. London: Phaidon.

Bayne, S. (2006) 'Temptation, trash and trust: the authorship and authority of digital texts', *E-learning*, 3, 1.

Bayne, S. (2010) 'Academetron, automaton, phantom: uncanny digital pedagogies', *London Review of Education*, 8, 1: 5–13.

Bazerman, C. (1981) 'What written knowledge does: three examples of academic discourse', *Philosophy of the Social Sciences*, 11: 361–387.

Becker, H. S., Geer, B., Hughes, E. C. and Strauss, A. L. (1961) *Boys in White: Student Culture in Medical School*. Chicago, IL: University of Chicago Press.

Beetham, H. (2009) 'Academic values and web cultures: points of rupture'. *Literacy in the Digital University*, ESRC Seminar, Edinburgh University, 16 October, http://kn.open.ac.uk/LiDU/Seminar1/Beetham_text.doc (accessed 9 March 2011).

Beetham, H., McGill, L. and Littlejohn, A. (2009) 'Thriving in the 21st century: learning literacies for the digital age' (LLiDA project report), http://www.academy.gcal.ac.uk/llida/LLiDAReportJune2009.pdf (accessed 17 July 2012).

Benkler, Y. (2006) *The Wealth of Networks: How Social Production Transforms Markets and Freedom*. New Haven, CT: Yale University Press.

Bennett, S., Maton, K. and Kervin, L. (2008) 'The "digital natives" debate: a critical review of the evidence', *British Journal of Educational Technology*, 39, 5: 775–786.

Berkenkotter, C. and Huckin, T. (1995) *Genre Knowledge in Disciplinary Communication*. New York: Lawrence Erlbaum Associates.

Bhabha, H. (1994) *The Location of Culture*. London: Routledge.

Biesta, G. (1998) 'Pedagogy without humanism: Foucault and the subject of education', *Interchange*, 29, 1: 1–16.

Biesta, G. (1999) 'Radical intersubjectivity: reflections of the "different" foundation of education', *Studies in Philosophy and Education*, 18: 203–220.

Black, R. W. (2007) 'Digital design: English language learners and reader feedback in online fanfiction'. In Knobel, M. and Lankshear, C. (eds), *A New Literacies Sampler*. Peter Lang.

Blackboard (2012) http://www.blackboard.com (accessed 4 April 2012).

Blair, K. L. (2007) 'Course management tools as "gated communities": expanding the potential of distance learning spaces through multimodal tools'. In E. P. Bailey (ed.) *Focus on Distance Education Developments*. New York: Nova Science Publishers.

Blommaert, J. and Rampton, B. (2011) 'Language and Superdiversity', *Diversities*, 13, 2: 3–21.

Borgman, C. (2003) *From Gutenburg to the Global Information Infrastructure*. Cambs MA: London: MIT Press.

Borgman, C. (2007) *Scholarship in the Digital Age. Information, Infrastructure and the Internet*. Cambs MA: London: MIT Press.

boyd, d. (2010) 'Social networking sites as networked publics: affordances, dynamics and implications'. In Papacharissi, Z. *A Networked Self: Identity Community and Culture on Social Network Sites*. New York: Routledge: 39–58.

boyd d., Golder S. and Lotan, G. (2010) 'Tweet, tweet, retweet: conversational aspects of retweeting on Twitter', HICSS-43. IEEE: Kauai HI, 6 January.

Boyer, E. L. (1990) *Scholarship Reconsidered: Priorities of the Professoriate*. Princeton, N.J., Carnegie Foundation for the Advancement of Teaching, https://depts.washington.edu/gs630/Spring/Boyer.pdf (accessed 13 December 2012).

Brandt, D. and Clinton, K. (2002) 'Limits of the local: expanding perspectives on literacy as a social practice', *Journal of Literacy Research*, 34, 3: 337–356

Brice-Heath, S. (1983) *Ways with Words: Language, Life and Work in Communities and Classrooms*. Cambridge: Cambridge University Press.

Brown, J. S. and Adler, R. P. (2008) 'Minds on fire: Open education, the long tail, and learning 2.0', *EDUCAUSE Review*, 43, 1: 16–32.

Brown, J. S., Collins, A. and Duguid, P. (1989) 'Situated cognition and the culture of learning', *Educational Researcher*, 18: 32–42.

Bruckman, A. and Jensen, C. (2002) 'The mystery of the death of Mediamoo: seven years of evolution of an online community'. In Renninger, K. A. and Shumar, W. (eds) *Building Virtual Communities: Learning and Change in Cyberspace*. Cambridge: Cambridge University Press: 21–33

Bruner, J. (1990) *Acts of Meaning*. Cambridge, MA: Harvard University Press.

Buckingham, D. (2007) 'Digital media literacies: rethinking media education in the age of the Internet', *Research in Comparative and International Education*, 2, 1: 43–55.

Burawoy, M. (2005) 'Provincializing the social sciences'. In Steinmetz, G. (ed.) *The Politics of Method in the Human Sciences: Positivism and its Epistemological Others*. Durhman, NC: Duke University Press: 508–525

Burton, G. (2009) *The Open Scholar. Academic Evolution*, http://www.academicevolution.com/2009/08/the-open-scholar.html (accessed 13 December 2012).

Calhoun, C. (2006) 'The university and the public good', *Thesis Eleven*, 84, 7: 7–43

Callon, M. (1986) 'Some elements of a sociology of translation: domestification of the scallops and the fishermen of St Brieuc Bay'. In Law, J. (ed.) *Power, Action and Belief: a New Sociology of Knowledge? Sociological Review Monograph*, 32. London: Routledge & Kegan Paul: 196–223.

Callon, M. (ed.) (1998) *The Laws of the Market*. Oxford: Blackwell.

Candy, P.C. (1991) *Self-Direction for Lifelong Learning: A Comprehensive Guide to Theory and Practice*. San Francisco: Jossey-Bass.

Carpenter, R. (2009) 'Boundary negotiations: electronic environments as interface', *Computers and Composition*, 26, 3: 138–148.

Carrington, V. and Robinson, M. (2009) *Digital Literacies: Social Learning and Classroom Practices*. London: Sage.

Castells, M. (1996 second edition 2000) *The Rise of the Network Society, The Information Age: Economy, Society and Culture Vol.1*. Oxford, UK: Blackwell.

Castells, M. (1999) *Critical Education in the New Information Age*, Oxford: Rowman and Littlefield.

Clarke, J. (2002) 'A new kind of symmetry: Actor-network theories and the new literacy studies', *Studies in the Education of Adults*, 34, 2: 107–122.

Colley, H., James, D., Diment, K. and Tedder, M. (2007) 'Learning as becoming in vocational education and training: class, gender and the role of vocational habitus', *Journal of Vocational Education and Training*, 55, 4: 471–496

Collini, S. (2012) *What Are Universities For?* London: Penguin.

Conole, G. (2012) ' Integrating OER into Open Educational practices'. In Glennie, J., Harley, K., Butcher, N. and van Wyk, T. (eds) *Perspectives on Open and Distance Learning: Open Educational Resources and Change in Higher Education: Reflections from Practice*. Vancouver: Commonwealth of Publishing, http://www.col.org/PublicationDocuments/pub_PS_OER_web.pdf (accessed 16 July 2012).

Cope, B. and Kalantzis, M. (eds) (2000) *Multiliteracies: Literacy Learning and the Design of Social Futures*, London: Routledge.

Cope, B. and Kalantzis, M. (2009) 'Signs of epistemic disruption: transformations in the knowledge system of the academic journal'. In *First Monday*, 6 April 2009 14, 4.

Courant, P. (2008) 'Scholarship: the wave of the future in the digital age'. In Katz, R. (ed.) *The Tower and the Cloud: Higher Education in the Age of Cloud Computing*, Educause, http://www.educause.edu/ir/library/pdf/PUB7202t.pdf (accessed 13 December 2012).

Cowan, W., Cowan, R. and Llerena, P. (2008) 'Running The Marathon', Working Papers of BETA 2008–10, Bureau d'Economie Théorique et Appliquée, ULP, Strasbourg, http://ideas.repec.org/p/ulp/sbbeta/2008-10.html (accessed January 2012).

Cranmer, S. (2006) 'Children and young people's uses of the Internet for homework', *Learning, Media and Technology*, 31, 3: 301–316.

Crystal, D. (2006) *Language and the Internet*, Cambridge: Cambridge University Press.

Cuddy, C. (2009) 'Twittering in health sciences libraries', *Journal of Electronic Resources in Medical Libraries*, 6, 2: 169–173.

Cummings, J., Butler, B. and Kraut, R. (2002) 'The quality of online social relationships', *Communications of the ACM*, 45, 7: 103–108.

Cushman, E. (2004) 'Toward a rhetoric of new media: Composing (me)dia', *Computers and Composition Online*, http://www.bgsu.edu/cconline/theory.htm (accessed 17 July 2012).

Czerniewicz, L., Williams, K. and Brown, C. (2009) 'Students make a plan: understanding student agency in constraining conditions', *The Association for Learning Technology Journal, ALT-J*, 17, 2: 75–88.

Danet, B. and Herring, S. C. (eds) (2007) *The Multilingual Internet: Language, Culture and Communication Online*. New York and Oxford: Oxford University Press.

Davis, E. and Hardy, S. (2003) 'Teaching writing in the space of Blackboard', *Computers and Composition Online*, http://www.bgsu.edu/cconline/DavisHardy/index.html (accessed 4 April 2012).

Dede, C. (2005) 'Planning for neomillennial learning styles', *EDUCAUSE Quarterly*, 28, 1: 7–12.

Deleuze, G. and Guattari, F. (1987) *A Thousand Plateaus*. Minneapolis: University of Minnesota Press.

Delphi Center (2012) 'What's new in Blackboard 9.1 Service Pack 7', https://louisville.edu/delphi/teaching-with-technology/training/whats-new-in-blackboard-9.1.html (accessed 28 March 2012).

Derrida, J. (1982) *'Différance', Margins of Philosophy*. Chicago and London: University of Chicago Press.

Derry, J. (2007) 'Epistemology and conceptual resources for the development of learning technologies', *Journal of Computer Assisted Learning*, 23: 503–510.

DeSanctis, G. and Poole, M. S. (1994) 'Capturing the complexity in advanced technology use: adaptive structuration theory', *Organization Science*, 5, 2: 121–47.

Dick, S. (2010) 'Open University'. *SCONUL Focus (news from member libraries)*, 50, http://www.sconul.ac.uk/publications/newsletter/50/37.pdf (accessed 16 March 2012).

Dickens, A., Borthwick, K., Richardson, S., Lavender, L., Mossley, D., Gawthrope, J. and Lucas, B. (2010) 'The HumBox Project: final report'. Higher Education Academy/JISC Open Educational Resources Programme, http://www.llas.ac.uk/resourcedownloads/3233/humbox_final_report.pdf (accessed 16 March 2012).

Downes, S. (2007) 'Models for sustainable open educational resources', *Interdisciplinary Journal of Knowledge and Learning Objects*, 3: 29–44.

Dubé, L., Bourhis, A. and Jacob, R. 'Towards a typology of virtual communities of practice', *Interdisciplinary Journal of Information, Knowledge, and Management* (1), 2006, 69–93.

Dyson, G. (2012) *Turing's Cathedral: The Origins of the Digital Universe*. London: Allen Lane.

Ebner, M., Schiefner, M. and Nagler, W. (2008) 'Has the Net-Generation arrived at the university?' – oder der Student von Heute, ein Digital Native? [or contemporary student – a digital native?]. In Zauchner, S. Baumgartner, P., Blaschitz, E. and Weissenbäck, A. (eds) *Offener Bildungsraum Hochschule, Medien in der Wissenschaft*, 48: WaxmannVerlag: 113–123.

Economic and Social Research Council (ESRC) (2012) Literacy in the Digital University, http://www.esrc.ac.uk/my-esrc/grants/RES-451-26-0765/read (accessed 15 January 2013).

Educause Learning Initiative (Nov. 2011) '7 things you should know about MOOCs', Educause, http://www.educause.edu/ir/library/pdf/ELI7078.pdf (accessed 4 September 2012).

Edwards, R. (2010) 'The end of lifelong learning: a post-human condition?', *Studies in the Education of Adults*, 42, 1: 5–17.

Edwards, R. and Usher, R. (2000) *Globalisation and pedagogy: Space, Place and Identity*. London: Routledge.

Elavsky, C. M., Mislan, C. and Elavsky, S. (2011) 'When talking less is more: exploring outcomes of Twitter usage in the large lecture hall', *Learning Media and Technology*, 36, 3: 215–233.

Ellison, J. and Eatman, T. K. (2008) *Scholarship in Public: Knowledge Creation and Tenure Policy in the Engaged University*. Syracuse, NY: Imagining America.

eMarketer (2011) 'Global media intelligence report (Asia Pacific)', cited in: *Digital Media across Asia*, Singapore Management University, https://wiki.smu.edu.sg/digitalmediaasia/Digital_Media_in_Hong_Kong (accessed 12 July 2012).

Engeström, Y. (1999) 'Communication, discourse and activity', *The Communication Review*, 3, 1–2: 165–185.

Engeström, Y. (2001) 'Expansive learning at work: toward an activity theoretical reconceptualization', *Journal of Education and Work*, 14, 1: 133–156.

Engeström, Y. (2009) 'Expansive learning: toward an activity-theoretical reconceptualization'. In Illeris, K. (ed.) *Contemporary Theories of Learning: Learning Theorists – In Their Own Words*. London: Routledge: 53–73.

Erickson, T. (1999) 'Persistent conversation: an introduction', *Journal of Computer Mediated Communication*, 4, 4, http://jcmc.indiana.edu/vol4/issue4/ericksonintro.html (accessed 23 May 2012).

Eshet-Alkalai, Y. (2004) 'Digital literacy: a conceptual framework for survival skills in the digital era', *Journal of Educational Multimedia and Hypermedia*, 1391: 93–106.

European Commission (2009) Commission of the European Communities, 'The governance challenge for knowledge policies in the Lisbon Strategy: between revolution and illusion'. Synthesis Report of Expert Group for the follow-up of the research aspects of the revised Lisbon Strategy (No. EUR 3469). Brussels: European Commission.

Evans, S. (2002) 'The medium of instruction in Hong Kong: policy and practice in the new English and Chinese streams', *Research Papers in Education*, 17: 97–120.

Facer, K. and Selwyn, N. (2010) 'Social Networking'. In Sharpe, R., Beetham, H. and de Freitas, S. (eds) *Rethinking Learning for a Digital Age*. London: Routledge: 31–42.

Fairclough, N. (1992) *Discourse and Social Change*. Cambridge: Polity Press.

Farr, M. (1993) 'Essayist literacy and other verbal performances', *Written Communication*, 10, 4: 4–38.

Feenberg, A. (2002) *Transforming Technology: A Critical Theory Revisited*. Oxford: Oxford University Press.

Fenwick, T. and Edwards, R. (2010) *Actor-Network Theory in Education*. London and New York: Routledge.

Fenwick, T., Edwards, R. and Sawchuck, P. (2011) *Emerging Approaches to Educational Research: Tracing the Sociomaterial*. London: Routledge.

Ferguson, R. (2012) 'The state of learning analytics in 2012: a review and future challenges'. Technical Report KMI-12-01, Knowledge Media Institute, The Open University, UK, http://kmi.open.ac.uk/publications/techreport/kmi-12-01 (accessed 8 June 2012).

Fernandez-Villavicencio, N.G. (2010) 'Helping students become literate in a digital, networking-based society: a literature review and discussion', *International Information and Library Review*, 42, 2: 124–136.

Fiedler, S. and Pata, K. (2009) 'Distributed learning environments and social software: in search for a framework of design'. In Hatzipanagos, S. and Warburton, S. (eds) *Social Software and Developing Community Ontologies*. Hershey, PA, USA: IGI Global: 145–158.

Flanders, J. (2009) 'The productive unease of 21st-century digital scholarship', *Digital Humanities Quarterly*, 3, 3, http://digitalhumanities.org/dhq/vol/3/3/000055/000055.html (accessed 7 September 2012).

Foucault, M. (1977; 2nd edn 1991) *Discipline and Punish*. Trans. Alan Sheridan (1977). New York: Random House.

Foucault, M. (1984) 'Of other spaces (1967)', Heterotopias, http://foucault.info/documents/heteroTopia/foucault.heteroTopia.en.html (accessed 8 February 2012).

Fransman, J. (2012) 'Re-imagining the conditions of possibility of a PhD thesis'. In Andrews, R., Borg, E., Boyd Davis, S., Domingo, M. and England, J. (eds) *The Sage Handbook of Digital Dissertations and Theses*, London: Sage: 138–157.

Freud, S. (2003) *The uncanny*, London: Penguin Classics.

FutureLab (2009) 'Digital participation, digital literacy, and school subjects: a literature review', http://archive.futurelab.org.uk/resources/publications-reports-articles/literature-reviews/Literature-Review1473 (accessed 17 July 2012).

Gallagher, M. (2010) 'The flaneur was here: mobile augmented reality and urban cultural heritage learning in Lower Manhattan', http://michaelseangallagher.org/flaneur-analysis/ (accessed 30 April 2012).

Garfinkel, H. (1967) *Studies in Ethnomethodology*. Oxford: Blackwell.

Garrett, R. (2004) 'The real story behind the failure of U.K. eUniversity', *Educause Quarterly*, 4: 4–6.

Garrison, D. R. and Anderson, T. (2003) *E-learning in the 21st Century: A framework for Research and Practice*. NY: RoutledgeFalmer.

Gaver, W. (1991) 'Technology affordances'. In *Proceedings of the ACM CHI 91 Human Factors in Computing Systems Conference*. Louisiana, New Orleans, 28 April–5 June: 79–84.

Gaver, W. (1996) 'Affordances for interaction: The social is material for design', *Ecological Psychology*, 8, 2: 111–129.

Gee, J. (1996) *Social Linguistics and Literacies: Ideology in Discourses*. Philadelphia, RoutledgeFalmer.

Gee, J. (1999) *An introduction to discourse analysis: Theory and Method*. New York and London: Routledge.

Gee, J. (2008) *What Video Games Have to Teach Us about Learning and Literacy*, 2nd edn. NY: Palgrave Macmillan.

Geser, G. (ed.) (2007) *OLCOS Roadmap 2012*. Open e-Learning Content Observatory Services (OLCOS), http://www.olcos.org/cms/upload/docs/olcos_roadmap.pdf (accessed 13 December 2012).

Gibson, J. J. (1977) 'The theory of affordances'. In Shaw, R. and Bransford, J. (eds) *Perceiving, Acting and Knowing*. Hillsdale, NJ: Erlbaum: 67–82.

Glennie, J., Harley, K. and Butcher, N. (2012) 'Discourses in the development of OER Practice and Policy'. In Glennie, J., Harley, K., Butcher, N. and van Wyk, T. (eds) *Perspectives on Open and Distance Learning: Open Educational Resources and Change in Higher Education: Reflections from Practice*. Vancouver: Commonwealth of Publishing:1–12, http://www.col.org/PublicationDocuments/pub_PS_OER_web.pdf (accessed 16 July 2012).

Goddard, A. and Geesin, B. (2011) *Language and Technology*. London: Routledge.

Goldhaber, M. H. (1997) 'The Attention Economy and the Net', *First Monday*, 2, 4, http://firstmonday.org (accessed 12 July 2012).

Goodfellow, R. (2005) 'Academic literacies and e-learning: a critical approach to writing in the online university', *International Journal of Educational Research*, 43,7–8: 481–494.

Goodfellow, R. (2011) 'Literacy, literacies and the digital in higher education', *Teaching in Higher Education*, 16, 1: 131–144.

Goodfellow, R. and Lea, M. R. (2007) *Challenging e-Learning in the University – a Literacies Perspective*. McGraw Hill/Open University Press, Studies in Research in Higher Education series.

Goodfellow, R., Morgan, M., Lea, M. and Pettit, J. (2004) 'Students' writing in the virtual university: an investigation into the relation between online discussion and writing for assessment'. In Snyder, I. and Beavis, C. (eds) *Doing Literacy Online: Teaching, Learning and Playing in An Electronic World. New Dimensions in Computers and Composition*. Cresskill, NJ: Hampton Press: 25–44.

Goodyear, P. and Ellis, R. (2008) 'University students' approaches to learning: rethinking the place of technology', *Distance Education*, 29: 141–152.

Gough, N. (2004) 'RhizomANTically becoming-cyborg: performing posthuman pedagogies', *Educational Philosophy and Theory* 36, 3: 253–265.

Gourlay, L. (2010) 'Multimodality, visual methodologies and higher education'. In Savin-Baden, M. and Howell-Major, C. *New Approaches to Qualitative Research: Wisdom and Uncertainty*. London: Routledge: 80–88.

Gourlay, L. and Deane, J. (2012) 'Loss, responsibility, blame? staff discourse of student plagiarism', *Innovations in Education and Teaching International*, 49, 1: 19–29.

Graff, H. J. (1995) *Labyrinths of Literacy, Reflection on Literacy Past and Present*. University of Pittsburgh Press.

Graham, L. (2008) 'Teachers are digikids too: the digital histories and digital lives of young teachers in English primary schools', *Literacy*, 42, 1: 10–18.

Grint, K. and Woolgar, S. (1997) *The Machine at Work*. Cambridge: Polity.

Hamilton, M. (2001) 'Privileged literacies: policy, institutional process and the life of the IALS', *Language and Education* 15, 2–3: 178–196.

Hamilton, M. (2011) 'Unruly practices: what a sociology of translations can offer to educational policy analysis'. In *Educational Philosophy and Theory*, 43, S1: 55–75.

Haraway, D. (1991) 'A cyborg manifesto: science, technology and socialist feminism in the late twentieth century', *Simians, cyborgs, and women: the reinvention of nature*. London: Free Association Books

Haraway, D. (1997) *Modest_Witness@Second_Millennium. FemaleMan©_Meets_Onco-Mouse™: Feminism and Technoscience*. New York and London: Routledge.

Hardt, M. and Negri, A. (2004) *Multitude*. London: Penguin.

Hargittai, E. (2005) 'Survey measures of web-oriented digital literacy', *Social Science Computer Review*, 23: 371–379.

Hargittai, E. (2009) 'An update on survey measures of web-oriented digital literacy', *Social Science Computer Review*, 27, 1: 130–137.

Hargittai, E. (2010) 'Digital na(t)ives? Variation in internet skills and uses among members of the "Net Generation"', *Sociological Inquiry*, 80, 1: 92–113.

Harkin, P. (2005) 'Excellence is the name of the (ideological) game.' In Williams, B. T. (ed.) *Identity Papers: Literacy and Power in Higher Education*. Logan, UT: Utah State University Press: 29–41.

Harland, T. and Pickering, N. (2011) *Values in Higher Education Teaching*. London: Routledge.

Hase, S. and Kenyon, C. (2000) 'From andragogy to heutagogy', http://ultibase.rmit.edu.au/Articles/dec00/hase2.htm (accessed 12 July 2010).

Hayes, N. and Introna, L. (2005) 'Cultural values, plagiarism and fairness: when plagiarism gets in the way of learning', *Ethics and Behaviour*, 15, 3: 213–231.

Hayles, N. (1999) *How We Became Posthuman: Virtual Bodies in Cybernetics, Literature, and Informatics*. Chicago: University of Chicago Press.

Hayles, N. (2006) 'Unfinished work: from cyborg to cognisphere', *Theory, Culture, Society*, 23, 7–8: 159–166.

Haythornthwaite, C. (2006a) 'Facilitating collaboration in online learning', *Journal of Asynchronous Learning Networks*, 10,1, http://sloanconsortium.org/jaln/v10n1/facilitating-collaboration-online-learning (accessed 20 May 2012).

Haythornthwaite, C. (2006b) 'Articulating divides in distributed knowledge practice', *Information, Communication and Society*, 9, 6: 761–780.

Haythornthwaite, C. (2008) 'Learning relations and networks in web-based communities', *International Journal of Web Based Communities*, 4, 2: 140–158.

Haythornthwaite, C. (2009) 'Crowds and communities: light and heavyweight models of peer production', *Proceedings of the 42nd Hawaii International Conference on System Sciences*. Los Alamitos, CA: IEEE Computer Society, https://www.ideals.uiuc.edu/handle/2142/9457 (accessed 18 December 2012).

Haythornthwaite, C. and Andrews, R. (2011) *E-learning Theory and Practice*. London: Sage.

Haythornthwaite, C. and Kazmer, M. M. (2002) 'Bringing the Internet home: adult distance learners and their Internet, home and work worlds'. In Wellman, B. and Haythornthwaite, C. (eds) *The Internet in Everyday Life*. Oxford, UK: Blackwell: 431–463.

Haythornthwaite, C. and Kazmer, M. M. (eds) (2004) *Learning, Culture and Community in Online Education: Research and Practice*. New York: Peter Lang.

Haythornthwaite, C., and Kendall, L. (2010) Internet and community. *American Behavioral Scientist*, 53, 8: 1083–1094.

Haythornthwaite, C., Kazmer, M. M., Robins, J. and Shoemaker, S. (2000) 'Community development among distance learners: temporal and technological dimensions', *Journal of Computer-Mediated Communication*, 6, 1, http://jcmc.indiana.edu/vol6/issue1/haythornthwaite.html (accessed 9 June 2012).

Hazemi, R. and Hailes, S. (eds) (2002) *The Digital University – Building a Learning Community*. London: Springer-Verlag.

Head, A. J. and Eisenberg, M. (12 October 2011) 'Project information literacy research report: Balancing act: how college students manage technology while in the library during crunch time', http://projectinfolit.org/pdfs/PIL_Fall2011_TechStudy_FullReport1.1.pdf (accessed 6 June 2012).

HEFCE (Higher Education Funding Council for England) (2005) *HEFCE Strategy for Elearning*. Bristol, UK: HEFCE.

Hemsley-Brown, J. and Oplatka, I. (2006) 'Universities in a competitive global marketplace: a systematic review of the literature on higher education marketing', *International Journal of Public Sector Management*, 19, 4: 316–338.

Hendrix, D. and Johannsen, G. (2008) 'A knowledge sharing and collaboration platform', *Inside Knowledge*, 11 (8), http://www.ikmagazine.com/xq/asp/sid.0/articleid.0A6EF1DD-1D6A-4CD0-94EA-DC872A5A708E/eTitle.Case_study_Shell_Wiki/qx/display.htm (accessed 17 July 2012).

'Hewlett Foundation, values and policies', http://www.hewlett.org/values (accessed 1 July 2012).

Hiemstra, R. and Brockett, R. G. (1994) *Overcoming Resistance to Self-Direction in Adult Learning*. San Francisco: Jossey-Bass Inc.

Hilton III, J., Wiley, D., Stein, J. and Johnson, A. (2010) 'The four "R"s of openness and ALMS analysis: frameworks for open educational resources', *Open Learning: The Journal of Open, Distance and e-Learning*, 25, 1: 37–44, http://dx.doi.org/10.1080/0268051 0903482132 (accessed 16 March 2012).

Holland, D., Lachicotte, W., Skinner, D. and Cain, C. (1998) *Identity and Agency in Cultural Worlds*. Cambridge, Mass: Harvard University Press.

Holliman, R. (2011) 'The struggle for scientific consensus: communicating climate science around COP-15'. In Wagoner, B., Jensen, E. and Oldmeadow, J. (eds) *Culture and Social Change: Transforming Society through the Power of Ideas*. Information Age Publishers, Charlotte, N.C: 185–207.

Hook, D. (2005) 'Monumental space and the uncanny', *Geoforum*, 36: 688–704.

hooks, b. (2004) 'Choosing the margin as a space of radical openness'. In Harding, S. (ed.) *The feminist standpoint theory reader: intellectual and political controversies*. New York: Routledge. 153–160.

Howe, J. (2006) 'The rise of crowdsourcing', *Wired* 14.06, http://www.wired.com/wired/archive/14.06/crowds.html (accessed 20 May 2012).

Howe, J. (2008) *Crowdsourcing: How the Power of the Crowd is Driving the Future of Business*. London: Random House Business Books.

Howe, N. and Strauss,W. (2000) *Millennials Rising: The Next Greatest Generation*. New York: Vintage Books, http://www.heterogeneities.net/publications/Law2009CollateralRealities.pdf (accessed 30 December 2009).

Hughes, J. and McKenna, C. (2012) 'The impact of developing OERs on novice OER developers', *Proceedings of OER 2012*, Cambridge, 318–388.

Hull, G. and Schultz, K. (2002) *School's out! Bridging Out-of-School Literacies with Classroom Practice*. New York: Teachers College Press.

Hutchby, I. (2001) 'Technologies, texts and affordances', *Sociology*, 35 (2), 451–456.

Hyland, K. (2006) *English for Academic Purposes: An Advanced Resource Book*. London: Routledge.

Introna, L. and Hayes, N. (2011) 'On sociomaterial imbrications: what plagiarism detection systems reveal and why it matters', *Information and Organization*, 21: 107–22.

Ito, M., Baumer, S., Bittanti, M., boyd, d., Cody, R., Herr, B., *et al.* (2010) *Hanging Out, Messing Around, Geeking Out: Living and Learning with New Media*. Cambridge, MA: MIT Press.

Ivanič, R. (1998) *Writing and Identity: The Discoursal Construction of Identity in Academic Writing*. Amsterdam: John Benjamins.

Ivanič, R. (2004) 'Discourses of writing and learning to write', *Language and Education*, 18, 3: 220–245.

Ivanič, R., Edwards, R., Barton, D., Fowler, Z., Mannion, G., Miller, K., Satchwell, C., Smith, J., Martin-Jones, M. and Hughes, B. (2009) *Improving Learning in College*, London: Taylor & Francis.

Ivanič, R., Edwards, R., Barton, D., Fowler, Z., Satchwell, C., Mannion, G., Miller, K. and Smith, J. (2008) 'Harnessing everyday literacies for student learning at college', Research Briefing No. 50, Teaching & Learning Research Programme, ESRC.

Ivanič, R., Edwards, R., Satchwell, C. and Smith, J. (2007) 'Possibilities for pedagogy in further education: harnessing the abundance of literacy', *British Educational Research Journal*, 33, 5: 703–721.

Jakupec, V. and Garrick, J. (2000) (eds) *Flexible Learning, Human Resource and Organisational Development: Putting Theory To Work*. London: Routledge.

Jenkins, H. (2006) *Convergence Culture: where old and new media collide*. New York: NYU Press.

Jenkins, H., with Clinton, K., Purushotma, R., Robinson, A. J. and Weigel, M. (2006) *Confronting the Challenges of Participatory Culture: Media Education for the 21st Century*. Chicago, IL: MacArthur Foundation.

Jensen, M. (2007) 'Authority 3.0: friend or foe to scholars?', *Journal of Scholarly Publishing* 39, 1: 33–43.

Jewitt, C. (2008) *Technology, Literacy, Learning: A Multimodal Approach*. Abingdon: Routledge.

Johnson, L., Levine, A., Smith, R. and Stone, S. (2010) *The 2010 Horizon Report*. Austin, Texas: The New Media Consortium, http://www.nmc.org/pdf/2010-Horizon-Report.pdf (accessed 16 March 2012).

Joint Information Systems Committee (JISC) (2007) *Student Expectations Study, July 2007*, http://www.jisc.ac.uk/media/documents/publications/studentexpectations.pdf (accessed 29 June 2011).

Joint Information Systems Committee (JISC) (2011a) Developing Digital Literacies: Briefing Paper in support of JISC Grant Funding 4/1, http://www.jisc.ac.uk/fundingopportunities/funding_calls/2011/04/grant411.aspx (accessed 1 November 2011).

Joint Information Systems Committee (JISC) (2011b) OER Impact Study blog, http://oerblog.conted.ox.ac.uk/ (accessed 1 July 2012).

Joint Information Systems Committee (JISC) (2011c) Open Educational Resources Infokit, https://openeducationalresources.pbworks.com/w/page/24836480/Home (accessed 14 April 2013)

Joint Information Systems Committee (JISC) (2012) *Digital Literacies as a Postgraduate Attribute?* http://www.jisc.ac.uk/whatwedo/programmes/elearning/developingdigitalliteracies/DigLitPGAttribute.aspx (accessed 14 August 2012).

Jones, C. and Dirckinck-Holmfeld, L. (2009) 'Analysing Networked Learning Practices: An Introduction'. In Dirckinck-Holmfeld, L., Jones, C. and Lindström, B. (eds) *Analysing Networked Learning Practices in Higher Education and Continuing Professional Development*. Rotterdam: Sense Publishers, BV: 1–28.

Jones, C. and Healing, G. (2010) 'Net Generation students: agency and choice and the new technologies', *Journal of Computer Assisted Learning*, 26, 5: 344–356.

Jones, C. and Shao, B. (2011) *The Net Generation and Digital Natives: Implications for Higher Education*. Higher Education Academy, York, http://www.heacademy.ac.uk/resources/detail/evidencenet/net-generation-and-digital-natives (accessed 12 July 2012).

Jones, C., Ramanau, R., Cross, S. and Healing, G. (2010) 'Net generation or digital natives: is there a distinct new generation entering university?', *Computers and Education*, 54, 3: 722–732.

Jones, C., Turner, J. and Street, B. (eds) (1999) *Students Writing in the University – Cultural and Epistemological Issues*. Amsterdam: John Benjamins.

Jones, S. and Lea, M. R. (2008) 'Digital literacies in the lives of undergraduate students: exploring personal and curricular spheres of practice', *Electronic Journal of e-Learning*, 6, 3: 207–216.

Junco, R., Heiberger, G. and Loken, E. (2011) 'The effect of Twitter on college student engagement and grades', *Journal of Computer Assisted Learning*, 27 (2), 119–132.

Kahn, R. and Kellner, D. (2005) 'Reconstructing technoliteracy: a multiple literacies approach', *E-Learning*, 2, 3: 238–251.

Kaptelinin, V. and Hedestig, U. (2009) 'Breakdowns, affordances and indirect design'. In Dirckinck-Holmfeld, L., Jones, C. and Lindström, B. (eds) *Analysing Networked Learning Practices in Higher Education and Continuing Professional Development*. Rotterdam: Sense Publishers, BV: 223–240.

Kassens-Noor, E. (2012) 'Twitter as a teaching practice to enhance active and informal learning in higher education: The case of sustainable tweets', *Active Learning in Higher Education*, 13, 1: 9–21.

Katz, R. (2010) 'Scholars, scholarship and the scholarly enterprise in the digital age', *Educause Review* March/April 2010, http://www.educause.edu/ero/article/scholars-scholarship-and-scholarly-enterprise-digital-age (accessed 20 December 2012).

Kazmer, M. M. (2007) 'Beyond C U L8R: disengaging from online social worlds', *New Media and Society*, 9: 111–138.

Kemp, B. and Jones, C. (2007) 'Academic use of digital resources: disciplinary differences and the issue of progression revisited', *Journal of Educational Technology and Society*, 10, 1: 52–60.

Kennedy, G., Dalgarno, B., Bennett, S., Judd, T., Gray, K. and Chang, R. (2008) 'Immigrants and natives: investigating differences between staff and students' use of technology'. In 'Hello! Where are you in the landscape of educational technology?', *Proceedings of Ascilite Melbourne 2008*, http://www.ascilite.org.au/conferences/melbourne08/procs/kennedy.pdf (accessed 12 July 2012).

Kenton, J. and Blummer, B. (2010) 'Promoting digital literacy skills: examples from the literature and implications for academic librarians', *Community and Junior College Libraries*, 16, 2: 84–89.

Kinzie, M. B., Whitaker, S. D. and Hofer, M. J. (2005) 'Instructional uses of Instant Messaging (IM) during classroom lectures', *Educational Technology and Society*, 8, 2: 150–160.

Kling, R., Rosenbaum, H. and Sawyer, S. (2005) *Understanding and Communicating Social Informatics*. Medford, NJ: Information Today.

Knox, J. (2010) 'Pedagogies of deferral and difference: tracing a rhizomatic connection to learning', http://deferralanddifference.atwebpages.com (accessed 10 May 2012).

Koschmann, T. (ed.) (1996) *CSCL: Theory and Practice of an Emerging Paradigm*. Mahwah, NJ: Lawrence Erlbaum.

Kress, G. (1999) 'Design and transformation: new theories of meaning'. In Cope, B. and Kalantzis, M. (eds) *Multiliteracies: Literacy, Learning and the Design of Social Futures*. London/New York: Routledge: 153–161

Kress, G. (2003) *Literacy in the New Media Age*. London: Routledge.

Kress, G. (2005) 'Gains and losses: new forms of texts, knowledge and learning', *Computers and Composition*, 22, 1: 5–22.

Kress, G. (2010) *Multimodality: A Social Semiotic Approach to Contemporary Communication*. London: Routledge.

Lam, W. S. E. (2009) 'Multiliteracies on instant messaging in negotiating local, translocal, and transnational affiliations: a case of an adolescent immigrant', *Reading Research Quarterly*, 44, 4: 377–397.

Landry, B. J. L., Griffith, R. and Hartman, S. (2006) 'Measuring student perceptions of Blackboard using the technology acceptance model', *Journal of Decision Sciences*, 4: 87–99.

Lane, A. (2012) 'Reuse and repurpose: the life story of an (open) educational resource', *OpenCourseWare Consortium Conference*, Cambridge 2012, http://oro.open.ac.uk/33244/1/OER_lifestory_paper.pdf (accessed 30 October 2012).

Lankshear, C. and Knobel, M. (2003) *New Literacies: Changing Knowledge and Classroom Learning*. Maidenhead and New York: Open University Press.

Lankshear, C. and Knobel, M. (2008) 'Introduction'. In Lankshear, C. and Knobel, M. (eds) *Digital Literacies*, New York: Peter Lang: 1–16.

Larkin, T. L. and Belson, S. I. (2005) 'Blackboard technologies: a vehicle to promote student motivation and learning in physics', *Journal of STEM Education: Innovations and Research*, 6, 1: 14–27.

Latour, B. (1987) *Science in Action: How to Follow Scientists and Engineers through Society*. Cambridge, Mass: Harvard University Press.

Latour, B. (2004) 'Why has critique run out of steam? From matters of fact to matters of concern', *Critical Inquiry*, 30: 225–248.

Latour, B. (2005) *Reassembling the Social: An Introduction to Actor-Network-Theory*. Oxford: Oxford University Press.

Latour, B. and Woolgar, D. (1979) *Laboratory Life: The Social Construction of Scientific Facts.* Beverley Hills: Sage Publications.

Lave, J. and Wenger, E. (1991) *Situated Learning – Legitimate Peripheral Participation.* New York: Cambridge University Press.

Law, J. (1991) *A Sociology of Monsters: Essays on Power, Technology, and Domination.* London: Routledge.

Law, J. (1992) *Notes on the theory of the actor network: ordering, strategy and heterogeneity.* Centre for Science Studies, Lancaster University, http://www.lancs.ac.uk/fass/sociology/ papers/law-notes-on-ant.pdf (accessed 13 November 2012).

Law, J. (2004) *After Method: Mess in Social Science Research.* London: Routledge.

Law, J. (2009a) 'Collateral realities', version of 29 December 2009, http://www.heterogeneities.net/publications/Law2009CollateralRealities.pdf (accessed 20 December 2012).

Law, J. (2009b) 'Actor network theory and material semiotics'. In Turner, S. (ed.) *The New Blackwell Companion to Social Theory.* Oxford: Blackwell.

Law, J. (2010) 'The double social life of method', Paper presented at the Sixth Annual CRESC conference on the Social Life of Method, 31 August–3 September, St Hugh's College, Oxford.

Law, J. and Hassard, J. (1999) *Actor Network Theory and After.* Oxford: Blackwell.

Lawrence, D. (2006) 'Blackboard on a shoestring: tying courses to sources.' *Journal of Library Administration*, 45: 245–265.

Lawton, P. and Montague, R. (2004) 'Teaching and learning online: LEEP's tribal gleanings'. In Haythornthwaite, C. and Kazmer M. M. (eds) *Learning, Culture and Community in Online Education: Research and Practice.* NY: Peter Lang: 197–213.

Lea, M. R. (2001) 'Computer conferencing and assessment: new ways of writing in higher education', *Studies in Higher Education*, 26, 2: 163–181.

Lea, M. R. (2007) 'Emerging literacies in online learning', *Journal of Applied Linguistics*, 4, 1: 79–100.

Lea, M. R. (2013) 'Reclaiming literacies: competing textual practices in a digital higher education', *Teaching in Higher Education*. DOI:10.1080/13562517.756465.

Lea, M. R. and Jones, S. (2011) 'Digital literacies in higher education: exploring textual and technological practice', *Studies in Higher Education* 36, 4: 377–395.

Lea, M. R. and Stierer, B. (eds) (2000) *Student Writing in Higher Education: New contexts.* Buckingham: Society for Research into Higher Education/Open University Press.

Lea, M. R. and Stierer, B. (2009) 'Lecturers' everyday writing as professional practice in the university as workplace: new insights into academic identities', *Studies in Higher Education*, 34, 3: 417–28.

Lea, M. R. and Stierer, B. (2011) 'Changing academic identities in changing academic workplaces: learning from academics' everyday professional writing practices', *Teaching in Higher Education*, 16, 6: 605–616.

Lea, M. R. and Street, B. (1998) 'Student writing in higher education: an academic literacies approach', *Studies in Higher Education*, 23, 2: 157–172.

LearnHigher (2006) 'Information literacies literature review', http://www.learnhigher.mmu.ac.uk/research/InfoLit-Literature-Review.pdf (accessed 17 July 2012).

Lee, C. (2007a) 'Affordances and text-making practices in online instant messaging', *Written Communication*, 24, 3: 223–249.

Lee, C. (2007b) 'Linguistic features of email and ICQ instant messaging in Hong Kong'.

In Danet, B. and Herring, S. C. (eds) *The Multilingual Internet: Language, Culture and Communication Online*. New York and Oxford: Oxford University Press: 184–208.

Lee, C. and Lien, P. (2011) 'Facebook group as a third space for teaching and learning', Paper presented at The Second International Conference on Popular Culture and Education, Hong Kong Institute of Education, 7–10 December.

Lewin, T. (2012) 'Instruction for masses knocks down campus walls', *New York Times*, 4 March 2012, http://www.nytimes.com/2012/03/05/education/moocs-large-courses-open-to-all-topple-campus-walls.html?pagewanted=all (accessed 27 September 2012).

Lewis, C. and Fabos, B. (2005) 'Instant messaging, literacies, and social identities', *Reading Research Quarterly*, 40, 4: 470–501.

Lewis, T. E. and Kahn, R. (2010) *Education out of Bounds: Reimagining Cultural Studies for a Posthuman Age*. New York: Palgrave Macmillan.

Lievrouw, L. A. (2010) 'Social media and the production of knowledge: a return to little science?', *Social Epistemology*, 24, 3: 219–237.

Lillis, T. (2001) *Student Writing: Access, Regulation, Desire*. London: Routledge.

Lillis, T. (2003) 'Student writing as "academic literacies": drawing on Bakhtin to move from critique to design', *Language and Education*, 17, 3: 192–207.

Lillis, T. and Curry, M. J. (2010) *Academic Writing in a Global Context: The politics and Practices of Publishing in English*. London: Routledge.

Lima, M. (2011) *Visual Complexity: Mapping Patterns of Information*. NY: Princeton Architectural Press.

Littlejohn, A., Beetham, H., McGill, L. and Falconer, I. (2011) 'Factors affecting the release of Open Educational Resources', *Technologie Didattiche*, 51 (1).

Littlejohn, A., Margaryan, A. and Vojt, G. (2010) 'Exploring students' use of ICT and expectations of learning methods', *Electronic Journal of E-Learning (IJEL)*, 8, 1, http://www.ejel.org/volume8/issue1 (accessed 17 July 2012).

Luckin, R. (2010) *Re-designing Learning Contexts: Technology-rich, Learner-centred Ecologies*. London: Routledge.

Luckin, R. and Hammerton, L. (2002) 'Getting to know me: helping learners understand their own learning needs through metacognitive scaffolding'. In Stefano, A., Gouardeeres, G. and Paraguacu, F. 'Intelligent tutoring systems', *6th International Conference*, ITS 2002 Biarritz, France, San Sebastian, Spain, 2–7 June 2002: 759–771.

Luckin, R., Clark, W., Logan, K., Graber, R., Oliver, M. and Mee, A. (2009) 'Do Web 2.0 tools really open the door to learning? Practices, perceptions and profiles of 11–16 year old learners', *Learning, Media and Technology*, 34, 2: 87–104.

McAvinia, C. (2011) *Investigating the adoption of a university virtual learning environment – an Activity Theoretic analysis*. Unpublished PhD thesis, Dublin Trinity University.

Macfadyen, L. and Dawson, S. (2010) 'Mining LMS data to develop an "early warning system" for educators: a proof of concept', *Computers & Education*, 54, 2: 588–599.

Macfarlane, B. (2004) *Teaching with Integrity: The Ethics of Higher Education Practice*. London: Routledge.

McGill, L. (2011) *Stakeholders and Benefits*. Open Educational Resources InfoKit. JISC and HEA, https://openeducationalresources.pbworks.com/w/page/24838012/Stakeholders_and_benefits (accessed 16 March 2012).

McGill, L., Currier, S., Duncan, C. and Douglas, P. (2008) 'Good intentions: improving the evidence base in support of sharing materials'. JISC Project Report [Unpublished], http://ie-repository.jisc.ac.uk/265/1/goodintentionspublic.pdf (accessed 16 March 2012).

McGrenere, J. and Ho, W. (2000) 'Affordances: clarifying and evolving a concept'. Proceedings of graphic interface 2000. 15–17 May, Montreal, Canada: 179–186.

McKenna, C. (2006) 'Disrupting the narrative: the hypertext essay as a challenge to academic writing', *Academic Literacies Annual Symposium*. University of Westminster, June 2006.

McKenna, C. (2012a) 'Digital texts and the construction of writerly spaces: academic writing in hypertext', *Pratiques: Litteracies Universitaires: Nouvelle Perspectives*, No. 153–154: 211–229.

McKenna, C. (2012b forthcoming) 'Digital writing as transformative: texts and process'. In Lillis, T., Harrington, K., Lea, M. and Mitchell, S. (eds) *Working with Academic Literacies: Research, Theory and Design*. Parlour Press.

Mackenzie, A. and Martin, L. (2010) *Making Content Open*. Edge Hill University, http://www.eshare.edgehill.ac.uk/1424 (accessed 16 March 2012).

McKenzie, D. and Ozler, B. (2011) 'Academic blogs are proven to increase dissemination of economic research and improve impact'. LSE: Impact of Social Sciences blog, http://blogs.lse.ac.uk/impactofsocialsciences/2011/11/15/world-bank-dissemination/ (accessed 1 April 2012).

MacKenzie, D. and Wajcman, J. (1999) *The Social Shaping of Technology*. 2nd edn. Buckingham: Open University Press.

Mann, S. (2000) 'The students' experience of reading', *Higher Education* 39, 3: 297–317.

Margaryan, A., Littlejohn, A. and Vojt, G. (2011) 'Are digital natives a myth or reality? University students' use of digital technologies', *Computers & Education*, 2: 429–440.

Margaryan, A., Milligan, C. and Littlejohn, A. (2011) 'Validation of Davenport's classification structure of knowledge-intensive processes', *Journal of Knowledge Management*, 15, 4: 568–581.

Martin, A. and Grudziecki, J. (2006) 'DigEuLit: concepts and tools for digital literacy development in ITALICS', *Innovation in Teaching and Learning in Information and Computer Sciences*, 5, 4, http://www.ics.heacademy.ac.uk/italics/vol5iss4/martin-grudziecki.pdf (accessed 17 July 2012).

Marwick, A. and boyd, d. (2011) 'I tweet honestly, I tweet passionately: Twitter users, context collapse, and the imagined audience', *New Media and Society*. 13, 1: 114–133

Masterman, L. and Wild, J. (2011) *JISC Open Educational Resources Programme: Phase 2 OER Impact Study. Research Report*. Oxford University and JISC, http://www.jisc.ac.uk/media/documents/programmes/elearning/oer/JISCOERImpactStudyResearchReportv1-0.pdf (accessed 16 March 2012).

Merchant, G. (2001) 'Teenager in cyberspace: an investigation of language use and language change in internet chatrooms', *Journal of Research in Reading*, 24, 3: 293–306.

Mills, K. A. (2010) 'A review of the "digital turn" in the new literacy studies', *Review of Educational Research*, 80, 2: 246–271.

Milojevic, I. (2003) 'Hegemonic and marginalised utopias in the contemporary western world', *Policy Futures in Education*, 1 (3): 440–466.

Modern Language Association (n.d.) 'How do I cite a tweet?', http://www.mla.org/style/handbook_faq/cite_a_tweet (accessed 1 April 2012).

Modern Language Association of America (MLAA) (2002) 'The future of scholarly publishing', http://www.mla.org/pdf/schlrlypblshng.pdf (accessed 2 October 2012).

Moje, E. B., Ciechanowski, K. M., Kramer, K., Ellis, L., Carrillo, R. and Collazo, T. (2004) 'Working toward third space in content area literacy: an examination of everyday funds of knowledge and discourse', *Reading Research Quarterly* 39, 1: 40–70.

Mol, A. (1999) 'Ontological politics: a word and some questions'. In Law, J. and Hassard, J. (eds) *Actor Network and After*. Oxford and Keele: Blackwell and the Sociological Review: 74–89.

Molesworth, M., Nixon, E. and Scullion, R. (2009) 'Having, being and higher education: the marketisation of the university and the transformation of the student into consumer', *Teaching in Higher Education*, 14, 3: 277–287.

Montague, R-A. (2006) 'Riding the waves: a case study of learners and leaders in library and information science education', unpublished doctoral dissertation. University of Illinois at Urbana-Champaign, Champaign, IL.

Morgan, W., Russell, A. L, Ryan, M. (2002) 'Informed opportunism: teaching for learning in uncertain contexts of distributed education'. In Lea, M. R. and Nicolls, K. (eds) *Distributed Learning: Social and Cultural Approaches to Practice*. London: Routledge: 38–55.

Morris, D. (2009) 'Encouraging more open educational resources with Southampton's EdShare', *Ariadne*, 59, http://www.ariadne.ac.uk/issue59/morris/ (accessed 16 March 2012).

Neff, G. and Stark, D. (2004) 'Permanently beta: responsive organization in the Internet era'. In Howard, P. E.N. and Jones, S. (eds) *Society Online: The Internet in Context*. Thousand Oaks, CA: Sage: 173–188.

Newkirk, T. (2009) *Hanging on To Good Ideas in a Time of Bad Ones: Six Literacy Principles Worth Fighting For*. Portsmouth: NH Heinemann.

Newman, T. (2009) *Digital Literacies: a Becta Literature Review*, http://www.timmus-limited.co.uk (accessed 17 July 2012).

Nicholas, D., Rowlands, I. and Huntington, P. (2008) *Information Behaviour of the Researcher of the Future – Executive summary*. London: JISC.

Nie, N. H. (2001) 'Sociability, interpersonal relations, and the Internet: Reconciling conflicting findings', *American Behavioral Scientist*, 45, 3: 420–35.

Norman, D. (1988) *The Psychology of Everyday Things*. New York: Basic Books.

Norman, D. (1999) 'Affordance, conventions, and design', *Interactions*, 6, 3: 38–42.

O'Bannon, B., Lubke, J., Beard, J. and Britt, G. (2011) 'Using podcasts to replace lecture: effects on student achievement', *Computers & Education*, 57, 3: 1885–1892.

O'Reilly, T. (2005) 'What is Web 2.0? Design patterns and business models for the next generation of software', http://www.oreillynet.com/pub/a/oreilly/tim/news/2005/09/30/what-is-web-20.html (accessed 8 June 2012).

Oblinger, D. and Oblinger, J. (2005) 'Is it age or IT: first steps towards understanding the net generation'. In Oblinger, D. and Oblinger, J. (eds) *Educating the Net Generation*, Boulder, CO: EDUCAUSE: 2.1-2.20, http://www.educause.edu/educatingthenetgen (accessed 21 October 2008).

OECD (2007) *Giving Knowledge for Free: The Emergence of Open Educational Resources*. Centre for Educational Research and Innovation, Organisation for Economic Cooperation and Development, http://www.oecd.org/document/41/0,3343,en_2649_201185_38659497_1_1_1_1,00&&en-USS_01DBC.html (accessed 16 March 2012).

Oliver, M. (2012) 'Learning with technology as coordinated sociomaterial practice: digital literacies as a site of praxiological study'. In Hodgson, V., Jones, C., de Laat, M., McConnell, D., Ryberg, T. and Sloep, P. *Proceedings of the 8th International Conference on Networked Learning*, 2–4 April 2012, Maastricht, NL: 440–447, http://www.networkedlearningconference.org.uk/ (accessed 16 July 2012).

Online College Courses (2011) '50 great ways colleges are using Facebook', http://www.onlinecollegecourses.com/2011/04/04/50-great-ways-colleges-are-using-facebook/ (accessed 12 July 2012).

Orlikowski, W. J. (2002) 'Knowing in practice: enacting a collective capability in distributed organizing', *Organization Science*, 13, 3: 249–273.

Palfrey, J. and Gasser, U. (2008) *Born Digital: Understanding the First Generation of Digital Natives.* New York: Basic Books.

Palmer, C. L. and Cragin, M. H. (2008) 'Scholarship and disciplinary practices', *Annual Review of Information Science and Technology*, 42, 163–212.

Parker, K., Lenhart, A. and Moore, K. (2011) 'The digital revolution and higher education', http://pewinternet.org/Reports/2011/College-presidents/Summary.aspx (accessed 7 September 2011).

Payne, D. (2005) 'English studies in Levittown: rhetorics of space and technology in course-management software', *College English*. 67, 5: 483–507.

Paynton, S. (2012) 'Developing digital literacies: briefing paper'. JISC, http://www.jisc.ac.uk/publications/briefingpapers/2012/developing-digital-literacies.aspx (accessed 16 July 2012).

Pearce, N., Weller, M., Scanlon, E. and Kinsley, S. (2010) 'Digital scholarship considered: how new technologies could transform academic work', *Education*, 16, 1, http://www.ineducation.ca/article/digital-scholarship-considered-how-new-technologies-could-transform-academic-work (accessed 20 December 2012).

Pedersen, H. (2010) 'Is the posthuman educable? On the convergence of educational philosophy, animal studies, and posthumanist theory', *Discourse: Studies in the Cultural Politics of Education*, 31, 2: 237–250.

Pegler, C. (2012) 'Herzberg, hygiene and the motivation to reuse: towards a three-factor theory to explain motivation to share and use OER', *JIME (Journal of Interactive Media in Education)*, Special Issue on Open Educational Resources, http://www-jime.open.ac.uk/jime/article/view/2012-04 (accessed 1 April 2012).

Peters, M. and Humes, W. (2003) 'Educational futures: utopias and heterotopias', *Policy Futures in Education*, 1, 3: 428–440.

Pew Internet (2011) 'Internet adoption over time', http://pewinternet.org/Reports/2012/Digital-differences/Main-Report/Internet-adoption-over-time.aspx (accessed 12 July 2012).

Pinch, T. and Bijker, W. (1987) 'The social construction of facts and artefacts: or how the sociology of science and the sociology of technology might benefit each other'. In Bijker, W., Hughes, T. and Pinch, T. (eds) *The Social Construction of Technological Systems*. Cambridge, Mass: The MIT Press: 17–50.

Piñuelas, E. (2008) 'Cyber-Heterotopia: figurations of space and subjectivity in the virtual domain', *Watermark*, 2: 152–169.

Poster, M. (2001) *What's the Matter with the Internet?* Minneapolis: University of Minnesota Press.

Prensky, M. (2001) 'Digital natives, digital immigrants'. *On the Horizon*. 9, 5: 1–6, http://www.emeraldinsight.com/journals.htm?issn=1074-8121&volume=9&issue=5 (accessed 20 December 2012).

Prensky, M. (2010) *Teaching Digital Natives: Partnering for Real Learning*. London: Sage Publishers.

Preston, C. J. (2008) 'Braided learning: an emerging process observed in e-communities of practice', *International Journal of Web Based Communities*, 4, 2: 220–243.

Rainie, L. (2012) 'The shifting education landscape: networked learning', http://pewinternet.org/Presentations/2012/Mar/NROC.aspx (accessed 6 June 2012).

Rainie, L. and Wellman, B. (2012) *Networked: The New Social Operating System*. Cambridge, MA: MIT Press.

Raymond, E. (1998) 'The cathedral and the bazaar', *First Monday*, 3, 3, http://firstmonday.org/htbin/cgiwrap/bin/ojs/index.php/fm/article/view/578/499 (accessed 20 May 2012).

Reed, A. (2005). 'My blog is me': texts and persons in UK online journal culture (an anthropology)', *Ethnos* 70, 2: 220–242.

Rheingold, H. (2000) *The Virtual Community: Homesteading on the Electronic Frontier* (revised edition). Cambridge, MA: MIT Press.

Rheingold, H. (2003) *Smart Mobs: The Next Social Revolution*, NY: Perseus Books.

Rinaldo, S. B., Tapp, S. and Laverie, D. A. (2011) 'Learning by tweeting: using Twitter as a pedagogical tool', *Journal of Marketing Education*, 33, 2: 193–203.

Rolfe, V. (2012) 'Open educational resources: staff attitudes and awareness', *Research in Learning Technology*. 20, 1–13, http://www.researchinlearningtechnology.net/index.php/rlt/article/view/14395/pdf (accessed 16 March 2012).

Romero, C., Ventura, S., Pechenizkiy, M. and Baker, R.S.J.d. (eds) (2011) *Handbook of Educational Data Mining*. Boca Raton, FL: CRC Press, Taylor & Francis.

Ross, C., Terras, M., Warwick, C. and Welsh, A. (2011) 'Enabled backchannel: conference Twitter use by digital humanists', *Journal of Documentation* 67, 2: 214–237.

Ross, J. (2012) 'Performing the reflective self: audience awareness in high-stakes reflection', *Studies in Higher Education*, 39, 7. Available online with iFirst: http://www.tandfonline.com/doi/abs/10.1080/03075079.2011.651450.

Ryberg, T.and Dirckinck-Holmfeld, L. (2008) 'Power users and patchworking: an analytical approach to critical studies of young people's learning with digital media', *Educational Media International*, 45, 3: 143–156.

Säljö, R. (1999) 'Learning as the use of tools: a socio-cultural perspective on the human-technology link'. In Littleton, K. and Light, P. (eds) *Learning with Computers: Analysing Productive Interaction*. London: Routledge: 144–161.

Säljö, R. (2010) 'Digital tools and challenges to institutional traditions of learning: technologies, social memory and the performative nature of learning', *Journal of Computer Assisted Learning*, 26, 1: 53–64.

Sample, I. (2012a) 'Free access to British scientific research within two years', *The Guardian*, 15 July 2012, http://www.guardian.co.uk/science/2012/jul/15/free-access-british-scientific-research (accessed 1 August 2012).

Sample, I. (2012b) 'Harvard says it can't afford to pay publishers' prices', *The Guardian*, 24 April 2012, http://www.guardian.co.uk/science/2012/apr/24/harvard-university-journal-publishers-prices (accessed 1 June 2012).

Scardamalia, M. and Bereiter, C. (1996) 'Computer support for knowledge-building communities'. In Koschmann, T. (ed.) *CSCL: Theory and Practice of an Emerging Paradigm*. Mahwah, NJ: Lawrence Erlbaum: 249–268.

Schön, D. (1995/2000) 'The new scholarship requires a new epistemology'. In DeZure, D. and Marchese, T. J. (eds) *Learning from Change: Landmarks in Teaching and Learning in Higher Education*. Sterling, VA: Stylus Publications: 32–34.

Schreibman, S., Siemens, R. and Unsworth, J. (eds) (2004) *A Companion to Digital Humanities*. Oxford: Blackwell, http://www.digitalhumanities.org/companion (accessed 20 December 2012).

Schulmeister, R. (2010) 'Students, Internet, eLearning and Web 2.0'. In Ebner, M. and
    Schiefner, M. (eds) *Looking Toward the Future of Technology-Enhanced Education: Ubiq-
    uitous Learning and Digital Native.* Hershey, PA: IGI Global: 13–36.
Seely Brown, J. and Adler, R. (2008) 'Minds on fire: open education, the long tail, and
    Learning 2.0', *EDUCAUSE Review*, 43, 1: 16–32, http://net.educause.edu/ir/library/
    pdf/ERM0811.pdf (accessed 17 July 2012).
Selfe, C. L. and Selfe, R. J. (1994) 'The politics of the interface: power and its exercise in
    electronic contact zones', *College Composition and Communication* 45, 4: 480–504.
Selwyn, N. (2009) 'Faceworking: exploring students' education-related use of Facebook',
    Learning, Media and Technology, 34, 2: 157–174.
Selwyn, N. (2011) *Schools and Schooling in the Digital Age: A Critical Analysis.* London:
    Routledge.
Senges, M., Brown, J. S. and Rheingold, H. (2008) 'Entrepreneurial learning in the net-
    worked age', *Paradigms*, 1, 1: 125–140.
Sharpe, R. (2010) 'Conceptualizing differences in learners' experiences of e-learning: a
    review of contextual models: Report of the Higher Education Academy Learner Differ-
    ence (HEALD) synthesis project', http://www.heacademy.ac.uk/assets/EvidenceNet/
    HEALD_Report.doc (accessed 17 July 2012).
Sheridan, M. P. and Rowsell, J. (2010) *Design Literacies: Learning and Innovation in the
    Digital Age*, London: Routledge.
Shortis, T. (2001) *The Language of ICT.* London: Routledge.
Siemens, G. (2006) 'Connectivism: a learning theory for the digital age. eLearnSpace',
    http://www.elearnspace.org/Articles/connectivism.htm (accessed 17 July 2012).
Siemens, G. (2010) 'What are Learning Analytics?', http://www.elearnspace.org/
    blog/2010/08/25/what-are-learning-analytics (accessed 8 June 2012).
Smith, J., Satchwell, C., Edwards, R., Miller, K. and Fowler, Z., with Gaechter, J., Know-
    les, J., Phillipson, C. and Young, R. (2008) 'Literacy practices in the learning careers of
    childcare students', *Journal of Vocational Education and Training*, 60: 363–375.
Snyder, I. (2001) 'A new communication order: researching literacy practices in the net-
    work society', *Language and Education*, 15, 2 & 3: 117–131.
Spiro, L. (2010) Blog: 'Digital scholarship in the humanities', http://digitalscholarship.
    wordpress.com/ (accessed 14 April 2013).
Stables, A. (2005) *Living and Learning as Semiotic Engagement: A New Theory of Educa-
    tion.* Lewiston, NY/Lampeter: Edwin Mellen Press.
Steinfield, C., DiMicco, J. M., Ellison, N. B. and Lampe, C. (2009) 'Bowling online: social
    networking and social capital within the organization', *Proceedings of the Fourth Com-
    munities and Technologies Conference.* New York: ACM: 245–254.
Steinkuehler, C. (2007) 'Massively multiplayer online gaming as a constellation of literacy
    practices', *E-Learning and Digital Media* 4, 3: 297–318.
Strauss, A. L. (1987) 'A social world perspective', *Studies in Symbolic Interactions*, 1:
    119–128.
Street, B. (1984) *Literacy in Theory and Practice.* Cambridge: Cambridge University
    Press.
Street, B. (1996) 'Academic literacies'. In Baker, D., Clay, J. and Fox, C. (eds) *Challenging
    Ways of Knowing: In English, Mathematics and Science*, London: Routledge: 101–134.
Street, B. (2003) 'What's "new" in the new literacy studies? Critical approaches to literacy
    in theory and practice'. *Current Issues in Comparative Education*, 5, 2: 77–91.
Stringer, E. T. (1999) *Action Research.* London: Sage.

Swan, K. (2006) 'Online collaboration', *Journal of Asynchronous Learning Networks*, 10, 1: Introduction to the whole issue, http://sloanconsortium.org/jaln/v10n1/online-collaboration-introduction-special-issue (accessed 20 December 2012).

Tapscott, D. (1998) *Growing Up Digital: The rise of the Net Generation*. New York: McGraw-Hill.

Tapscott, D. (2009) *Grown Up Digital: How the Net Generation Is Changing Your World*. New York: McGraw-Hill.

Tapscott, D. and Williams, A. (2008) *Wikinomics: How Mass Collaboration Changes Everything*. New York: Penguin.

Tapscott, D. and Williams, A. (2010) 'Innovating the 21st century university: it's time', *Educause Review*, 45, 1: 17–29.

Terras, M. (2012) 'Is blogging and tweeting about research papers worth it? The Verdict', http://melissaterras.blogspot.co.uk/2012/04/is-blogging-and-tweeting-about-research.html (accessed 1 April 2012).

Thesen, L. and Van Pletzen, E. (2006) *Academic Literacy and the Languages of Change*. London: Continuum.

Thoma, M. (2011) 'New forms of communication and the public mission of economics: overcoming the great disconnect', http://publicsphere.ssrc.org/thoma-new-forms-of-communication-and-the-public-mission-of-economics (accessed 1 June 2012).

Thomas, M. (ed) (2011) *Deconstructing Digital Natives*. New York: Routledge.

Thurlow, C. (2007) 'Fabricating youth: new media discourse and the technologization of young people'. In Johnson, S. and Ensslin, A. (eds) *Language in the Media*. London: Continuum: 213–233.

Trinder, K., Guiller, J., Margaryan, A., Littlejohn, A. and Nicol, D. (2008) *Learning from digital natives: integrating formal and informal learning*. Final project report. Higher Education Academy, UK, http://www.heacademy.ac.uk/projects/detail/projectfinder/projects/pf2969lr (accessed 17 July 2012).

Tummons, J. (2010) 'Institutional ethnography and actor-network theory: a framework for researching the assessment of trainee teachers', *Ethnography and Education*, 5, 3: 345–57.

Tuominen, K., Savolainen, R. and Talja, S. (2005) 'Information literacy as a sociotechnical practice', *The Library Quarterly*, 75, 3: 329–345, http://www.jstor.org/stable/10.1086/497311 (accessed 16 March 2012).

Turnbull, M., Littlejohn, A. and Allen, M. (2011) 'Preparing Graduates for the 21st Century Workplace', *7th International Conference 'New Horizons in Industry, Business and Education' (NHIBE 2011)*. 25–26 August, Chios Island, Greece.

Turner, J. (1999) 'Academic literacy and the discourse of transparency'. In Jones, C., Turner, J. and Street, B. (eds) *Students Writing in the University: Cultural and Epistemological Issues*. Amsterdam: John Benjamins: 149–160.

Turner, J. (2011) *Language in the Academy: Cultural Reflexivity and Intercultural Dynamics*. Bristol, Buffalo, Ontario: Multilingual Matters.

Tyack, D. and Cuban, L. (1995) *Tinkering Toward Utopia: A Century of Public School Reform*. Cambridge, MA: Harvard University Press.

Tyma, A. (2011) 'Connecting with what is out there!: Using Twitter in the large lecture', *Communication Teacher*, 25, 3: 175–181.

UK Government Report (2009) *Digital Britain*, http://interactive.bis.gov.uk/digitalbritain/report (accessed 17 July 2012).

UNESCO (2012) Open Educational Resources, http://www.unesco.org/new/en/

communication-and-information/access-to-knowledge/open-educational-resources (accessed 16 March 2012).

Unsworth, J. (2000) 'Scholarly Primitives': what methods do humanities researchers have in common, and how might our tools reflect this?' In symposium on 'Humanities Computing: formal methods, experimental practice', King's College, London, 13 May, http://people.lis.illinois.edu/~unsworth//Kings.5-00/primitives.html (accessed 14 April 2013).

van Barneveld, A., Arnold, K. E., and Campbell, J. P. (2012) 'Analytics in higher education: establishing a common language', *Educause Learning Initiative Paper 1*, http://www.educause.edu/ir/library/pdf/ELI3026.pdf (accessed 8 June 2012).

van Leeuwen, T. (2005) *Introducing Social Semiotics*. London: Routledge.

van Meter, P. N. and Firetto, C. (2008) 'Intertextuality and the study of new literacies: research critique and recommendations'. In Coiro, J., Knobel, M., Lankshear, C. and Leu, D. J. (eds) *Handbook of Research on New Literacies*. New York: Erlbaum: 1079–1092.

Van Wyk, T. (2012) 'Taking OER beyond the OER communities: policy issues and priorities'. In Glennie, J., Harley, K., Butcher, N. and van Wyk, T. (eds) *Perspectives on Open and Distance Learning: Open Educational Resources and Change in Higher Education: Reflections from Practice*. Vancouver: Commonwealth of Publishing, http://www.col.org/PublicationDocuments/pub_PS_OER_web.pdf (accessed 16 July 2012).

Vold Lexander, K. (2012) 'Analyzing multilingual text-messaging in Senegal – an approach for the study of mixed language SMS'. In Sebba, M. *et al.* (eds) *Language Mixing and Code Switching in Writing*. London: Routledge: 146–169.

Vygotsky, L. (1978) *Mind in Society*. Cambridge MA: Harvard University Press.

Wagner, C.S. (2008) *The New Invisible College: Science for Development*. Washington, DC: The Brookings Institute.

Wang, H. and Wellman, B. (2010) 'Social connectivity in America: changes in adult friendship network size from 2002 to 2007', *American Behavioral Scientist*, 53, 8: 1148–1169.

Warschauer, M. (1995) 'Heterotopias, panopticons, and internet discourse', *University of Hawai'i Working Papers in ESL*, 14(1), http://www.gse.uci.edu/person/warschauer_m/heterotopias.html (accessed 22 February 2012).

Weller, M. (2010) 'Big and little OER'. In *Open ED2010: Seventh Annual Open Education Conference*. 2–4 November 2010, Barcelona, Spain.

Weller, M. (2011) *The Digital Scholar: How Technology Is Transforming Scholarly Practice*. Bloomsbury Academic, http://www.bloomsburyacademic.com/view/DigitalScholar_9781849666275/book-ba-9781849666275.xml (accessed 16 March 2012).

Weller, M. (2012a) 'The ed techie', http://nogoodreason.typepad.co.uk/

Weller, M. (2012b) 'Digital scholarship, tenure & barometers' (blog post), http://nogoodreason.typepad.co.uk/no_good_reason/2012/09/digital-scholarship-tenure-barometers.html (accessed 4 October 2012).

Weller, M. (2012c) 'The openness-creativity cycle in education', *Journal of Interactive Media in Education*, 2, http://www-jime.open.ac.uk/jime/article/view/2012-02 (accessed 20 December 2012).

Weller, M. (2012d) 'The virtues of blogging as scholarly activity', *The Chronicle of Higher Education*, 29 April 2012, http://chronicle.com/article/The-Virtues-of-Blogging-as/131666/ (accessed 1 July 2012).

Wenger, E. (1998) *Communities of Practice: Learning, Meaning and Identity*. Cambridge Cambridge University Press.

Wentzel, K. R. and Wigfield, A. (1998) 'Academic and social motivational influences on students' academic performance', *Educational Psychology Review*, 10, 2: 155–174.

Whatmore, S. (2006) 'Materialist returns: practising cultural geography in and for a more-than-human world', *Cultural Geographies*. 13, 4: 600–609.

White, D. and Manton, M. (2011) *JISC Funded OER Impact Study*. University of Oxford, http://www.jisc.ac.uk/media/documents/programmes/elearning/oer/OERTheValueOfReuseInHigherEducation.pdf (accessed 16 March 2012).

Williams, B. T. (2007) 'Trust, betrayal, and authorship: plagiarism and how we perceive students', *Journal of Adolescent & Adult Literacy*, 51, 4: 350–354.

Williams, B. T. (2009) *Shimmering Literacies: Popular Culture and Reading and Writing Online*. London, Peter Lang.

Williamson, O. E. (1981) 'The economics of organizations: The transaction cost approach', *American Journal of Sociology*, 87: 548–577.

Wolfe, C. (2010) *What Is Posthumanism?* Minneapolis: University of Minnesota Press.

Young, J. (8 January 2012) '"Badges" earned online pose challenge to traditional college diplomas', *The Chronicle of Higher Education*, http://chronicle.com.ezproxy.library.ubc.ca/article/Badges-Earned-Online-Pose/130241/ (accessed 9 June 2012).

Zimmerman, B. J. (1989) 'A social cognitive view of self-regulated academic learning', *Journal of Educational Psychology*, 81, 3: 329–339.

Zwagerman, S. (2008) 'The Scarlet P: plagiarism, panopticism, and the rhetoric of academic integrity', *College Composition and Communication*, 59, 4: 676–710.

Index